Uncertain Tastes

Uncertain Tastes

Memory, Ambivalence, and the Politics of
Eating in Samburu, Northern Kenya

Jon Holtzman

UNIVERSITY OF CALIFORNIA PRESS
Berkeley • Los Angeles • London

University of California Press, one of the most
distinguished university presses in the United States,
enriches lives around the world by advancing
scholarship in the humanities, social sciences, and
natural sciences. Its activities are supported by the UC
Press Foundation and by philanthropic contributions
from individuals and institutions. For more
information, visit www.ucpress.edu.

University of California Press
Berkeley and Los Angeles, California

University of California Press, Ltd.
London, England

Library of Congress Cataloging-in-Publication Data

Holtzman, Jon.
  Uncertain tastes : memory, ambivalence, and the
politics of eating in Samburu, northern Kenya /
Jon Holtzman.
      p.   cm.
  Includes bibliographical references and index.
  isbn 978-0-520-25736-8 (cloth : alk. paper)
  isbn 978-0-520-25737-5 (pbk. : alk. paper)
  1. Samburu (African people)—Food.   2. Samburu
(African people)—Domestic animals.   3. Samburu
(African people)—Social conditions.   4. Food habits—
Kenya—Samburu District.   5. Food preferences—
Kenya—Samburu District.   6. Food—Symbolic
aspects—Kenya—Samburu District.   7. Culture
conflict—Kenya—Samburu District.   8. Social
change—Kenya—Samburu District.   9. Samburu
District (Kenya)—Social conditions.   10. Samburu
District (Kenya)—Economic conditions.   I. Title.

DT433.545.S26H653   2009
641.30089'965—dc22   2009003368

Manufactured in the United States of America

18   17   16   15   14   13   12   11   10   09
10   9   8   7   6   5   4   3   2   1

Contents

Acknowledgments

One style of acknowledgments lists the notables who have commented on and presumably anointed the manuscript. The second is an exhaustive list of everyone—perhaps including the author's dog—who has contributed to the grand undertaking that has ultimately resulted in a book. I aim for the second, while apologizing to those who may inadvertently be forgotten. Thankfully, those forgotten will not include my dog.

My greatest debt is to the many Samburu who have opened their lives to me, and whose human gifts I hope these pages do at least partial justice to. Leanoi Lekeren and his family have been gracious hosts since 2001, and Lenyuki Leekachula was my first Samburu friend, whom I met while I was an undergraduate, and without whose humor and warmth I might have been less inclined to choose Samburu for graduate study. Lemujel Lekutaas is the best neighbor on any continent. Many individuals have acted as formal research assistants but also friends. Adamson Lanyasunya was my first Samburu research assistant and has remained a friend and a brother. His brother Barnabas has been a source of great wit, wisdom, and insight, and has as much as anyone enriched these pages. Robert Lelesengei remains a delightful friend, and A.K. Lengerded's humor, stories, and energy cannot be separated from the joy and outcomes of research. Sammy Letoole has

been able and loyal since we began working together in 2001, while
Benson Leparmorijo and Simon Leekachula played key roles at earlier times. Mamai Lekpanapan, Lopelu Lekupano, Stimu Lekeren, and
Mpaayo Lepariyo are generous friends who also worked briefly at various stages. I also thank Lekarrero Lepariyo, Otan Lentiyo and family, the Lemarash family, Timothy Loishopoko, Musa Letuaa and the
people of Lodokejek Group Ranch, Lodungokwe, and Ndonyo Nasipa.
Michael and Judy Rainey first took me to Samburu, with the St. Law-
rence University Program led by Paul Robinson and Howard Brown.
Their inspiration fostered the love of East Africa that has continued to
draw me over the years.

I thank the government of the Republic of Kenya for extending permission for research, and the Institute of African Studies of the University of Nairobi for providing affiliation. Funding for research was
provided in 1992–94 by grants by a National Science Foundation Dis-
sertation Improvement Grant and a fellowship from the Population-
Environmental Dynamics Project. Research in 2001–2 was funded by
a Grant for Senior Research from the National Science Foundation.
Annual trips back since that time have been funded by grants from
the National Science Foundation and Western Michigan University.
A number of colleagues have generously provided comments on this
manuscript, in part or whole, including Conrad Kottak, Tom Fricke,
Sidney Mintz, Carole Counihan, Sarah Hill, Bilinda Straight, as well
as reviewers at University of California Press. A version of chapter 7
previously appeared in *American Ethnologist*; parts of chapters 1 and
2 appeared in *Annual Reviews in Anthropology*; chapter 6 contains
material from articles published in *Food and Foodways* and the *Journal of East African Studies*. Chapter 8 contains material that appeared
in the *American Anthropologist* and *Postcolonial Studies*. I thank
these journals for the permission to reprint this material.

On a different note, I wish to thank Katie Lendia, who has been my
most loyal companion from start to finish. I also remember KXZ 625,
whom I still miss as a sister, as a lover.

My brother, Jeremy Holtzman, suggested that I take an archeology class as an interesting elective. It was interesting, though not life-
changing, so I thank Bryn Mawr College for requiring students to
take the cultural course to get credit for the archeology one. Evidently,
the cultural course was life-changing. I particularly thank Phil Kil-
bride and Jane Goodale at Bryn Mawr for the inspiration to pursue
anthropology.

My parents, Jordan and Joyce Holtzman, have provided more and varied support than anyone could hope for. The role of BS must also be acknowledged. Janet Mills assisted with the final photographic production. Clare (Naisula) Holtzman and William (Nkampit) Holtzman have been the most wonderful children an anthropologist could ask for.

Introduction

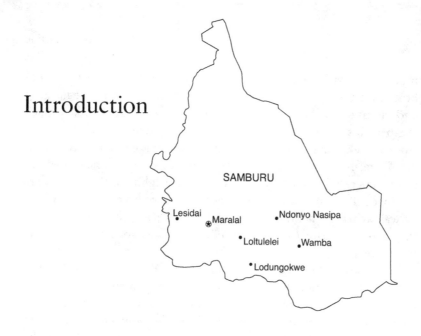

SAMBURU

Lesidai
⊛ Maralal
• Ndonyo Nasipa
• Loltulelei   • Wamba
• Lodungokwe

I walked behind Barnabas in the cool morning air, approaching his home in Lesidai. Nearly on the equator, but more than 7,000 feet high on the Leroghi Plateau, Lesidai's weather year-round is reminiscent of early autumn in the American Midwest—perpetually on the cusp between warmth and briskness—and, over the past two decades or so, farming has assumed a growing importance in an area previously devoted wholly to subsistence pastoralism. As I followed Barnabas along a path through his brother's field of ripening maize, he gestured to the surrounding crops and exclaimed with characteristic drama, and his best ethnographic English: "This is the Samburu's staple food!" I was caught off-guard by his surprising pronouncement, which so essentialized Samburu culture at the same time that it was markedly at odds with carefully constructed Samburu ideals of a diet garnered from the family herds of cows, sheep, and goats. I managed the fieldworker's well-practiced riposte of echoing these surprising words in question form: "This is the Samburu staple food?" I asked. "No milk, no meat, no blood!" he declared. "We just survive on grains."

What do we make of Barnabas's commentary on early twenty-first-century Samburu eating in the context of current and historical Samburu eating practices, salient forms of Samburu historical consciousness, and his own personal biography? His words reflect contradictions and ambivalences that to a degree parallel those in his own life. Now in his early thirties, he is a high school graduate from a prominent family in an area of Samburu District that is a bastion of Protestant forms of Christianity which advocate Western education and cultural change. Yet he is at the same time the drunken black sheep in his family of born-agains—as he spoke, he was just back from a week spent on a drinking safari who-knows-where. Although his Western-style clothes were emblematic of a commitment to Western practices advocated by his family and neighbors, the particulars hardly conformed to the squeaky clean image of his church or family: he was wearing a denim jacket and ill-fitting jeans so dirty and faded they appeared ready to rot off his body, the loose soles of his Saucony tennis shoes flopping hobolike as he walked.

His proclamation was no less full of such contradictions. He was not merely describing how, in his observation, Samburu now eat but, rather, rendering a complex iteration of his views on the state of the Samburu world, marked both by a pride in "development" and a sense of loss resulting from the decline of Samburu culture as reified in the pastoral culinary complex of milk, meat, and blood. If Barnabas held a sense of pride for his Developed way of life—and indeed, he viewed less Developed Samburu from lowland areas as "almost a different tribe"—he also felt a profound tension between these changes and his sense of identity and culture. The fields of maize were closely identified by Barnabas, his family, and his neighbors with the ideological triumph of Development, typified by the adoption of enlightened agriculture and the renunciation of a life of ignorance based in pastoral conservatism. Yet on this day he did not highlight the fields of maize as a symbol of the victory of reason over folly. Rather, for him the maize symbolized what, in his view, had been lost: a culturally salient and nutritionally superior diet of milk, meat, and blood, exchanged for an era when development goes hand in hand with poverty, when the taste of enlightenment is *nchata natotoyo*, the "dry stick" descriptive of a bowl of boiled maize lacking the tasty additions of milk or fat.

Let us now compare Barnabas's comments with those of another Samburu friend, from a very different area: Lekanapan, a junior elder from the remote lowland area of Ndonyo Nasipa, where the pastoral economy is still at its strongest and where agriculture is impossible on the hot, stark landscape of bare soil and acacia scrub. Here pastoral foods are still the most valued, with purchased foods a less desirable supplement even as they become a necessity with the decline of the pastoral economy. Though roughly the same age as Barnabas, he

FIGURE 1. Barnabas, ironically well armed. Photo by the author.

cuts an entirely different figure. He has never been to school, though he speaks reasonably good Kiswahili. With a *kikoi* cloth wrapped around his waist and a tartan blanket draped over his upper body, he presents a fashionably up-to-date version of traditional dress. As we rested and sheltered ourselves from the blazing sun in his small, low house of sticks, leaves, mud, and dung, I noticed the bow and arrow he uses to collect blood from his goats when milk is scarce, and we talked about how Samburu responses to nutritional deficits had changed from even the recent past. He noted the reticence of many Samburu today to rely, as they had in the past, on blood, stored fat, and wild plants to get them through droughts and famines. Now, he asserted, they preferred to sell livestock and "buy town foods, like rice" in the shops to get them through hard times. That he chose rice to make his point—rather than the more common maize meal—was telling, for to Samburu (as well as other Kenyans), rice is the most effete of starches, not suitable for satisfying a manly hunger and much more closely associated with a town way of life, with education and development. He was not extolling development as a form of enlightenment, but rather indicting it as a slavish, irrational adherence to a cultural model with origins distant from Samburu values, a model out of step with the logic of pastoral practice. Mustering as much contempt as he could from his gentle manner, Lekanapan exclaimed, in a tone suggestive of disbelief: "You sell your wealth to buy food—*this* is Development!"

To Lekanapan the logic of such a strategy was lacking. Food is a transitory thing; as the Samburu proverb says, "Ndaa naidaiya" (Food gets finished). It is foolish to sacrifice your wealth—which endures and carries long-term significance—to the passing need for food. If it is sometimes necessary to slaughter, or nowadays to sell, a goat to push your family nutritionally until better times, this should be viewed as an odious drain on the resources necessary for the family's survival, not as a strategy embraced in the neophilia of Development. And yet, this was more or less the life Lekanapan lived. Although residing in a remote, relatively wealthy pastoral area, he was even less the ur-pastoralist surviving on the historically validated cuisine of milk, meat, and blood than most of his neighbors—themselves regular marketers of livestock. Rather, he was, by his community's standards, rather poor, with only a modest flock of sheep and goats to rely on for his family's survival; without relief food doled out by the World Food Program and the occasional sale of a goat or some skins, his family could not have fed themselves for long. And indeed, his very location belied his words. Less than a year earlier a simple road had been cut through the bush to allow mobile health clinics to visit the area. Whereas during my previous research (in 1992–94), this area could be accessed only through a half-day walk (and this from a remote, rough-hewn road), the area was now accessible to four-wheel-drive vehicles. The director of the NGO that ran the mobile clinics had built a small house and a shop, from which he sold such basic goods as maize meal and sugar. And Lekanapan had now resituated his own house so that he was the shop's closest neighbor, just down the hill from where these "town foods" (or "government foods," "gray foods," or "poverty foods") could be purchased. Thus, even if the idea of "selling your wealth to buy food" fostered a degree of contempt in Lekanapan, through a decision born both of necessity and choice, this was how he himself lived.

For all that distinguishes Barnabas and Lekanapan, there is, then, also something important that they share, namely, ambivalence and contradiction in how they view and experience their world and how they are constituted as persons within it. In this sense, they should be viewed less as opposite poles of a continuum—no matter how much they might at first glance appear to be so or characterize themselves as such—but rather as subjects constituted through a differing, but for each uneasy, mix of largely shared elements concerning how they valuate, negotiate, and experience the mundane and profound realities of their present through an understanding of the past. Consequently, there are several related arguments that I develop here and throughout the book concerning the relationship of food, memory, and ambivalence among Samburu pastoralists in northern Kenya: that the kinds of ambivalences and contradictions exemplified by Barnabas and Lekanapan are not unique but rather central to the ways Samburu have experienced the transformations of the past seventy or eighty years and how they make sense today of their present through the past, inflected in varying ways based on gender, age, location, education, and the like; that food is for Samburu a particularly potent nexus for the disparate strands of material and moral transformations that have remade both the social and the person; and finally that, while affording Samburu the specificity of the ethnographic richness they deserve, the way food in general condenses independent but intersecting strands—sensual, symbolic, psychological, social, material,

FIGURE 2. Lekanapan sifts through donated maize. Photo by the author.

and so on—renders it a particularly compelling site for the construction of complex, contradictory forms of memory and the ambivalent subjectivities that arise from them.

The backdrop for this analysis is a shift over approximately the past seventy years away from a diet centered predominantly on the products of their herds. At a rate accelerating markedly over the last three or so decades, their long-standing diet of milk, meat, and blood has lost viability as the mode of normal subsistence, as Samburu have experienced a severe and steady decline in the livestock economy coupled with perhaps a tripling of the human population. There has been a trend, consequently, toward a diet dependent on nonpastoral foods, and a challenge to the broad-reaching Samburu cultural framework concerning an array of values and practices centered upon eating (Holtzman 2001, 2003b). Since patterns of provisioning, eating, and food sharing have long constituted a domain densely packed with core cultural values and thickly entangled webs of social relations, recent trends away from a pastoral diet have problematized these wide-ranging social and cultural domains closely entwined with food and eating.

In explicating the significance of these processes, this book interweaves a focus on both history and memory, a distinction I will take up with greater specificity in the next chapter. Briefly, I am concerned with understanding the historical processes in colonial and postcolonial Kenya that have reworked Samburu configurations of eating practices in ways that are social, symbolic, nutritional, and the like, while also examining the ways in which these form a lens through which Samburu, ambiguously and ambivalently, valuate the past and the present. I will on one hand draw on archival, oral historical, and ethnographic sources to make an argument concerning events and processes that occurred over time and at particular times, piecing together with as much precision as possible why these changes occurred, how these processes were shaped both by a Samburu dynamic and by its interplay with regimes of power at the local, national, and global level, and what these transformations meant to varying Samburu at particular historical moments. For instance, how and why has tea (laden with both a traditional staple, milk, and a recent import, sugar) become both a dietary staple and one of the very few nonlocal items Samburu-ized as part of a self-defined "traditional culture"—linked in different historical periods to varying indigenous Samburu categories, and employed by varying actors to distinct symbolic and nutritional ends? In a society that until the 1950s was characterized by only small-scale and intermittent alcohol use, how did the needs of the colonial regime and the anxieties of the postcolonial regime contribute to the emergence of alcohol as a potently ambivalent signifier, standing for and constructing a dense and conflicting array of strands in new forms of Samburu moral—and immoral—personhood for both elders and women? And how does a seemingly simple transformation in the process of cooking associated with new foods and new dietary patterns problematize core relations in the age-gender system, particularly in regard to the central institution of murranhood, in which young men live for over a decade as bachelor-warriors, unmarried and eschewing foods seen by women? Yet, beyond understanding these as historical processes, this book is centrally about the present, concerned with understanding how a real or idealized past, constructed disproportionately around changes in eating, becomes a lens through which Samburu think about, express, and experience a politics of everyday life. Thus, the mundane but intimate and profound minutiae of daily experience provide a compelling arena through which Samburu understand the contests and joys within their own changing lives, experienced both in their immediacy and their historicity.

What is most compelling about the processes and meanings centered on changes in eating is not simply the kinds of structural contradiction and contestation—based on age, gender, wealth, class, religion, and the like—that have long since become a staple of social analysis. Although these are present, what is more intriguing is the dissonance, ambivalence, and ambiguity that not only blur and crosscut simple lines between social categories in Samburu valuation of food changes but construct individual subjectivities rife with internal contradictions. Indeed, two prominent and opposed master narratives inform Samburu readings of their history through food, along with a host of individual and collective permutations to these broad themes. While the predominant tendency is for Samburu to view changes in eating as a form of cultural decay, there are also significant numbers—particularly among younger, educated Samburu—who view this as being of a piece with "Progress," in line with long-standing antipastoralist development ideologies. But more tellingly, rarely do advocates of either of these two master narratives of history through food understand or express their positions in unambiguous terms; rather, they speak in ways that suggest affective ambivalence and internal contradiction. Consequently, my aim here is to consider these ambivalences in terms of what they say about memory in general and about food as a particularly telling and complex site of memory.

For a variety of reasons, many anthropological studies of how societies remember have constructed overly unidimensional renderings of history and memory, which end up showing how a set of memories conglomerated by our subjects or ourselves may ultimately be understood to be about a particular thing—whether it be identity, resistance, colonialism, or the state, and so on. Yet there is a paradox in this. For if the stuff of memory may be used to construct particular stories—used by particular actors for particular ends—memories are not linear in the way that stories we construct out of them (consciously or unconsciously) typically are. Like dreams, memories do not always fit neatly together as coherent narratives, except to the extent that we narrativize them, often quite consciously and deliberately. The experiences that gave birth to these memories are rarely themselves without their ambiguities and ambivalences. When something is gained, something else may be lost, and when something is lost, something else may be gained.

If ambivalence and dissonance are underexplored (but broadly characteristic) aspects of memory, food has dimensions that lend special complexity to the forms of memory that surround it. Although in the last decade or two there has been a veritable explosion in the study of food within anthropology and related fields, I suggest in chapter 2 that its salience as a powerful and complex cultural field remains to be fully realized. Food studies have blossomed, highlighting diverse nutritional, symbolic, social, and historical dimensions (e.g., Counihan and Van Esterik 1997; Dettwyler 1993; Kahn 1986; Mintz 1985, 1996; and Weismantel 1988, to name just a handful of the better known examples). However, I suggest that what is so significant about food— what makes food *food*—is that its salience emanates not only from its material centrality as the nutritional source of life but from how this key facet articulates with densely intersecting lines of causality and meaning in ways that are deeply symbolic, sensuous, psychological, and social.

Food has a powerful capacity to inscribe both identity and difference, as well as to forge or elide salient relationships based on such factors as gender, generation, class, and ethnicity. Food has the uncanny ability to tie the minutiae of everyday experience to broader cultural patterns, hegemonic structures, and political-economic processes. It can structure experience in ways that are logical and outside of logic, in ways that are conscious, canonized, or beyond the realm of conscious awareness. Food is thus a particularly poignant arena for constructing memories characterized by multiple levels and multiple textures (see Sutton 2001 and Counihan 2004). A history and a historical consciousness constructed in this way are neither linear nor shapeless but are constituted as a terrain of practices and meanings that are both affectively ambivalent and socially contested but also lacking some degree of coherence or integration. Thus, the ultimate configuration may be understood less as a coherent, cohesive whole than as a bricolage of often independent but intersecting paths.

The theoretical possibilities of food, which this book aims to further, lie in its ability to distill—but not erase—an array of intersecting but disparate social and individual needs, motivations, emotions, aesthetics, and the like. These dimensions of food make it a particularly promising arena for developing a perspective on memory—and the subjectivities constructed through it—that takes affective ambivalence and internal contradiction as defining features. This argument is developed through a varied and richly ethnographic account of the social, material, and symbolic contours of Samburu eating, today and in their transformations over the past seventy years, taking food as a poignant, yet ambivalent, site of social action, historical transformations, and historical consciousness.

Part 1 develops analytical perspectives on both food and memory. Chapter 1 elaborates the complex ethnographic dimensions of Samburu memory and further develops theoretical perspectives on the ambivalent and contradictory aspects of memory. Highlighting the widespread and profound Samburu ambivalence concerning the construction of memory through changes in eating practices, I consider treatments of the concept of memory in anthropology and related fields, with particular attention to a variety of analytical issues that mask the dissonance, ambivalence, and incoherence intrinsic to the fabric of both individual and collective memory.

In chapter 2, I discuss the qualities of food that render it a uniquely complex subject of social analysis, considering the expanded theoretical possibilities of food and its significance as a site for complex, multilayered, and ambivalent memory. Arguing that a full understanding of the power and complexities of food—what makes food *food*—lies in the interplay between varying forms of analysis that are increasingly treated as incompatible, I consider how the growing emphasis on embodiment and "sensuous scholarship" present a promising bridge between varying poles of analysis, but one that requires a deliberate break with Western constructions of food and the body.

Part 2 focuses on the ways in which the Samburu social universe is constituted through food. Chapters 3 and 4 are primarily ethnographic, aimed at detailing the social and cultural complexities of Samburu eating. Chapter 3 centers on the ways Samburu social relationships and forms of moral personhood are constituted through food, with particular attention to the constitution of gender and age through eating,

eating avoidance, and food sharing. Chapter 4 focuses more squarely on diet and cuisine, considering what and how Samburu eat and the cultural logic underlying these patterns. Despite the seemingly simple traditional pastoral diet of milk, meat, and blood, there is a surprisingly wide variety of forms through which this pastoral triad can be consumed, and a complex cultural logic governs exceptions to strict adherence to a pastoral diet that are dictated by nutritional deficits of the past and the present.

Chapter 5 examines Samburu food and eating practices as a site of strategic ambiguity and veiled contestation. Arguing that morality is the cornerstone of memory, I focus on the core moral concept of *nkanyit* (a sense of respect) to understand how food provides a lens on the past. Although *nkanyit* implies even-handedness and selflessness, what it actually mandates is maintaining a *plausible façade* of this virtue, enforced by a belief in often fatal curses that are commonly associated with denying a hungry person food. Consequently, the ability to conduct artful duplicity is itself only a thinly veiled social value.

Part 3 focuses on specific foods and practices that saliently detail the significance of eating changes to both Samburu history and memory. Chapter 6 considers how the act of cooking—not a daily necessity in a pastoral diet but increasingly important with the widespread adoption of agricultural products—has become a focal site of tension resulting from transformations in contemporary Samburu life, as formerly discrete age-gender groups are increasingly brought together to eat around a common hearth. Taking cooking as a central arena through which Samburu understand and experience their transformations highlights how mundane, everyday activities may provide lenses for understanding change in ways that neither rely on convenient Euro-American categories, such as modernity or "the global," nor reinforce essentializing views of a primitive Other.

In chapter 7, I return to questions of history and memory by employing a particular beverage—tea—as a lens to explore twentieth-century Samburu history. The enthusiastic Samburu adoption of tea as part of self-defined traditional culture is in some ways surprising, both because it contrasts with the Samburu tendency to devalue new foods and because "drug foods" such as tea are viewed in classic anthropological analyses as emblematic of the types of global transformations against which Samburu construct this "traditional culture." Tracing historical transformations in practices and meanings associated with tea use, I consider the processes underlying its acceptance and their importance in explicating broader processes through which Samburu have negotiated contexts of change.

Chapter 8 considers alcohol as a potently ambivalent signifier that stands for and constructs a dense and conflicting array of strands in new forms of Samburu moral—and immoral—personhood for both elders and women. Recreational drinking emerged only in the 1950s, with the colonial introduction of commercial beer halls, and intensified as home brewing became a surreptitious cottage industry in which Samburu women brew for sale to elders, including their own husbands. In material terms, women gain access to a predominantly male resource—cash—while men are able to self-provision by purchasing calorically rich brews. Yet beyond these material dimensions, alcohol's capacity to transform both actual and socially constructed expectations of behavior has led to new forms of masculine and feminine personhood characterized by great moral ambiguity and viewed by Samburu with marked ambivalence.

Chapter 9 considers how particularly Samburu configurations of the use and meaning of money, and the formal properties of money, have catalyzed the reworking of food-centered social, material, and symbolic relations concerning commensality, age, and, in particular, gender. How food is exchanged depends to a great extent on the degree to which particular forms of eating are viewed as being commodified. Here the meaning of commodification is defined less by abstract Western understandings of money than by how money engages with practical and symbolic aspects of pastoral exchange. The politics of food and money have particular significance for gender relations, with money holding both opportunities and losses for women and men by eliding some historically validated behaviors and meanings while reinforcing others.

In my conclusion, I synthesize a variety of issues developed in the preceding chapters, concerning food as a site of complex processes of social transformation and of the intricate, ambivalent, and dissonant forms of historical consciousness accompanying such transformations. In doing so, the conclusion aims to develop key theoretical issues concerning food and memory, as well as to highlight the ethnographic significance of what they mean for varying Samburu living in contexts of change.

Currently about 150,000 Samburu inhabit the semiarid lands of north central Kenya. Most live in Samburu District, though smaller numbers live in neighboring Laikipia District to the south, and Marsabit District to the northeast. Culturally they are closely related to the better-known Maasai, speaking a mutually intelligible dialect of Maa. Historically the Samburu were among the world's wealthiest livestock keepers and survived almost exclusively on the products of their animals (Spencer 1965). There are significant ecological differences in the areas where Samburu live, which affect patterns of pastoralism and responses to change. The most significant distinction is between the lowlands *(lpurkel)* and the highlands *(ldonyo)* of the Leroghi Plateau (Holtzman 2004). The *lpurkel* constitutes the largest portion of Samburu land and is composed of semiarid to arid acacia scrub lying at around 4,000 feet above sea level. There, population density is low and pastoralism tends to be much more nomadic, with towns, trading centers, and schools fewer and farther between. In contrast, the Leroghi Plateau (5,500–8,000 feet) is much cooler and wetter, characterized by open grasslands with substantial forested areas at higher altitudes. Population densities are much higher, and today human migratory movements have largely ceased, though seasonal transhumance with the herds remains the norm. On Leroghi, the ideologies and practices of Development have been embraced more fully, though this varies widely by community, age, education, gender, and individual.

The aspect of Samburu life that has received the most attention is the age-gender system, of which the most striking feature is the institution of murranhood. Youths are initiated into manhood through circumcision and associated rituals between the ages of fifteen and twenty, and spend the next ten to fifteen years as murran, or bachelor-warriors. Murran are visually distinctive, allowing their hair to grow into long braids *(lmasi)*, which are decorated with red ochre. They are primarily responsible for the most difficult and dangerous jobs in Samburu life, such as long-distance herding and warfare, but also are considered the most glamorous sector of Samburu society, cultivating both physical beauty and ability in singing and dancing. Murran are expected to stay at the fringes of domestic life; the most salient aspect of this is the *lminong* (prohibitions) that forbid them to eat food which has been seen by women. Murran move through life with their age set and typically do not marry until initiations have begun for a new age set. Women do not have formal age sets, though their social status is closely tied to the age of their husbands and children, particularly their sons.

Sustained European contact with the Samburu began in the first decade of the twentieth century, on the heels of indirect contact through the caravan trade and sporadic contact with European explorers. A

FIGURE 3. Cleaning day at a "modern" house. Photo by the author.

permanent administrative presence was established by the British in
the 1920s (Holtzman 1996; Straight 1997a; Fumagalli 1977). Colonial political-economic interests in the district were much less significant than in other parts of Kenya, due to the small population and the
low productivity of most Samburu land. Labor flows from the district
were highly restricted, and Samburu purchased few consumer goods.
The export of cattle from the district was important, but maximizing
Samburu beef production was neither a central concern of the colonial
state nor a central facet of local policy toward the Samburu. In the
absence of clear and compelling political-economic objectives, policy
frequently took on the idiom of a moral project but without clear moral
objectives. Apart from initial concern with establishing security in the
district—particularly in regard to the murran—British administrators foresaw the possibility of improving the quality of life through
Western-style clothing, housing, health, hygiene, and education. At the
same time, there was a perception that, despite various problems, the
Samburu were basically a good, if backward, tribe. The district commissioner, for instance, noted in 1928 that while Samburu were "on
the whole a law abiding and inoffensive tribe," he had met only two

"who I should call truly civilized. . . . They are a released murderer and a prostitute" (Colony and Protectorate of Kenya 1928). In pushing change, the colonial authorities were ever concerned that their actions not serve to "change an honourable tribe into a dishonourable one." For their part, Samburu showed little enthusiasm for most forms of change that colonialism had to offer and sought to evade or oppose those they found most directly threatening. Generally convinced of the superiority of their way of life over the alternatives offered by colonialism, they vigorously opposed such impositions as forced culling and grazing control.

Kenyan independence changed Samburu life in many ways. While Samburu welcomed such changes as the end of grazing control, they were not highly politicized in regard to the independence movement, and indeed Samburu proxies enthusiastically served the colonial government in killing Kikuyu during the Mau Mau Emergency (Colony and Protectorate of Kenya 1952; Chenevix-Trench 1993). Samburu consequently did not widely view the transition in terms of their own independence, but more in terms of a change in the color of a government imposed upon them from the outside. This change was not unambiguously positive. While resentful of the British administration in many ways, Samburu tended to view it as honest and well organized, whereas the independent government was plagued by corruption and perceived hostility toward the Samburu, who had fought against them during Mau Mau. Moreover, independence largely coincided with major shifts in the pastoral economy, foretelling the poverty that would ensue. The early independence period was marked by a major drought, as well as attacks by heavily armed Somalis in the Shifta War and by Turkana Ngoroko bandits, leading to a downward trend in the pastoral economy.

Thus, whereas colonialism was characterized by unprecedented pastoral wealth, the independence period has seen a steady decline in the livestock economy. During the colonial period, Samburu averaged around seven cows per capita, but the subsequent combination of drought, livestock disease, and a steady rise in human population has now reduced that to around two cattle per capita. Not only is this far fewer livestock than are needed for pastoral subsistence, but they are not distributed evenly among Samburu, such that large numbers of Samburu are now entirely or nearly stockless. This has resulted in a diversification of economic activity, including widespread migratory wage labor by young men (Holtzman 2003a), brewing by many women (Holtzman 2001), and small-scale agriculture by Samburu living in areas sufficiently watered to make these often futile attempts at cultivation at least plausible (Holtzman 1997; Lesorogol 2003). These transformations have created not only conditions of scarcity but major shifts in diet and in the broad social and cultural dynamic surrounding food. It has become increasingly difficult to survive on a diet composed largely of the pastoral triad of milk, meat, and blood; instead, Samburu have been forced to rely more and more on purchased foods, such as maize meal. This has not simply resulted in eating different foods, valued by Samburu in differing ways, but has altered the dynamic of acquisition and preparation, and most significantly the social relations enacted, created, and reinforced through food. This book explores the implications of these developments, framed by their material conditions and the extent to which they are situated within Samburu cultural configurations surrounding food and the profound historical consciousness that ambivalently informs Samburu readings of changes in food.

This book is based on several periods of fieldwork, including research undertaken over the course of about two and a half years in 1992–94, an additional year in 2001–2, and subsequent stints of summer research. Because of the significant differences among Samburu, even those living in nearly adjacent areas, I have employed a multisited approach to fieldwork, working in both highland and lowland primary field sites, and spending additional time in a number of secondary locations. In this research I have used a range of methods and analysis that is perhaps more broad than those now employed by most anthropologists in a field that is not only increasingly specialized but increasingly polarized between scientific approaches and interpretive, postmodernist perspectives. In addition to long-term participant observation, I have relied heavily on qualitative interview methods, oral history, and archival research. At the same time, I have found it essential when studying economic—and, indeed, nutritional issues—to incorporate more overtly empirical methods, ranging from quantitative socioeconomic and demographic data to biometric measurements used to assess the effects of contemporary transformations in food on a range of differing Samburu.

In considering the style and substance of the book, I am reminded of a recent conversation with a journal editor who, in persuading me to remove an epigraph, told me that, unfortunately, there are some anthropologists today who will refuse to read an article if it contains an epigraph, while there are others who will refuse if it contains a number. If this book leans more heavily towards an epigraph-friendly sensibility, there is also to be found the occasional number, along with a range of conclusions and understandings concerning the material dimensions of contemporary Samburu life that could not be reached with confidence in the absence of quantitative data drawn from study of a large number of diverse Samburu. I take what I hope is a more inclusive approach, not only because I feel that the polarization of the field is counterproductive in general, but because, as I will argue in the course of the chapters that follow, it is impossible to adequately account for the power of food without understanding the complex interplay between varying and sometimes countervailing strands of causality and meaning, which run the gamut from abstract symbolism to the vulgarly material. If we may appreciate the artful play of signs in Samburu cultural understandings of the changing configurations of eating, we must not lose sight of the fact that it is also deep play, as actors struggle to remake integral social relationships and secure vital resources—and the ultimate result of these struggles may be how much porridge is in someone's bowl, or how thick the fat is on the back of their arm.

PART ONE

Orientations

CHAPTER I

Memory, Ambivalence, and Food

ONE MAN, TWO HISTORIES OF FOOD

"Would you like to see a film of the time when you Kimaniki were murran?" I asked Lekutaas, our colorful next-door neighbor in Loltulelei. A member of the Kimaniki age set, who were murran from 1948 to 1960, hundreds of his age mates were captured on film in 1951 in the John Ford classic *Mogambo*. Ford was purportedly lured to Samburu District by the blustering district commissioner Terence Gavaghan, with the promise of "a thousand pig-tailed, ochre-smeared, spear-toting moran as extras" and all the charging rhinos and elephants he cared to film. Gavaghan delivered, while also providing hospitality to stars Clark Gable, Grace Kelly, and (especially, according to both Chenevix-Trench [1964] and Gavaghan's [1999] memoirs) Ava Gardner. Three hundred or so murran were brought down to a spot near what is now Samburu Game Reserve, feted in slaughtered oxen, and paid handsomely in cloth and other goods. The result was a rather corny five-minute sequence in which Clark Gable's safari party—he was hired by Grace Kelly's (subsequently cuckolded) anthropologist husband to lead him to gorillas—decides to stop their riverine odyssey to see the Samburu. The Gable party alight from their dugout canoes and walk through an eerily empty village toward the house of the district commissioner. Samburu warriors begin appearing menacingly from behind the odd conical huts of which the village is composed (bearing no resemblance to actual Samburu houses), and the party hurries into the commissioner's house to find him in bed dying of malaria. The commissioner explains that the Samburu rebelled after he caught them poaching ivory. No hope for him, he explains, but please help get his two African policemen out—they are "good boys." Gable's party exits between masses of angry Samburu, spears poised to strike, and jump into their canoes just in time to safely avoid a small group that, without explanation, suddenly decides to run after them and hurl some spears.

I discovered this classic but hokey film sometime after my doctoral fieldwork, and when I prepared to return in 2001 I copied the Samburu sequence onto my laptop to show to interested informants. Some had actually been in the filmed group; all were amused by oddities in the film—the strange houses, the fact that though threatening with their spears, the murran are not actually holding them in a way that would allow them to be thrown. Among members of the Kimaniki age set in particular, there was considerable interest in seeing themselves during their glory days as murran. When I told Lekutaas that he was going to see his age set when they were young, he was excited and replied in his characteristic half-joking manner, "Now we will see some real murran," grunting, flexing his muscles, and practically strutting about. "These ones who ate meat [grunting again]—not like these ones these days who eat . . . I don't know what." After he watched the film clip on the laptop, I was curious if he noticed changes in dress, ornaments, and the like. When I asked him to compare the murran in the film with those of today, he had more on his mind than such superficial differences. "Are those murran different?" I asked. "Very different," he replied. "Those ones [in the film] were fools. They wouldn't even eat things at home."

In this short exchange, Lekutaas captured the essence of the two master narratives employed by Samburu to discuss their history through food. In the first instance, murran of today—and by extension all Samburu—were seen to be essentially degraded from their former glory. Where once they ate meat, garnishing not only physical strength but self-discipline and self-restraint, today they eat peculiar, unimaginable things—characterized, as Lekutaas's words trailed off in befuddled disbelief, simply as "I don't know what". Yet within minutes Lekutaas transposed his condemnation of the current, degraded murran eating practices to its mirror image: the murran of his time clung foolishly to cultural beliefs that the Enlightened life of today shows to have no practical basis.

FIGURE 4. Lekutaas with the author. Photo by Sammy Letoole.

That Lekutaas encompassed both sides of this reality is not as surprising as it might first appear. While on the surface he appears to
be, like many of his age mates, highly oriented toward what Samburu
regard as "traditional" culture—always seen wearing tartan blankets,
focused on his herd, prominent at local meetings and ceremonies but
rarely venturing to town—at the same time his extended experience
outside the district in the King's African Rifles is central to his self-
construction of a worldly and forward-looking persona. In the 1950s
he spent two years in the jungles of Malaysia, fighting communist
insurgents but also "learning about white things." Thus, while he is
very knowledgeable about Samburu traditions, he is often more enthusiastic about discussing World War II based on films he saw while in
the service, contemplating the fate of Hitler, and sometimes imitating
the goose-stepping Nazi troops.

Yet these seeming contradictions vis-à-vis food are not unique to
Lekutaas's mildly eccentric persona but are, indeed, characteristic of
how Samburu live and remember through food. For if eating practices
remain central to self-definitions rooted in the superiority of a pastoral
way of life, they also form the basis for a self-critique rooted in the

impracticality of "traditional" cultural practices. There is little sound basis for the long-standing stereotype of pastoralists as "naturally conservative" and resistant to change (e.g., Schneider 1959), but Samburu, like many other African pastoralists, have been historically quite circumspect in embracing forms of development that they view as undermining core cultural values and the economic basis of their existence. Thus, while there is no question that a host of significant processes of transformation have been ongoing since the earliest days of colonialism, Samburu have accepted change only piecemeal and on their own terms, fusing it to their own notions of tradition, in contrast to "government" (that is, European) ways. However, severe declines in the livestock economy over the past few decades have changed these views. They have left many Samburu destitute and struggling to find alternatives, open to embracing the notion that current patterns of widespread poverty are empirical proof that perhaps they had been wrong about Development all along.

THE GASTRONOMICAL MASTER NARRATIVES OF SAMBURU HISTORY

Comments such as Lekutaas's criticism of traditional eating are in many ways a contemporary and culturally specific instantiation of long-standing discourses and debates. How pastoralists eat has long been a source of interest and unease to observers in East Africa and elsewhere, as well as a source of self-definition for pastoralists, both in its own right and in contrast to these external discourses. Pastoralism, as practice and diet, has long been marked as a problematic aspect of the lives of East African pastoralists. From quite early in the colonial period, travelers, missionaries, and administrators drew stark boundaries based on the economic practices of pastoralism and agriculture, and the resulting dietary practices. Thus, for example, Karl Peters emphasizes the distinctive psychological makeup of pastoral peoples.

> The continual flesh diet on which they live has physiologically increased their natural savageness, and the brutalising of the feelings that must ensue with people who are in the habit of slaughtering and devouring, in a cold-blooded manner, the domestic animal they themselves have reared, appears here in a very decided manner. . . . This law has always explained why the herdsmen of the nomadic races have constantly furnished the most savage phenomena in the world's history, as we have seen them embodied in Europe, in personages like Jhengis Khan and Attilla. In addition to this psychological law comes the fact, that such races are prevented

by the peculiarity of their employment, from establishing themselves anywhere permanently. The possession of great herds necessitates a continual
change of domicile. While the agriculturalist is obliged to remain on his
soil, to which his heart becomes attached, the nomad is indifferent to the
charms of owning a home. (Peters 1891, 224–25)

This distinction was not merely economic but was layered with connotations that were ethnic, racial, and evolutionary as well. Pastoral peoples
were viewed as more savage and more conservative than agricultural ones,
yet they were often accorded a racial status more akin to European races.
Indeed, despite their greater savagery, they were by and large viewed as
savages of a decidedly noble variety. As Peters continues:

> But if all the conditions are present that tend to bring to full development
> the wild and brutal qualities of the man, on the other hand, among the
> Massais there may be recognized the ennobling influence which is pro-
> duced in every people by the inherited consciousness of rule. Accustomed
> to see all around them tremble at the name of Massai, the warriors of the
> race have acquired a natural pride, which cannot be designated otherwise
> than as aristocratic. From the first the Massais assumed towards me the
> deportment of young, haughty noblemen. (225)

Within the framework of colonialism, this opposition of cultiva-
tor and pastoralist provided a crucial distinction in understanding
processes of change. While agriculturalists have been seen as quite
ready to engage with Progress—through education, missionization,
and the like—pastoralists are seen as uninterested, even disdainful
of change, content in the nobility of their traditional ways. In this
sense, they were seen as the inevitable victims of progress, swept away
in the maelstrom of change—change that was most prominently seen
as the spread of cultivation to their pastoral lands. Take, for example,
H.H. Johnston, writing about the closely related Maasai in 1886:
"They must turn their spears into spades and their swords into reap-
ing hooks—or starve. . . . Soon there will be no cattle left to raid and
the Masai will range the wide deserted plains in all their splendid,
insolent bravery and die of inanation. The inhabitants of the walled
cities or lofty hills will dwell secure from attack, and the wretched
remnants of vanquished tribes still lingering in unprotected haunts
will not be worth robbing. Then the proud Masai must turn to and
wring from the soil the sustenance which only comes as the reward of
honest labor" (Johnston 1886, 406–7).

Like many discourses and images of East African pastoralists, these
are uncommonly resilient, coming forth into the twenty-first century,

seemingly altered little by the intervening 150 years. While in the colonial period authorities throughout East Africa pushed cultivation as a means of bettering pastoral peoples (e.g., Galaty, Aronson, and Salzman 1981; Little 1992; Fratkin 1994), the transition to cultivation continues to be viewed as an inevitable step that will finally be undertaken on the road of reluctant pastoral peoples toward modernity. Indeed, some read cultivation (and eating crops) as having a unique, civilizing influence. Looking at other parts of Africa, Gordon (1992) notes the widespread Namibian belief that to tame a Bushman you simply needed to chain him to a post and force-feed him mielie (maize) meal, the infusion of cultigens presumably transforming his wild nature. Both NGOs and governmental agencies continue to push agriculture as the key to the future of pastoral peoples, bringing the benefits of a more stable and economically viable way of life, as well as successful integration in the economies and polities of East Africa. While we must be cautious of too readily glossing the cultural specificity of what such perspectives mean in particular historical contexts, the kinds of issues to which they become fused and the agendas they support or contradict, their resilience is nonetheless significant.

These discourses form an important backdrop for understanding contemporary Samburu collective memory through the lens of food. They may be read in two different and important ways. These discourses provide an external critique of the cultural and economic forms of East African pastoralists, such as the Samburu, and are an important part of long-standing and ongoing external efforts to modify pastoralist societies. Yet they now have become part and parcel of a Samburu landscape of memory in which food is prominent. In an era of pastoral poverty, it has become increasingly common for Samburu to conceive of their current predicament with a degree (albeit misplaced) of self-blame, alleging that their reticence to embrace Development is at least partially responsible for the struggles they now face. There is thus a growing tendency to intermingle an identity based on the cultural superiority of pastoralism with an identity based on underdevelopment (Gupta 1998; Holtzman 2004), and to ambivalently embrace—sometimes in speech, less often in action—the very economic and cultural alternatives they have struggled against for decades. Consider the comments of Leirana, a junior elder from Lodokejek who has never attended school. His views are by no means atypical, as he compares the Samburu with the Kikuyu, the agricultural group from central Kenya that was affected most profoundly by colonialism, and which in the independent period has been considered the most "developed" Kenyan ethnic group. Scanning the dry grasslands around his home in Lodokejek, Leirana mused on how different things would be if these were Kikuyu lands rather than Samburu: "If this place had been theirs [the Kikuyu's] this land would be filled up with food. But these people here, they only know how to look after the animals."

As Leirana's comments suggest, a notion of Development and Progress informs one major discourse concerning the division of agricultural and pastoral peoples: if Samburu were more Enlightened (or if a more Enlightened group occupied their lands), things might be different—and better. While such discourses are considered with increasing degrees of acceptance by Samburu themselves, not surprisingly, Samburu discourses typically differ. Long-standing cultural values of East African pastoralists—and of Maa speakers such as Samburu and Maasai—construct the opposition between agricultural and pastoral foods as a central feature of their value systems. A reliance on a pastoral diet of meat, milk, and blood, and a general avoidance of cultivated food has long been noted to be of central importance in constructing the identity of Maa-speaking pastoralists (e.g., Galaty 1982). This is summarized neatly in the title of Arhem's (1987) "Meat, Milk and Blood," which emphasizes that while such a diet has never been easy to fully realize, it forms an important means through which Maa speakers construct their identity. Pastoral products are seen as the only proper foods, and the need to consume other foods—be they cultigens or wild foods—is viewed as a consequence of poverty, of having inadequate herds to provide proper food. Beyond these issues of ethnic self-definition, food is profoundly linked to an array of practices and values that are fundamental to pastoral life in areas such as the age-gender system, religious beliefs, and moral forms of sociability.

The centrality of a pastoral diet has been significantly problematized, however, by severe and steady declines in the livestock economy, beginning in the 1960s and accelerating through the present. In tandem with a more than doubling in human population, Samburu livestock holdings have declined from seven cattle per capita in the 1950s (the approximate threshold for a purely pastoral diet) to around two cattle per capita today. Thus, it is only a small, wealthy minority who can rival even the average livestock holdings of the 1950s, while large numbers of Samburu are virtually stockless. The immediate consequence is that Samburu have been forced to rely more and more heavily on nonpastoral foods—particularly maize meal—usually purchased

FIGURE 5. Author's host, Lekeren, with his cattle. Photo by the author.

with cash acquired through livestock sales, remittances from wage labor, or mercantile activities. As is elaborated in detail in the chapters that follow, this has resulted in transformations in practices and values surrounding eating that are generally held to have had negative consequences on social, moral, and physical well-being. Drawing on the contrast between a culturally salient diet of milk, meat, and blood, and the unappetizing, unhealthy, and symbolically empty "gray foods" or "poverty foods" of the present, a seemingly endless litany of complaints target the new ways of eating: These foods have made women promiscuous. Children's stomachs are made "hot," resulting in symptoms reminiscent of ADHD. Too much maize meal gives you liver disease. And most notably, new foods and new patterns of cooking and consumption have made warriors weak and shameless, the most salient expression of a loss of the sense of respect and social distance central to the age-gender system, seen across all social categories.

Two gastronomical master narratives, then, form the scaffolding of Samburu collective memory through food. On the one hand, a transition away from a pastoral diet is a form of Progress, leaving behind antiquated nonrational practices grounded in a cultural love of cattle. On the other hand, an agricultural diet is a form of cultural decay, eroding core aspects of ethnic self-definition and fundamental practices central to a construction of Samburu moral personhood. These two discourses represent what appear to be diametrically opposed models of memory concerning food. Each contains a historical metanarrative that employs the past to speak to present realities. Yet what is most compelling about the relationship of these two discourses is not their opposition but rather their interplay. Indeed, Samburu food-centered collective memory is characterized neither by consistency nor by unambiguous lines of contestation based on age, social status, gender, and the like. Rather, individuals may collage bits and pieces from each to make sense of their lives in ways that can be wildly ambivalent, as Samburu engage in everyday forms of meaning creation concomitant with critical daily struggles to feed themselves.[1]

THE WHAT AND WHY OF MEMORY

Despite the recent surge in interest concerning memory in general and more specifically collective memory, scholars analyze—indeed, even define—*memory* in radically different ways. These differences center around a number of fundamental but often unacknowledged questions, particularly concerning the social life of memory: To what extent can we extrapolate the individual faculty of memory to groups and institutions? How, or to what extent, should we extend the concept of memory beyond those things that are consciously remembered (accurately or inaccurately) to unconscious, perhaps unembodied, residues of the past inscribed in thought, practices, landscapes, and the like? Does the significance of memory lie principally in what it tells us about actual beliefs, relations, and processes of the past, or rather as an ideology that employs an imagined past toward present ends? The problem is not that any of these approaches (or any blend of them) is necessarily better than another, but rather that there is frequently considerable slippage in these terms, such that very different phenomena come to be homonymically labeled "memory," although they are grounded in very different processes, in very different sites of agency, and with very different kinds of social importance. Without greater clarity and specificity regarding the meaning of *memory* and the interrelation of various memory processes, we risk reducing it to little more than an odd-job word.

The notion of *collective memory* stands to gain, in particular, from close reading. The term is somewhat problematic—as Wertsch (2002) argues, "a term in search of a meaning." In many ways it conjures up the kind of anthropomorphic, extrasomatic beast that anthropologists seem determined to purge in attacks on the notion of culture through the 1980s and '90s. The notion of collective memory takes a process (memory) that is a property of the mental and corporeal faculties of humans and other sentient beings, and locates it in an abstracted collective body that does not have (indeed could not have) parallel faculties for storing, recalling, and in particular experiencing memory.[2] In the varying contexts where we extend the concept of memory beyond the sentient being, it is always essentially metaphorical. We say that a spring has "memory" because the process of repeated compression and expansion affects the metal in ways that affect future compressions and expansions. Viewing a computer as an electronic brain leads us to say that before an essay is printed, it is stored in "memory"; in contrast, after printing converts the essay to paper, the shelf upon which it rests is afforded no similar faculty for remembering. Thus—contra Connerton (1989)—societies *do not* remember in a literal sense, and extending "memory" to a social group is arguably just as metaphorical as applying it to other nonsentient entities.

This is not to dispense with the cultural and social—that is, collective—aspects of memory. Individual memory is created and given meaning in the context of a social group, and valuated and mobilized in light of sets of shared meanings (Connerton 1989). Yet even as we embrace the role of the social and cultural in shaping memory, we must adequately differentiate the often very different phenomena we characterize as collective memory. For instance, social practices may foster individual memories that share varying degrees of resemblance to one another (e.g., as elaborated by Connerton and, in a different way, by Bourdieu). Societies (or individuals or factions within societies) may seek to inscribe events or to mark time. They may seek to create events or practices that never existed, or inscribe wholly novel, presentist meanings to ones that did, perhaps at odds with individual memories of those same occurrences. Thus, what we label as "memory" often refers to an array of very different processes—from monumental architecture to the reminiscences evoked by the smell of coffee—that have a totally different dynamic, that we may (or may not) care to understand for very different reasons, and that may or may not significantly overlap with one another. The interrelations among these varying phenomena may be most interesting, yet such interrelations are largely masked by labeling them all under the rubric of *memory,* implying that they are somehow all of a piece within the same phenomenon. Constructing the relationships between these phenomena is, however, the analyst's work; these relationships do not intrinsically inhere in the fact that we may conveniently call all of them memory.

Some of the lack of precision in use of the term *memory* may stem from its ontogeny in contemporary scholarly jargon. The recent scholarly excitement over the study of memory places the concept in juxtaposition (though sometimes without total clarity) with its older, frumpier sibling *history.* Though some (e.g., Samuel 1994; Jordanova 2000) contest and problematize the distinction, *history* is frequently tied to empiricism, objectivity, and, as Hodgkin and Radstone note, "a certain notion of truth (2003, 3)." In contrast, *memory* is associated more closely with poststructuralist approaches to the production of knowledge, concerned with the subjective construction of understandings of the past linked to present issues. To an extent, there is a real difference in the kinds of understanding one aims to produce and the varying sources one may draw on, with history aiming to piece together a more or less accurate record and analysis of the past and memory aiming to view the past through subjective, imperfect, and conflicting lenses rooted in the experiences, understandings, and agendas of the present. Consequently, where history seeks to understand the facts of past processes, memory is less concerned with facts than with what is now made of the past by individuals or social groups. Yet this distinction is far from clear-cut,[3] and the invocation of memory may at times owe less to carefully constructed notions of what memory is than it does to signposting the brand of knowledge production a scholar aims to engage in—that is, one congenial to a postmodernist, literary turn, with a destabilized notion of truth.

Jing (1996) provides a useful distinction between several approaches to social memory, emphasizing differences in the social or political dynamic. First, collective memory (using Connerton [1989] as a central exemplar) concerns how memory is created and inscribed as a shared property of what is construed as a relatively cohesive social group (i.e., "the kind of people anthropologists used to study"), à la Durkheim via Halbwachs (1992). In contrast, official memory concerns how constructions of the past are used to validate the positions of those in power. Indeed, a tremendous amount of what is currently billed as memory studies in anthropology centers on public memory, constructed by political elites for purposes of contesting or establishing the legitimacy of power (e.g., Baker 1990; Deacon 1998; Verdery 1999; Hobsbawn 1983; Lane 1981). Popular memory is the mirror image of official memory, the historical discourses of the downtrodden, the unheard voices of the disenfranchised and oppressed (e.g., Scott 1985; Hofmeyr 1994; Minkley and Rassool 1998; Bozzoli and Nkotsoe 1991). This schema is useful in locating the varying forms of "memory" along lines of power. Where collective memory inheres in groups without reference to power and contestation, official (or public) memory is concerned with understanding how visions of the past are invoked for purposes of domination, while popular memory relates to the disempowered and is frequently linked to their resistance to domination.

Apart from these distinctions, the *kinds* of memories that are deemed worthy of scholarly explication can be problematic. Like most social science categories, the construct of memory is rooted in Western commonsense ideas and colloquial practice, which prefigure the form and content of our analyses. Consequently, there is a distinct if unsurprising tendency for memory studies to focus on the kinds of things that Western "common sense" construes as important forms of memory, most notably traumatic events, experienced collectively and in their individual manifestations. Not unlike psychoanalysis, in which individuals deal with issues from their traumatic past through a process of structured reminiscence, a significant body of memory literature is concerned with understanding processes of collective trauma, most notably the Holocaust (Young 2000; Wood 1999) and apartheid (e.g.,

Botman and Peterson 1996; Antze and Lambek 1996). Such a position seems problematic, since although the extreme and the sensational may form very important forms of memory, they do not broadly characterize memory as such. That is, memory may be a productive means of understanding processes of collective trauma, but collective trauma may be a less useful lens for understanding memory as a general process. In counterpoint, memory is also commonly approached through a lens of nostalgia. This has the advantage of bypassing the extreme in favor of the more mundane aspects of everyday remembering and the phenomenological experience of reminiscence (e.g., Casey 1987). Yet there remains a basic issue of how people remember, particularly since this can differ significantly even among Euro-American groups (Seremetakis 1996).

One further important issue, which bears significantly on memories of the sensorial experience of eating, concerns the contrast between discursive and practical memory (Shaw 2002). Paralleling Giddens's notion of discursive versus practical consciousness,[4] some suggest a broadening of the definition of memory to include practices and meanings that have been historically sedimented, though not necessarily remembered in a conscious, concrete, narrativized sense. For instance, James (1988) contends that Udduk maintained a "cultural archive" from their foraging past—in ritual practice, cosmology, language, and moral knowledge—long after the practice of foraging had disappeared. More recently, Rosalind Shaw (2002) has provocatively examined how the slave trade shaped West African lives over the past several centuries in ways that, if not consciously remembered, resonate in novel expressions up through the present. Thus, contemporary rumors and discourses concerning politicians who commit ritual murders were shaped by colonial human leopard rumors, which in turn were shaped by cultural memories of the slave trade. Although making clear that the subsequent discourses are not simple reformulations of previous ones, she compellingly argues for the value of examining continuities over the long term.

These and related studies are important for a number of reasons in extending our gaze to nonverbal aspects of memory, such as bodily memory, as described in the work of Connerton (1989) and Stoller (1995),[5] or to types of memories that, though unlikely to reach a narrativized collective memory, become part of the taken-for-granted aspects of daily practice (e.g., Comaroff and Comaroff 1991; Cole 2001).[6] Attention to such phenomena, which are not always directly and consciously accessible to our subjects, allows us to consider their engagement with conscious forms of memory—that is, how sublimated or hitherto forgotten phenomena may bear on the affective assessment of the past and the present in ways that may not be straightforward and that our subjects themselves may not even be fully conscious of.

From this discussion I draw two conclusions. From a more scholastic perspective, we need greater specificity in how authors apply memory to an array of very different phenomena, so as to preserve its meaningfulness as an analytical concept. At the same time, however, this multiplicity of uses is to a great extent driven by the very complexity of the phenomena we seek to analyze. That is, there are indeed very different forms of memory, very different types of processes that we tend to gloss (often rightly, sometimes wrongly) under the rubric of memory. How these phenomena interact and whether these different processes coalesce—in experiences of remembering subjects or merely in the minds of analysts—into a complex whole that we may label memory is a point I turn to now.

COHERENCE AND DISSONANCE IN COLLECTIVE MEMORY

Noldirikany, a Samburu woman of about thirty, presented a fairly standard and multifaceted indictment of the present mode of Samburu eating when I interviewed her at her home in the remote lowland site of Ndonyo Nasipa. Citing both physical and social maladies arising from the movement away from a pastoral diet, Noldirikany explained:

> Diseases used to be rare when people didn't have food from the shops. Now diseases have increased. Samburu did not have a lot of killer diseases when these foods were not in use, these foods that are killing the Samburu. The old foods did not have diseases. . . . Milk has no disease, and even wild fruits cannot bring disease. So we think, and we conclude, that the old foods suit people's health. . . . [Also] Samburu no longer love each other, and they used to love each other very much. When a person had a problem, people solved that problem together out of love. When you were sick, or had a certain problem, or if you were starving—but now Samburu no longer love each other very much. . . . That's what we see these foods are bringing to Samburu nowadays.

This indictment is consistent with images of a pastoral good life most Samburu readily evoke, as is her assessment of the toll exacted by changes in eating on Samburu physical and social well-being. Food changes are at the core of patterns of decay that have resulted in a

diminishment in everything from physical stature to moral personhood, leading to increased susceptibility to disease and degraded patterns of commensality. Yet just moments later she added:

> There is a lot of food today, and that is better. Because people no longer
> need to go to the bush to look for fruits from trees. People no longer have
> to scatter in different directions, and people are no longer dying of hun-
> ger. Like when times would get hard and a drought finishes the cattle, the
> government now takes care of people and gives them relief food. People
> have been spared, they no longer die of hunger. And it is easy to get maize
> meal these days, you don't have to struggle a lot to get it. It's easy to get
> it from a shop when you've sold your goat. Nowadays it is so easy to buy
> food from a shop.

In a somewhat puzzling way, then, in Noldirikany's view there is
much to redeem those same "gray foods" that she had referenced but
moments earlier as "these foods that are killing the Samburu." However odd this juxtaposition, it is broadly typical. The value Samburu see
in these foods goes beyond the simple fact that they save lives during
famines, though that is far from trivial. In her account, like many others, there is intertwined in these discourses a notion of lazy repose—in
an odd and ambivalent way, a kind of good life in which one struggles
far less for the now seemingly boundless food, even if this food is virtually empty of nutritional content and cultural meaning. In essence,
there are several stories that Noldirikany has to tell here; each may
separately make sense vis-à-vis her lived experience but fail to mesh
cleanly with the premises and valuations of the other.

As this chapter concludes, and through the remainder of the book,
I will attend to the complexities of change that make these issues profoundly ambivalent, creating dissonance in regard to collective memory. Ambivalence and dissonance have not figured prominently in
memory studies in anthropology and related fields. In the infrequent
instances where they are noted, they are not engaged with deeply as
fundamental to the fabric and texture of memory (e.g., Jackson 1995;
Ong 2003; Ganguly 2001), though some recent studies of post-Soviet
states are a notable exception in their attention to the ambivalence
and contradictions in identity that have frequently characterized
this transition (e.g., Chatwin 1997; Berdahl 1999; Berdahl, Bunzl,
and Lampland 2000). Elsewhere, Smith's (2004) recent analysis of
the contradictory narratives of former colonists in Algeria is a theo-
retically productive attempt to engage with ambivalence as a fundamental characteristic of memory, arguing that collective memory is

frequently heteroglossic, as individuals retain multiple and often conflicting viewpoints concerning the events that they have experienced and now remember.

Smith's approach fits well with Samburu food-centered memory, in that the varying strands of remembrance similarly form a heteroglossic memory invested with more ambivalence and less coherence than typically characterizes accounts of change. Such heteroglossic memory is constituted less by incoherence in the Derridean sense of endless seemingly random possibility, and more by a concern for thickness in a Geertzian sense, of richly accounting for the varying, and sometimes countervailing, strands of causality and meaning that structure sociocultural life at particular times and through time—of, in Sherry Ortner's terms, "producing understanding through richness, texture and detail rather than through parsimony, refinement . . . and elegance" (1995, 174) . Such a history is neither linear nor shapeless but is constituted as a terrain of practices and meanings that are both affectively ambivalent and socially contested but also lacking some degree of coherence or integration, in which the ultimate configuration may be more bricolage of independent but intersecting paths than a design ultimately determined by some underlying master cause or meaning.

Needless to say, some argument concerning coherence is essential in any analysis, lest it become *in*coherent. The problem, however, comes from the fuzziness of the lines drawn between analytical coherence—as authors seek to distill some salient meaning from the messiness of the lives of their subjects—and empirical coherence, in which the particular subject or topic upon which the analyst focuses is held to be relatively devoid of that messiness. Thus analytical coherence may be seen as a necessity (dubious or otherwise) in the observer's process of constructing a comprehensible account, while empirical coherence is a *possibility* that may (or may not) be present in varying degrees. For a variety of reasons, the lines between these are often less than sharply drawn. The danger in this is not only ethnography that risks disservice to our subjects, but theories that by their structure imply an overly coherent view of the world, thus relegating messiness to noise outside or tangential to a coherent model, rather than as a dimension of social life fundamental to the model itself.

Factors related both to styles of presentation and analysis and to theoretical perspectives that lean toward worldviews of empirical coherence play a role in overly coherent renderings of ethnography and history. A key influence is the effect of narrative structure on our accounts. That is, a history is always a history *of* something and that *of* in essence prefigures the content and structure of the account. In another way, a *history* is a kind of *story,* with a beginning, middle, and end and with key characters, actors, processes that are the engine that drives the plot. At any given moment, many different things are going on. To take a mundane and immediate example, I am now typing at the computer, while I am thinking, while I am drinking a cold soda, while I am wearing pants and a shirt and my semidress shoes, while I occasionally click on Yahoo News to see what's going on in the world, while I hear footsteps in the office hallway, while I am watching the clock, thinking that I will walk home in about an hour and wondering how cold it is and how dark it will be. Asked what I'm doing, now or later, I would probably give the account of my behavior that would most readily validate my time—working on a book manuscript—but I am doing a lot of other things that could just as easily form a singular account of my behavior. A soft drink manufacturer might see the real story in the large number of diet soda cans ferreted in various places around my office. An environmentalist, a transportation specialist, or a physical fitness expert might be more fascinated by my meditations on whether I will walk home, though not for the same reasons. Odd, seemingly random turns can change the whole course of events and abruptly refocus what is important—perhaps a major news event as, in procrastination, I click on Yahoo, or perhaps an accident, as I spill my soda on an embarrassing part of my trousers moments before the dean of the college passes my office. The passage of one, or five or thirty or a hundred years would doubtless cast today's afternoon of writing in a very different light.

In a similar vein, author Terry Pratchett muses:

> Suppose an emperor was persuaded to wear a new suit of clothes so fine that, to the common eye, the clothes weren't there. And suppose a boy pointed out this fact in a loud, clear voice. . . .
>
> Then you have The Story Of The Emperor Who Had No Clothes.
>
> But if you knew a bit more, it would be The Story Of The Boy Who Got a Well-Deserved Thrashing From His Father For Being Rude To Royalty, And Was Locked Up.
>
> Or the Story of the Whole Crowd That Was Rounded Up By The Guards And Told "This Didn't Happen, Okay? Does Anyone Want To Argue?"
>
> Or it could be a story of how a whole kingdom suddenly saw the benefits of the new "clothes" and developed an enthusiasm for healthy sports in a lively and refreshing atmosphere that gets many new adherents every year, which led to a recession caused by the collapse of the conventional clothing industry.

It could even be a story about The Great Pneumonia Epidemic of '09.
It all depends on how much you know. (Pratchett 2001, 3)

The point here is that there is a seemingly infinite number of ways
to describe the events of a particular moment and an equally infinite
number of ways to interpret, structure, and characterize events after
the fact. This is as true of anthropologists and historians as it is of
our subjects. Indeed, a frequent critique of "traditional" anthropology in the 1980s was the extent to which a scientific, realist writing style influenced the kinds of knowledge produced (Stoller 1989;
Marcus and Cushman 1982). While many of what were viewed as the
most problematic issues in anthropological writing have now been to
a great extent purged—or at least apologetically deemphasized in contemporary work—the absence of the ethnographer from the text, the
portrayal of anthropologists' subjects as nameless and characterless,
an emphasis on generalizing towards norms, writing in the "ethnographic present"—their replacement with other conventions does not
vitiate the extent to which our narrative structure influences the meaning of the text. In a historical analysis, how we make interpretations,
how we organize events, and how we select what persons and events
to include and exclude remain dependent to a disproportionate degree
on a conventional narrative structure that is not wholly dissimilar to
conventional literary forms. Most typically this is organized around a
linear progression of time covering a duration that is within established
conventions (e.g., the interwar years in Germany; the colonial period in
eastern Africa; the Renaissance) and is neither so lengthy as to include
material irrelevant to the thesis nor so short as to not allow sufficient
action to take place. There are main characters (individuals or groups)
and a main plot informed both by events and by a thesis grounded in
theoretical or empirical concerns of the discipline.

My aim here is not to erase these conventions; indeed, I will make no
heroic efforts to write outside of them. Just as Mueggler (2001) justifies his reliance on conventional Western chronological sequencing as a
clearer mode of explicating an alternative model of Yi temporality (see
Pandolfo 1997), what is more significant than uprooting these conventions (which inevitably gives rise to other conventions) is to recognize
them and their influence on the content of our analysis. I am, consequently, most concerned with the difficulties a conventional narrative
structure poses in recognizing and taking seriously an array of differing strands of causation and meaning, which may or may not bear a

necessary relationship to the central orientation of the text. Thus it is not simply a matter of recognizing that one's main analytical strand is composed of different strands, but that the ultimate focus of one's project may be composed of quite disparate processes, some of which do and some of which don't have a clear, organic relationship to one another except in the sense that they converge on the phenomena that one, as the observer, has found it worthwhile to explicate.

The effects of narrative structure, rather than being minimized, are frequently exacerbated by theory in anthropological writing. Most significant in this regard is anthropologists' tendency sometimes to overly conform their data to the theoretical interests of a discipline at a particular time. This problem is well known historically in anthropology—in any first-year graduate theory course, a student will learn of the circularity of structural functionalism, where whatever the processual and political complexities of a particular society, inevitably these serve to preserve and reinforce the social structure. Yet this tendency has not disappeared in contemporary ethnography, as I will highlight through two examples that are notable not only for the lucidity of their critiques of anthropological treatments of particular concepts, but for the system of knowledge production they see as responsible for the problematic analyses.

The first of these centers on critiques of the concept of resistance in the mid-1990s and related critiques undertaken by Ortner (1995) and Brown (1996). While each is congenial to the appropriate use of "resistance," they share a concern about the flattening of complex ethnographic processes that occurs in the application of the concept. Ortner attributes this not simply to ethnographic failure but to "ethnographic refusal," in which insufficient attention is paid to the social complexities that constitute the context in which resistance to domination is seen to occur, as well as the affective and motivational complexities in those agents purported to be engaging in resistance. Similarly, in the thoughtful essay "Resisting the Rhetoric of Resistance," Michael Brown takes issue with the overemphasis on issues of power found in anthropological analysis. Drawing on his own case study of shamans and Peruvian guerillas, he acknowledges that, although the case may to some extent be understood through the then trendy notion of resistance, this approach would fail to "fully address or comprehend the specificity of Ashinanka dreams of world transformation or the internal struggles that these touched off within Ashinanka society itself" (1996, 731). Brown concludes that notions of power have assumed such centrality in social analysis that they risk becoming not only reductionist but circular and meaningless—in Sahlins's (1993) words, "a new functionalism."

In a more recent example, Englund and Leach (2000) make a similar, and equally strident, critique of anthropological uses of the concept of *modernity*. They suggest that modernity has become a powerful metanarrative that prefigures anthropological understandings of contexts of social change. Drawing on examples from New Guinea and Malawi, they argue that notions of modernity employed in anthropological analysis frequently mask very different sets of meanings that would otherwise emerge from detailed ethnographic analysis. As with Brown's analysis of resistance, what is most troubling to Englund and Leach is not that their case studies *don't fit* with a concern with modernity but rather that they can *be fit*. They warn of a preexisting metanarrative becoming a convenient device for structuring anthropological analysis, made all the more insidious by a failure to make this orienting principle transparent in the organization of the analysis. Thus, although it is frequently worthwhile to examine modernity (or "resistance," or "social solidarity") as a transcultural phenomenon— shared concepts are an intrinsic part of the comparative project of anthropology—it becomes problematic when the concept prefigures the forms of ethnographic understanding rather than the ethnography informing our understanding of the concepts.

These two examples highlight a significant means through which excessive coherence can enter anthropological analyses of memory, and other topics. In essence, they suggest, there is a tendency for concepts to drive analysis, rather than concepts being treated merely as potential tools for ordering data that ultimately may or may not correspond to ethnographic realities.

ACCOUNTING FOR TASTE: COHERENCE AND DISSONANCE IN THE HABITUS

In many ways, theories that posit coherence are the least troubling, since coherence is a transparent component of the model. In respect to memory, the most prominent example is Bourdieu's notion of the set of internalized bodily practices that he labels "the habitus," and in a similar vein Connerton's (1989) approach to bodily memory. Though dealing with different foci, each posits a significant degree of consonance between those aspects of memory that can be cognitively understood or verbally narrativized and those aspects of memory that are rooted in unreflected-upon bodily practices or dispositions.

The notion of the habitus is central to Bourdieu's attempt to develop a theory of practice and of social reproduction that moves beyond mentalistic rules for structuring behavior while also having important implications for memory. The habitus is a set of relatively durable dispositions created out of the social conditions of a subject's upbringing and which, conversely, leads to practices that reproduce those same conditions. Your gait, your bearing, your tastes, and subtle aspects of language are embedded in the habitus, reflecting and reproducing aspects of the social environment. This has direct implications for the study of memory, for it allows us to look for memory in embodied practices that may or may not be clearly reflected in conscious memory (e.g., Stoller 1989; Bahloul 1996).

Two of the best recent works on memory in anthropology—Jennifer Cole's *Forget Colonialism?* and Eric Mueggler's *The Age of Wild Ghosts*—illustrate the value of a focus on these less obvious, unnarrativized aspects of memory making, while treading close to oversynthesizing these complexities into an analytically prefigured conception of what memories mean. It should be noted that neither author explicitly makes heavy use of Bourdieu, though the assumptions—and thus the concerns—are largely of a piece. Cole sets the stage for her study by explaining the contradictions and difficulties she faced in her first efforts to study memories of colonialism among Betsimakara inhabitants of Ambodiharina, Madagascar. Although she began her fieldwork convinced of the centrality of the colonial experience to contemporary Malagasy life, she was quickly struck by the extent to which Ambodiharina seemed less a dynamically constituted site of complex historical and political economic forces than the stereotypical "traditional" village of classic anthropology. As she writes:

> During my first few months of fieldwork, however, my contemporary anthropological preconceptions seemed distressingly at odds with the situation I encountered. . . . What I found when I first arrived in Ambodiharina was a world where people's relationships to one another were constituted through an elaborate moral economy of cattle sacrifice.
> It was also a world that—in its tone and tenor, its concerns with the ancestors, its enthusiasm for cattle sacrifice and its agricultural mode of subsistence—evoked classic anthropological accounts of African societies from the 1930s and 1940s. It was a world that Meyer Fortes (1945) and Evans Pritchard (1956) might well have invented for an essay exam for Oxbridge undergraduates.

Cole's response to this, however, was to delve more deeply into how memory is constructed. Broadening the scope of her analysis, she argues that colonial memory may be found less in neatly constructed narratives of the experience of colonialism than in a host of historically sedimented practices, ideas, and institutions that shape the contours of daily life—whether or not Betsimakara think of them through a lens of colonialism in everyday practice.

Mueggler's study of memory among the Yi ethnic minority in China shares with Cole an emphasis on exploring memory through its less obvious, visible, conscious forms. Mueggler focuses directly on the ways broader political economic forces have gained meaning through their insinuation in the intimacies of everyday experience, such as birth, mortuary rites, and spatial configurations. Through these practices, Yi form alternative visions of their experience over the turbulent decades encompassing the radical transformations of the Cultural Revolution, as well as their collective identity vis-à-vis the Chinese state. As Mueggler eloquently outlines his project:

> The ritual techniques examined here imagine such a state: a constitutive presence at the center of the social world with an intimate relation to loss. In these rites, the state is found to be a strange image, abstract and uncanny, divided from this world as shade is from sunlight, as insubstantial as it is omnipresent. . . . The body of the nation can be mapped onto individual bodies, the digestive flow of its rivers onto corporeal digestive tracts. Ritual techniques for healing find the body and the national landscape to coexist as a single, extended "collective unity of habitations." To heal physical or psychic pain is to reorder this unity. It is to release the knots or reversals in the body's flows; it is to locate a habitable place in a morally ordered national landscape and to guide violence and loss back toward their origins at the rivers' ends. (Mueggler 2001, 6–7)

There is much to commend in both these works, though also room for circumspection. The insights of Cole and Mueggler in illuminating the uncanny links between both everyday and extraordinary practices and forms of memory to which they do not have an obvious relationship are important in complexifying approaches to understanding processes of memory-making. Conversely, however, these insights ironically run the risk of flattening and oversimplifying those memories. That is, through a focus on meanings of memory that are simultaneously less transparent and more consonant with one's thesis, one may neglect both the highly potent significance of the more obvious aspects of these memories and practices (which may not be consonant with one's thesis), as well as other meanings that suffer from being less obvious and not resonating with one's thesis. With Cole, the conundrum lies in the fact that colonialism *appears* to a great extent to be forgotten. While she is convincing in demonstrating the ways in which it remains salient, what might be more contentious is how these colonial memories she has excavated might be ordered in relative significance to other kinds of meanings Betsimarkara derive from these same processes. In Mueggler's case, one might take the example of Yi exorcisms, which he potently links to salient tensions with the Chinese state. Yet it is also consistent with Mueggler's richly textured approach to recognize that not only are there myriad connections, meanings, and significances to which such exorcisms are also related but these dense, complex—and not necessarily logical, conscious, or straightforward—connections are central to the memory's power. Ironically, it is precisely the complexity that gives power to memory which is at risk when the anthropologist proposes that a set of memories may ultimately be understood analytically as about a particular issue or set of closely related issues.

Bourdieu's habitus is a means for considering why these seemingly disparate meanings might coalesce into a more coherent piece, but it also compounds the issues at hand. The habitus has obvious applicability to Samburu in providing a means through which the bodily practice of eating may become a salient site for particularly compelling forms of memory. One might suppose, for instance, that the powerful positive valuation Samburu attribute to a pastoral diet is grounded in a set of sedimented dispositions rooted in a lifestyle centered on pastoralism. To a degree this is axiomatic—and indeed, as I will explore in greater detail in chapters 4 and 5, Samburu experience different foods with varying sets of nonetheless quite powerful emotions. Yet if this may, then, serve to account for the coherence between Samburu social values or practices and bodily preferences for a pastoral diet, it does little to account for the dissonances, ambivalences, and inconsistencies in Samburu valuations of changes in eating practices.

This concern is somewhat different from the oft-repeated criticism that Bourdieu's theory is overly determinative or rigid.[7] This criticism suggests that if dispositions are the product of a history that then reproduces the practices, which will reinforce and recreate these dispositions, there is no room for social and cultural change, individual agency, and the like, barring significant external forces. My critique of Bourdieu is somewhat different—concerned more with the tight coherence between social conditions and dispositions rather than what

the implications might be for the determinative nature of his theory—
but potentially subject to the same countercharge leveled against these
other critiques. Certainly Bourdieu does not argue that humans are
automatons, but rather seeks a way that is "not locked in the dilemma
of determinism and freedom, conditioning and creativity" (1977, 95)
by constructing a system with its foundations in human agency, but
agency composed of agents whose motivations are by and large not
of their own making. Such agents may freely choose to do what they
want to do, but do not freely choose *what* they want to do. As he
concludes his oft-cited section on embodiment: "Because the habitus is an endless capacity to engender products—thoughts, perceptions, expressions, actions—whose limits are set by the historically
and socially situated conditions of its production, the conditioned and
conditional freedom it secures is as remote from a creation of unpre-
dictable novelty as it is from a simple mechanical reproduction of the
initial conditionings" (95).

The facets of Bourdieu's writing that imply a less deterministic, or
more fragmented, reading of his work are laudable; they should be
read as caveats, footnotes—evidence of his ability to speak to the limitations of his nonetheless brilliant system. They should not be read
as license to in essence "play it both ways," by drawing on a system
that roots its central significance in its elucidation of a mechanism of
social reproduction in ways that create a significant level of coherence
between social processes and the bodily practices they engender, while
denying that these implications for the system exist. In a (fragmented)
word, all of Bourdieu isn't overly coherent—just the Bourdieuian
parts.[8] The real question, then, is not whether Bourdieu's system is
totalistic. Rather—given that any fully totalistic system will render an
unrealistic or incomplete picture of some aspects of the world—what
kinds of processes interact with the mechanism he has postulated to
work against this grain under particular circumstances or in particular
arenas? Bourdieu's great insight is in identifying a significant mechanism for social reproduction that relies not on mentalistic adherence to
a set of codified cultural rules but on dispositions that are internalized,
embodied, through the act of living in the context of a particular set of
social conditions. The negative side is that it is untenable to hold that
all dispositions correspond neatly to those social conditions. Consequently the question is how neatly the habitus and the social conditions
that produce it fit together, and what kinds of factors may produce dissonance between them.

Ultimately, Bourdieu's project seeks to account for that which, according to Western folk wisdom, there is no accounting for—taste. Certainly, it is not the case that tastes or preferences cannot be explained. As Bourdieu has artfully shown, there is no question that one's cultural and social milieu is central to the internalization of individual dispositions. Yet it does not fully explain individual dispositions. What processes underlie these dissonances, and how do they import the role of the habitus?

Certainly there is the question of simple individual variation. Samburu—despite unanimously regarding pastoral foods as intrinsically more desirable—may have profound distastes for foods that their peers hold to be delicious. Consider, for instance, Yaniko Lesopiroi, a woman of about forty, describing her dislike for soup: "As for me, since long ago I have not drunk soup. And so it was [as a child], every time, I had to be beaten when a goat died so that I could be forced to drink soup [made from its meat]. But I would not drink it. Even now I will only drink soup [out of social obligation] when I give birth. But other times I still don't want it. . . . Finally they agreed to not give me soup."

The question is the extent to which such individual preferences may be discounted as mere fuzziness or noise in the system, or whether memory plays an important role in otherwise unaccountable preferences, as psychologists have suggested. Associations with negative events can play a particularly important role in creating aversions to particular foods—for instance, eating food in association with a sickness, or forced feeding episodes in which authority figures compel children to eat an undesirable food (Batsell 2002). Psychoanalytical perspectives, most notably in the work of Anna Freud (1930), similarly emphasize the unconscious ways in which dispositions toward food are influenced by nonlogical connections related to sex, excretion, aggression, and the parental relationship (Counihan 1999).

This shaping of tastes in ways that may be illogical or nonlogical, conscious or unconscious, challenges a notion of the habitus constructed around a strongly unified self with a set of highly coherent dispositions. Yet at the other end of the spectrum, we cannot ignore the inherent properties of the activities or items around which these dispositions form. That is, if the notion of the habitus rightly suggests that our dispositions come into being principally through cultural construction, it is not the case that the materials out of which they are constructed are equal and interchangeable. Thus, in the realm of food, considerable research suggests that certain qualities of food render them intrinsically more or less desirable, based on such factors as taste and the relative presence of an array of macro- and micro-nutrients—for instance, people tend to like sweet things and fatty things. This is, in fact, a key facet of Mintz's classic argument concerning the rise of sugar in England. Though sugar use on a grand scale articulated with political-economic developments in both the metropole and colony, underlying this was the fact that the sweetness of sugar makes it supremely appealing, owing to basic human—perhaps even primate—preference. Although the taste of sugar is only a piece of the puzzle of why sugar became such a necessity to the British during the Industrial Revolution, the powerful bodily experience of intensely sweet things was nonetheless significant to the developments most central to Mintz's arguments.

Thus we may not assume that all sets of dispositions are equally likely, equally resilient, or equally coherent. This is particularly the case in regard to food, because it resonates at multiple but not necessarily wholly intersecting levels. Stated simply, dispositions regarding food may be rightly interpreted to a significant degree to be part of a habitus structured by one's social milieu—yet this habitus is at the same time subjected to, as it were, the taste test. Thus although educated Samburu may typically make a favorable association between new ways of eating and Development and Progress, they nonetheless find the new ways unpalatable when they come in the form of plain boiled maize. By contrast—irrespective of age or ideology—modernity may seem like a good thing when you are spooning into the new, enlightened, and tasty dish of fried meat and vegetables.

Today when Samburu eat, cook, or, indeed, want for food, there is always some extent to which these prosaic, everyday activities are invested with meaning about the past and readings of the present through the past. Yet they are simultaneously—as they always have been—about other things, whether fulfilling one's basic bodily needs, caring for one's children, engaging in commensality with one's friends and neighbors, performing one's masculinity or femininity, recovering health and building one's body, or just enjoying a nice, hot drink. If Samburu subjects experience their history through food in ways that are deeply visceral, these experiences may be ambivalent, ambiguous, illogical, and nonlogical. We thus need to account for memory in ways that acknowledge that the fundamental texture of memory is not simply about a particular thing but more likely about many—perhaps unrelated, perhaps conflicting—things. This does not dilute the power of memory in shaping collective experience or individual subjectivities but may render it all the more salient through the resonance of its intersecting paths at an array of levels.

The terrain of Samburu memory through food is less, however, one of contestation or contradiction than of ambivalence. It is not wholly inaccurate to map the two central master narratives of food onto sectors of Samburu society differing vis-à-vis forces of change, and also onto our own convenient analytical dichotomies. Thus, the "progress of agriculture" might be read as the discourse of the global, the modern, the colonizer, the European, the secular. The counterposed discourse of social and cultural decay is the local, the traditional, the colonized, the indigenous, the mystical. There are strands of such characterizations that contain some truth. Certainly, one has its intellectual pedigree in European discourses at least centuries old, and the other is grounded in long-standing practices and values of Maa-speaking peoples centered on a pastoral lifestyle. It is, moreover, the case that the strongest Samburu adherents of each discourse vary in their engagement in everyday practice with aspects of Euro-American culture—for instance, in Western education, clothing, housing structures, languages spoken, and so forth. But far more telling is how unusual it is to find adherents of either of the two master narratives of food who unambiguously promote discourses either promoting or denigrating the changes in eating Samburu have experienced with increasing intensity over the last two or three decades. That Samburu may creatively blend these seemingly irreconcilable discourses is not because the issues incumbent in these discourses matter so little that they may freely piece them together, as in some glib, postmodern collage. Rather each discourse contains a core that to virtually all Samburu is both so true and so weighty that its rejection bristles against commonsense assumptions fundamental to their lived experience.

The very intertextuality that exists between the two discourses is in many ways central to the ambivalence of experience. Clearly, whatever each of these discourses owes to other places or other times, each is of this place and this time, shaped and made meaningful in the context of diverse Samburu lives in the late twentieth and early twenty-first centuries. As is by now commonplace in anthropological and historical analysis, even if a discourse of Progress or modernity has a particular intellectual, cultural, or political history, the specific Samburu actors who find these discourses meaningful employ them for reasons and to ends that are of their own time and place. Conversely, although discourses and practices concerning food are of long-standing import to Maa-speaking pastoralists, these values and practices should not be essentialized as part of an ossified "traditional" culture but understood as a construct that contains new dimensions and new meanings in contemporary life. And, indeed, it bears emphasizing that part of this context is the presence of these opposed narratives. The Samburu instantiation of global discourses valorizing Progress takes on specific meaning and significances by virtue of its relation to its counterdiscourse, just as long-standing values and meanings concerning food are shaped in counterpoint to the former.

This intertextuality is fundamental to the construction of these competing discourses as more than simple ideas or affiliations—as lived, and deeply visceral, meanings. "Modernity" and "tradition" may insinuate themselves in different Samburu subjects' eating practices in very different ways, but they are somehow always there, even though they may mean very different things to even very similar people. Food is so deeply embedded at many levels that it need not resonate in ways that are wholly consistent. It may be true that a diet lacking in animal products contributes to poor health, and even erratic behavior if nutritional needs are rarely wholly satisfied: these are phenomena that a belief in Progress cannot inoculate you against, and which the countervailing master narrative explains. It is also true that a flexible approach to economic life is desirable in the context of contemporary poverty, even if it is largely a caricature when those who have gone to school attribute this poverty to an overly rigid adherence to a livestock-centered economy by "traditional" Samburu, and this notion that their unenlightened outlook has contributed to contemporary conditions can also resonate even with victims of poverty themselves. The present and the past can mean very different things even to neighbors living side by side in the same community. For a thirty-year-old woman who has always been poor, subsisting predominantly on maize meal porridge, the idea of living on a predominantly pastoral diet may have the unreal quality of a historical dream-time. Older people may have lived that dream; wealthier neighbors or immigrants from other areas may still be striving to live it. The poor may welcome the availability of "gray foods" as a means of avoiding dependency on one's neighbors, and especially the mass deaths promised by famines of the past; others who have successfully embraced "modernity," through the market or employment, may feel that they are able to eat a better, more varied diet, which still includes pastoral foods when they choose, supplemented with tasty chapatis or stews when they wish.

In the next chapter, I turn to considering the nature of food itself, both as an object in the social life of Samburu (and humans more generally) and as an object of scholarly inquiry. In doing so, I consider what it is about food specifically that renders it a particularly potent arena for such ambiguous, ambivalent, and conflicting forms of memory.

CHAPTER 2

Food as Food

Naliapu Letoole, a Samburu woman in her mid- to late thirties, recalled a time when food had been especially plentiful. The memory was in some ways bittersweet, for it described events that many Samburu take to be a turning point in the vitality of their pastoral lifestyle, the coming of *lipis*, the East Coast Fever epidemic that began in the late 1970s and remains a chronic threat to livestock to this day. But what it represented to Naliapu was not the decisive moment of an epochal shift. Rather it represented a massive amount of meat—and not from emaciated cattle starving to death during droughts but fat, healthy cattle. At that time the herds remained plentiful, so that along with all this meat, there were also large amounts of milk. As she explained:

> Me, I can remember during those days of Lipis. Us children who were looking after the animals, once the sun began to dip a bit in the sky, we would bring the animals closer to the settlement and drink milk, so that there was room in the calabashes at the evening's milking. And along with this milk there was a lot of meat too—every kind of meat, whether you want the fat one or the lean one. People might even just sip a little fat soup, and pour it away, even though Samburu usually think it is unlucky to do so. Even meat was just thrown away. . . . As for warriors, they were eating meat [in the bush] and they knew again that the home was just full of milk. Meat could just be thrown away, or left [hanging on thorn trees]. So, you might be walking and—you could be walking and just bump into some here, bump into it there, or bump into some dry meat over there, and just bring it home.

Naliapu's account highlights not only the nutritional wonders of this time but its social and affective aspects. For alongside this extraordinary nutritional experience—calabashes full of milk and meat practically growing on the trees—came effects that were profoundly social and emotional. Thus she contends that despite the death of many cows,

> people were just happy. Their hearts were just full of spirit. And as for the murran, they just shined, enjoying their murranhood so much, and they sang. . . . [At times like that] I see that people just become good. They get fat, and they don't go circulating around from settlement to settlement like they are driven by hunger. They just stay around their homes—you can't find one person who is not at home. . . . You don't find people who are just wandering around aimlessly. They just stay quietly. But when you talk to them, it is like their hearts have become good.

What I find most notable in Naliapu's commentary is how she condenses seemingly distinct (or at least analytically distinguishable) aspects of food's significance around this single event. While what is most prominent in her account is the extreme bounty of that moment, she describes more than a nutritional state. The emotional response is compelling, as people's "hearts were just full of spirit," and murran were singing. Social friction was minimized as people no longer struggled to find food. And in some senses this bounty of food created an enhanced moral environment: "[People's] hearts have become good."

Like Naliapu, I aim to collapse and condense various crucial facets of food. As the scholarly literature on food has blossomed, particularly in the past two or so decades, diverse approaches have highlighted the bountiful ways through which food offers an rich entry point into understanding what it means to be human. My analysis is congenial to all these approaches—yet beyond this I seek to build upon them in ways that I hope suggest further directions for the theoretical possibilities of food. Food studies have shown us ways to understand not only the nutritional but the social, cultural, psychological, emotional, political economic, religious, gendered, symbolic, and sensuous aspects of food (and this list is not exhaustive). Yet, unlike Naliapu (and Samburu more generally), the scholarship on food tends to disaggregate these threads, which for our subjects may be of a single piece. This may mask what is, in fact, so powerful about food—what makes food *food*: its significance as a site for condensing these varying facets of food.

Such a perspective is in many ways more holistic but, as emphasized in the previous chapter, in no sense more seamless. Rather, food in many ways typifies the Althusserian notion of overdetermination

(Althusser 1962), where something (in this case, food) is the locus of such powerful, distinct threads of causality and meaning that ultimate causality and meaning become indeterminate. In moving toward such a view, I focus critically on food as a subject of social analysis. Focusing on a variety of tendencies that have tended to disaggregate food—issues of ethnographic writing, the gulf between scientific and interpretive approaches, and the insinuation of Western cultural constructions of food and eating into the anthropology of food—I suggest an approach that may more fully encompass the power of food.

WHAT IS FOOD?

This is not a stupid question. If the answer seems obvious—we can point to food; we have all eaten food—we would do well to consider the extent to which one thrust of the anthropological enterprise has been to destabilize categories that are part of the obvious, everyday architecture of Western thought. Thus food—like, for instance, the family, gender, religion, and personhood—must be understood as both a cultural construct and a site of social action in which analytical categories rooted in Euro-American cultural categories may prove inadequate for a full and culturally appropriate analysis. Perhaps food studies have in some sense grown too fast, enjoying a veritable renaissance over the past decade or two, while outpacing the development of theoretical frameworks for food's analysis. For though well-established anthropological subjects, such as kinship, sexuality, and religion, have the advantage of decades of scholarship concerned with overcoming our cultural constructions of these domains, the anthropology of food has not always moved convincingly beyond Western constructions of food—and indeed much of the academic food literature feeds on these constructions.

In this vein I consider a number of analytical and theoretical tendencies that have limited the theoretical possibilities of an anthropology of food and the illumination of its broader significance to social analysis. Some are broad tendencies within anthropology and related fields—for instance, aspects of ethnographic writing and the estrangement of materialist and meaning-centered approaches—while others more directly relate scholarly food studies to Western cultural constructions of food. As Sutton (2001) notes, food studies are often viewed less as serious scholarship than as "cute," "neat," or "fun." That they often are all those things is not a scholastic sin, but food is much more than that, as anyone who has gone hungry or lived alongside people for whom food is a daily concern knows full well. Indeed, if Woody Allen could once quip that his brain was his second favorite organ, it is only because he has never had to worry seriously about his stomach. Yet it is not merely that food is serious business—a fact well documented in nutritional studies of famine and food security (e.g., Dettwyler 1993; Pottier 1999)—but that the power of food comes precisely from the extent to which it serves as a site of articulation for powerful, if seemingly disparate, threads of causality and meaning. Consequently, I turn first to a discussion of tendencies that have contributed to disaggregating food, focusing on why and how we might reintegrate it in our analyses.

DISAGGREGATING FOOD

Two loosely related tendencies in current anthropological analysis have the shared effect of disaggregating the salient strands that provide food with its central significance. First, ethnographic writing and the ways in which the story arc around which contemporary ethnographic accounts are conventionally built serve to trivialize food as a detail that is important principally in its capacity to illuminate something else. Second, the polarization of more "mental" and "material" approaches—characterized less by great antipathy than by each camp's caring less and less what the other is doing—has further hampered an anthropology of food. What is most important about food, however—what makes food *food*—is how it simultaneously ties together disparate threads of causality and meaning. Consequently, these analytical tendencies are problematic because they separate varying facets of food, when what is most interesting about food is that it serves as a locus for articulating these disparate strands.

Writing Food

The anthropological formula in recent decades has increasingly drawn on the relationship between seemingly minor details and a broader process whose significance is more readily apparent. We have thus become a discipline that focuses less on a "big picture" than on the hidden but telling ways in which the big picture is illuminated through the minutiae of everyday experience. We are a discipline that sees the world in a grain of sand, or more ethnographically, sees the Balinese world in the bloody scraps between their chickens (Geertz 1973; for discussion of this formula of ethnographic writing, see, for example, Marcus and Cushman 1982; Stoller 1989). A brief perusal of *American Ethnologist,* the premier journal for cultural anthropology, confirms the continuing hegemony of this formula, where a detail from one morning in the village, a telling offhand comment from a friend and key informant, becomes a stepping-stone to illuminating a dimension of the latest trend in anthropological theory.

The anthropology of food has perhaps been particularly beholden to this type of story arc in constructing ethnographic accounts—and this tendency may be misleading and stifling to food's theoretical possibilities. It is not that this construction is intrinsically problematic. Who among us has failed to write in this mode, and how long might most of us continue to write successfully in defiance of this convention? My objection is that, as Marcus and others pointed out long ago, how we write matters (e.g., Marcus and Clifford 1985; Marcus and Cushman 1982). Our style defines ontological relations and directions of causality. And our story line typically marches upward: a seemingly trivial detail provides an illuminating window to some really important process. Consequently, when we write about one thing, we are, in a sense, always really writing about something else, a tendency particularly apparent in the study of food. Food becomes a sort of triviata that provides a window onto something more important. Gourmet coffee tells us about class (Roseberry 1996). Patterns of meat consumption tell us about constructions of masculinity (Orlove 1994). The preparation of obento snacks tell us about gender and the state in Japan (Allison 1991). Or, most famously, sugar tells us about the world system (Mintz 1985).

The insights of such studies can be brilliant, and my point is not to criticize their particulars. Their power is in revealing uncanny linkages between seemingly disparate aspects of cultural life and demonstrating how broader processes are tellingly located in everyday experience. Yet these studies should not, as a body, be taken to construe food as the unimportant side of the equation. Such an interpretation feeds the tendency to not take food as a serious object of study in its own right. By placing the significance of the argument on the " nonfood" side of the equation, one effectively disaggregates compelling aspects of food when what may be most important is the ways in which these are part of a complex, if contradictory, whole.

Mental and Material

The tendency to disaggregate food, driven by the conventions of ethnographic writing, is also in many ways a notable consequence of the end of anthropological debates concerning what might be roughly termed the "mental" and the "material." At the height of these debates, food played a prominent role, though debates between materialist and symbolic analysts of food have long ago run their course. In looking back at such academic frays, it can be difficult to discern why, in intellectual terms, the issues at the center of these brawls were really of such theoretical interest. I am not certain, however, that this is the case in regard to materialist and symbolic debates concerning food, where, if anything, the central issues remain important and highly debatable. While there is often a tendency in such polarized academic debates to generate more heat than light,[1] this particular debate left substantive issues in the anthropology of food less than fully resolved. That it has exited from anthropology's center stage owes less to fruitful resolution than to the growing distance between materialist and meaning-centered approaches in a discipline internally divided by the so-called Science Wars. It is not that, via Leviticus, Mary Douglas (1966) has convinced all of anthropology of the abominations of Marvin Harris–style materialism (1986), nor for that matter the inverse. Rather, it is an aspect of the ever-widening rift between positivistic materialists and meaning-centered interpretivists, with one side dismissing the other as fuzzy-minded postmodernists or as burdened by antiquated, simplistic scientistic thinking. It thus reflects less a triumph of ideas than a growing tendency, in a field characterized increasingly by subspecialization, to not feel the need to take seriously anthropologists with views significantly different from one's own.

Scholars (or groups of scholars) are, of course, free to chart the intellectual courses that they find most engaging and productive. It is in the spirit of the free intellectual endeavor for anthropologists of disparate perspectives to creatively build interdisciplinary bridges with literary theorists, neuroscientists, or economists rather than rehashing historically validated commonalities with anthropologists of differing persuasions. Whether the relative absence of a debate at the center of anthropology is more than compensated by lively intellectual life at its edges is a matter of opinion. What I am arguing, however, is that food can only, ultimately, be engaged with at that center—that it is its very simultaneity as material, social, and symbolic that makes food food.

What can be so useful pedagogically about pairing readings such as Harris's (1966) discussion of the sacred cow in India and Mary Douglas's (1966) famous chapter, "The Abominations of Leviticus" is not only that they are diametrically opposed but in reading either one it is easy to be drawn to a commonsensical conclusion that they have made an important point. Yet, irrespective of whether one feels they are on or near the mark, one does not necessarily feel compelled to conclude that they have told the whole story (and that, consequently, their rivals are clearly and utterly wrong). Though Harris argues convincingly that there are sound ecological reasons for banning the killing of cows, it is less believable when central aspects of Hindu thought are reduced to a mentalistic artifice whose real import is in securing an adequate supply of manure. Nor might one readily conclude—regardless of their similarity in Douglas's symbolic analysis—that Hebrew prohibitions on eating the opulent and widely prized flesh of the domestic pig share anything more than structural categorical equivalence with taboos on eating the rock hyrax (a creature whose tiny bones and stringy flesh are gnawed upon only in the odd foraging society where the animals are prevalent). Such debates are not useful if their intent is to demonstrate the ultimately materially determined nature of culture or, conversely, the ultimately mental underpinning of seemingly materially significant phenomena. These debates are useful rather as windows onto food as a complex, overdetermined aspect of human life that defies analysis framed in unnuanced renderings of the mental and the material, or the scientific and the interpretative. However polarized contemporary anthropology may be along these lines, a gesture toward either pole ultimately hinders the goal of understanding food as food. Food is a giver of life and, in its absence, the harbinger of death. Food ties us together, and it drives us apart. We share food and compete for food. It can define our deepest memories, our most cherished experiences, and the moments of our deepest ignominy. It is at once compellingly "good to think" and "good to eat." It is simultaneously the stuff of our most transcendent symbols and meanings and the stuff of our bodies, consumed as fuel in support of our trophic selves. What is so compelling about food is the extent to which it is complexly interwoven in webs of the symbolic, psychological, biological, and cultural. It is, in essence, overdetermined, in the sense of being an intersection of such powerful threads of causation and meaning that ultimate causation and meaning become indeterminate.

Such a view allows us to take seriously the ways in which changes in eating represent a historical development with materially serious implications, without reducing them to this. The Samburu case makes this starkly clear—there are startling material dimensions to the dietary changes that have accompanied the deterioration of the livestock economy over the past forty years. Thus, for instance, Sambu measured in 2002 were on average more than an inch and a shorter than a sample measured in 1960 (Shaper 1962), most likely due to changes in growth and development related to the shift from a high protein diet to one based heavily in simple carbohydrates. Yet if the rapidly shrinking Samburu vividly illustrate the material dimensions of these changes, it does not mean that such material issues represent the only—or even the most telling—lens for analyzing these transformations. Nor does it mean that this is the idiom most meaningful to the Samburu themselves, nor that the fact of material want signifies the same things to Samburu as it might to us. That is, we need to be prepared to take the material seriously without drifting into unmitigated materialism, to understand that these developments are part of our subjects' basic everyday realities—laden with significance beyond our anthropological imaginations and powers of analysis—without using this as a rationale to deny their intricacies and subtleties.

THE ETHNOGRAPHY OF TASTY THINGS

In *The Taste of Ethnographic Things,* Paul Stoller calls for a shift in anthropological practice toward forms of ethnographic fieldwork and writing that are attuned to the full range of human sensory experience. Rooted in phenomenological inclinations, which aim for "experience near" ethnography, Stoller argues: "Considering the senses of taste, smell and hearing as much as privileged sight will not only make ethnography more vivid and more accessible, but will render our accounts of others more faithful to the realities of the field—accounts which will be more, rather than less scientific" (1989, 9).

Stoller's call, here and elsewhere, for a more sensuous anthropology is in line with a tremendous interest, particularly in the 1980s and 1990s, in an anthropology of the body and of embodiment (e.g., Csordas 1994; Lakoff and Johnson 1999; Lupton 1996; Strathern 1996; Stoller 1995; Classen 1997), in understanding the ways previously abstracted aspects of human social life are realized and experienced in the site of the body. This is a particularly promising approach to food, with the body serving as a key site for mediating an array of analytically (though not necessarily empirically) distinguishable strands. But for the study of food, sensuousness also can be—and perhaps too often has been—a trap. "The body" and the sensuousness that is part and parcel of embodiment are a highly culturally constructed phenomenon (e.g., Geurts 2002). The notion of *sensuousness* is constituted in Euro-American thought in regard to historically particular mind-body oppositions (Straight 2006). Indeed, it is notable that we even have such a category as *the sensuous*— which tends to be structured around certain types of referents, defined by certain types of intrinsically culturally defined contexts. The sensuous is not just about sensation, but tends to be characterized by *strong* sensations. Often these are strongly positive—sex, eating—even to the point of being revelatory or a form of entertainment. Conversely, Western notions of the sensuous may also be defined as strongly negative, as in experiences of pain (e.g., Daniels 1996).

This particular construction of sensuousness informs much (though certainly not all) of the scholarly study of food. That is, food studies have grown synergistically with the interest in food that is emerging from Euro-American constructions of food and eating; this ranges from the specialized eating of epicurean gourmands to lay constructions and everyday experiences surrounding eating. The gourmand, in its professional and lay forms, is, of course, a particular historical construct, encompassing culturally specific ways of examining, interpreting, and valuing the sensuous qualities of food (Falk 1994). While the synergy between scholarly food studies and nonacademic gourmandism or food writing have spurred the development of scholarly food studies, they have at the same time worked against garnering respect for this rising field. Thus, Sutton (2001) notes, for instance, the wariness with which many academics have greeted the study of food, citing a 1999 article in the *Chronicle of Higher Education* and subsequent Internet debate on whether food studies are really just "scholarship lite."

Like Sutton, I find these criticisms to be largely misplaced. Yet at the same time, it is useful to consider their foundations, which rest in large part on the failure of much of the food literature to satisfactorily move beyond our own cultural assumptions concerning food and the experience of eating. Indeed, not infrequently the scholarly literature on food can be a small step from literature, travel, and cookbooks evoking the epicurean sensuousness of fresh-baked bread, pungent olives, and tangy soups. Consider, for instance, the intriguing new journal *Gastronomica,* whose vision combines "luscious imagery" and "a keen appreciation for the pleasures and aesthetics of food" with "smart, edgy analysis" and "the latest in food studies" (alongside sponsorship from KitchenAid and Bertolli Lucca olive oil). *Gastronomica*'s vision is commendable in many ways, demonstrating a commitment to an intriguing and compelling exploration of Western gastronomic epistemologies of an epicurean persuasion. Yet it does so largely synergistically with a model of the Euro-American gourmand, rather than challenging the extent to which this is a cross-culturally useful lens for exploring the relationship of food and culture.

In a similar vein, Hensel's (1996) study of Yup'ik cuisine is a fascinating example of the tendency to situate food scholarship within Western aesthetic constructions of food. Hensel explodes Western aesthetic sensibilities, along with such fundamental culinary categorizations as "the raw and the cooked," through an intriguing discussion of such dishes as fermented seal flipper and aged salmon heads. Yet, somewhat ironically, he does so in a well-meaning attempt to demonstrate that Yup'ik do not eat rotten food because of nutritional difficulties encountered in their challenging environment, but rather because they are sub-Arctic gourmands reveling in a cuisine of putrefied meat and fish, a cuisine that now constitutes an important element of their cultural identity. Hensel's case is well argued and well documented, yet he feels compelled to frame his fascinating case study of such a unique system of eating with nearly explicit references to the experience of "ethnic eating" found in French or Chinese restaurants.

In advancing the study of food-centered research, we would do well to more deliberately distance ourselves from Western constructions of "ethnic food" that have formed in a particular configuration of colonialism, immigration, epicureanism, and cultures of distinction, to name just a few of the strands in this complex (e.g., Narayan 1995). It is crucial to bear in mind that both westerners' experience of "ethnic food" and the character "ethnic food" takes on in immigrant communities in the United States and elsewhere may owe far more to Western constructions of food and the Other than it does to any non-Western logic of eating. Indeed, the meanings constructed around the Western notion of "ethnic food" may bear little relation to the meaning of eating even in the places from which these ethnic foods derive. I am reminded here of the scene in *Waiting for Guffman* in which Eugene Levy's dentist character, recalling his trip to China, confides that in Beijing they are for some reason unable to make a sauce as sticky and sweet as what they are able to make at the Chinese restaurant in Blaine, Missouri. Along these lines, writer Dean Lenane (2002) recently quipped, "Chinese restaurants are Chinese restaurants and are similar worldwide. Only in China are Chinese restaurants different."

This critique bears directly on the veritable explosion in studies highlighting the relationship between food and identity. This burgeoning literature in anthropology and other fields documents how ethnic identity is constructed in terms of food and eating, particularly for immigrant communities and other groups undergoing social change (e.g., Buckser 1999; Comito 2001; Diner 2003; Gabbacia 1998; Humphrey and Humphrey 1988; Kelly 2001; Kugelmass 1990; Lockwood and Lockwood 2000; Mankekar 2002; Singer 1984). Though a full discussion of this literature is beyond my present scope (see Holtzman 2006a), we should consider whether resilient ethnicity is expressed through food because particular qualities of food render it a poignant site for the construction of collective memory or because Western cultural constructions of food render it an innocuous site of identity in the context of a carefully tended and well-stoked melting pot. This is certainly not the case in all contexts—one need only consider oft-cited cases of Jews who were killed for making chicken soup during the Spanish Inquisition (Gitlitz and Kay 1999). Thus we might consider more incisively what it is about this particular cultural-historical moment that allows food to play a central role in such diverse ethnic groups as Italian Americans, Greek Americans, and diasporic Indians. In the West, food is "culture"—not in the sense of Tylor's complex whole, nor in the sense of those peculiar customs one teaches in Anthropology 101 (and which some less enlightened students silently hope that the foreigners will have the good sense to quickly abandon when they come over here)—but rather in the sense of arts and culture, of the new Peruvian restaurant where you dine before taking in the Cirque du Soleil, culture as aesthetics and entertainment. Western notions of food construct ethnic identity in a way that is no more threatening than the Bolshoi Ballet or a Ukrainian Easter egg, where the world becomes a menu to sample in an epicurean, emotive sensuousness.

OTHER SENSUALITIES

My goal here is not to deny the sensuousness of food. It is axiomatic that food is sensuous, and it is intrinsically "of the body," regardless of the ways in which the body is culturally constructed in differing milieus. In line with the notion that we must take food seriously *as food,* I aim to elucidate eating as a dense nugget of the material, social, and symbolic, of which its sensuousness is an intrinsic part. Indeed, a number of intriguing and diverse examples illustrate the ways food constitutes an important engine for the construction of bodily memories, illuminating its capacity to form special kinds of memory. Powles's

(2002) recent study of refugees in Malawi argues that the collective memory of displacement is constructed less around issues of traumatic violence—as for instance, in Malkki's (1995) groundbreaking study of Rwandan refugees—than it is through the corporeal experience of the absence of fish. Robert Batsell (2002) has found that in the United States memories of forced eating, in which children are required to clean their plate of some undesirable food, form compelling "flashbulb memories," preserving in vivid detail aspects of early childhood when little else may be remembered. Counihan (2004) shows how food-centered life histories can provide a vivid window into a wide array of processes in societies undergoing change. In a different vein, David Sutton (2001)—in service of his argument that synesthesia causes food to be remembered in particularly compelling ways—shows how food forms a pervasive and subtle form of memory for the inhabitants of the Greek island of Kalymnos. Memories are often expressed in reference to the food one was eating at particular times—an apricot or a particular meal—while long-term changes may be chronicled through changes in food. In much the same way, Seremetakis (1996) takes the change in the taste of peaches—once the "breast of Aphrodite," now tasteless and insipid—as the centerpiece for an extended meditation on erasure of unconscious memory in the context of the homogenization incumbent in the trade policies of the European Union.

What I take issue with, then, is not the sensuousness of food per se but positing a sensuousness overly burdened with Euro-American constructions of it. Certainly food is sensuous—but we can take for granted neither the body experiencing this sensuousness nor the cultural construction of this sensuousness. The experience of a Greek from Kalymnos recalling the sweet, moist delights of eating a fig in decades past (Sutton 2001) is a construction of sensuality that Westerners can perhaps appreciate. Yet a Samburu murran at *loikar* (meateating camp)—gorging himself in the bush on cattle he and his age mates have stolen, then consuming strong herbs to purge his bowels so he can stuff himself with more of the strength-giving meat is a construction of sensuousness quite outside commonplace Western notions. We need to take account of food as a subject of bodily experience but also remain wary of falling into the trap of viewing food studies through Western epicureanism.

It is notable in this regard that Samburu views of food—in autochthonous culinary systems or their recent transformations—are not especially sensuous from a Western standpoint. The comments of Lekutaas, a senior elder of the Kimaniki age set, are typical when he asserts, "All foods are just the same in taste. So long as the food is cooked well, it is a must that all food will taste delicious." Indeed, it is difficult to imagine a Samburu meditation on food on the order of Seremetakis's discussion of the nostalgia of peaches. Linguistically, Samburu taste vocabularies are relatively underdeveloped in comparison to Western ones. Only five main words are used to describe the tastes of foods, and these are fairly vague. *Kemelok* is often translated as "sweet," yet its meaning is less a physical sensation of sweetness than the positive experience of eating something tasty. Thus *kemelok* is used to describe not only honey but also especially tasty meat. Even fermented milk may be described as *kemelok,* if it has been soured well. *Kemelok* is also used metaphorically to refer to positive things in life. Thus, in the stylized home report that is central to Samburu greetings, it is common to say that at home there is *sirian namelok,* or "sweet peace."

Apart from *kemelok,* only one other taste word describes a positive sensation. *Keisiisho* denotes saltiness, particularly in sour milk. All other taste words are, to varying degrees, negative. *Kesukut* is used for fresh milk that has started to go sour but has not curdled. This is considered to be a serious defect in milk, though not one that renders it undrinkable. A parallel term for meat, *kesagamaka,* describes meat that has started to go bad—though meat has to become quite putrid by Western standards before people will refuse it. *Ketuka* refers to food that is tasteless, such as meat from animals that have not been fed salt. Today, porridge eaten without additives such as fat or milk is also referred to as *ketuka,* or may be described as tasting like *nchata natotoyo,* a dry stick. An additional taste term is *kedua,* or bitter, though this is not applied to food per se but is used for medicinal herbs and bile.

Samburu taste terminology is thus relatively nonsensuous. Of the six taste terms, only two are positive (*kemelok* and *kesiisho*), and only one of these refers exclusively to a taste sensation rather than a judgment on the merits of the food. Of the remaining four, one is strongly negative (*kedua,* bitter), two refer to food that tastes bad (*kesukut,* sour, and *kesagamaka,* putrid), and one *(ketuka)* refers to the absence of taste.

This lack of epicureanism is evidenced in a relatively low level of attention to preparing foods in ways that enhance their flavor. Desirable foods—milk and meat—are seen as intrinsically desirable, and there is no strongly developed notion that they should be prepared in special ways to render them more tasty. It is notable that very few foods are eaten as prepared dishes, in a Western sense. Certainly we must remain wary of relying too heavily on Western notions of cooking in considering the complexity of food preparation; as Hensell (1996) notes, a great deal of preparation may go into food long ahead of its time of eating—as in Yup'ik fermented seal flipper or Euro-American cheese—even if relatively little occurs at the time of eating. This does not, however, bear particularly on Samburu food. For Samburu, most food is eaten in its basic form, without extensive preparation beyond cooking (or, in the case of milk, fermentation). Dishes that combine different foods are relatively rare, and combining meat and milk is highly discouraged (though, as I discuss in chapter 4, milk is combined with blood). This is not a religious prohibition, as in the Jewish tradition, but is based on a belief that combining milk and meat can cause a disease known as *lkuposhoi,* characterized by infection with parasitic worms.

Obviously food—and hence the subject of this book—is quintessentially sensuous, and we cannot understand the meaning and power of food without taking into account the extent to which it is "of the body." Yet we cannot take for granted our understanding of food, the body, or the sensuousness with which they come together, particularly to the extent that these are influenced by peculiarly Euro-American configurations of epicureanism and the gourmand.

When there is a lot of food, explains Senteku Lekimaroro, an Lkshilli elder, "There is happiness in the land." He continues:

> The place is full of happiness, people sing. And warriors decorate themselves, and girls also decorate themselves. And they smear themselves with red ochre. As for women, they put on their *mporo* [marriage beads], and they sit in the shade sewing and making strings of beads. And so, all is happiness. . . . [But when there is no food] nobody will decorate themselves. It is just like recently when we climbed the wild olive trees [to cut branches for the cows to eat when there was no grass during the drought] and so people were removing their ornaments, and decorations, so as not to be caught on the trees.

This chapter has presented a view of food that is in many ways more holistic but in no sense more seamless than other approaches to the anthropology of food. What is so powerful about food is that it is constituted through complexly interwoven webs of causality and meaning that are simultaneously symbolic, psychological, social, emotional, biological, and cultural. These webs are not merely a part of how we as scholars analyze food but are fundamental to how our subjects *experience*—and consequently, remember—food. Our informants may make no clear distinction between what we identify as analytically distinguishable threads, not only because they experience them together but because the experience of each is intrinsically shaped by its relationship to food's other dimensions.

Senteku continues to muse on the psychological effects of pastoral foods, particularly on murran when meat is plentiful:

> As for the side of the murran, they get the fatness of young people, and their youthful vigor is apparent. . . . Isn't it that which sends the murran into trance? And so the warriors go into trance as they sing. Also, as a consequence of that meat, murran come so that they cannot feel the cold weather. . . . He goes and becomes strong and cannot fear anything. He becomes strong and there is nothing that can terrify him at all. It is just the trance which becomes too much. If you become too strong then, for instance—you know how bulls usually are. Isn't it that it just stays as a calf, and finally grows up. And then there is an old bull. And [the young one] starts fighting the old bull, because it has become very strong.

Having pastoral foods in plenty is thus seen—not surprisingly—as contributing to nutritional well-being, healthy weight gain, higher activity levels, and greater resistance to the elements. Yet it is far more than this, for having plenty of pastoral foods, and especially meat, is seen as leading to intense emotional states, indeed to what are ostensibly altered states of consciousness. The excessive strength the Samburu associate with meat consumption leads them, particularly murran, to be seized by *ltauja* (literally "hearts"), a form of trance. Samburu do not attribute such trancing (which involves violent shaking similar to epileptic seizures) to a supernatural cause, such as spirit possession. Rather, it is an intense emotional response in such contexts as circumcision rituals, marriages, or commonplace dancing of murran and their girlfriends—or brought on by excessive strength from having eaten well.

These varying facets of food are, then, of a piece. But though they are *simultaneously* of a piece, the direction of causation is flexible and indeterminate. That is, this interconnectedness does not suggest reductionism, in which the significant dimensions of food are located in one of these strands and other dimensions construed as epiphenomenal to its central meaning. This might be seen, for instance, in Marvin Harris–style cultural materialism, particular strands of Marxian thought, and to varying degrees within perspectives of cultural ecology. Such perspectives do not find surprising the convergence of the material with meaning and emotion. It is predictable because in their view the material plays an ultimate and determining role in shaping these "softer" facets of human existence. Alternatively, others may write outside of these material dimensions of food. If no one denies the material significance of food—without food, you die—this is little more than an axiomatic fact, which may be looked past as one moves on to the "really interesting questions" concerning the symbolic, social, or sensual aspects of food. Belaboring the material aspect of food may thus be dismissed as little more than a simple-minded descent into vulgar materialism.

The key question here is not whether one of these roughly hewn alternatives is the correct one. As Sutton (2001) asserts in regard to the Harris-Douglas debate on the sacred cow, most anthropologists today would agree that they are both in some senses right. The issue then becomes not *if* it is one or the other but *how* it is both, in what *ways* these varying facets express themselves and interrelate, what this *means* for how we study food. Food is not good to think (Levi-Strauss 1969) simply because it is good to eat (Marvin Harris 1986), but it would be foolish to suggest that these facts are unrelated. And it is sensuous, and symbolic, and social. And many other things. These facts do have something to do with each other, and they also don't; they are independent but also intersecting, reinforcing but sometimes contradicting.

How we understand these facets to fit together or how we put them together in essence defines food. In another sense, there is an implied epistemology of food in how one writes about it, whether one is concerned with the pungent aroma of a smoked olive or the amount of fat on the back of someone's arm. It is not that any one individual must synthesize these two disparate facts, but the collective definition of food as an object of study must of necessity take stock of these interrelationships, not least because this is how our subjects experience food, in the simultaneity and contradiction of its intersecting threads. And as we delve deeper into the structuring of memory through food, they provide it both with its power and with its ambivalences.

PART TWO

Worlds of Food

CHAPTER 3

The Alimentary Structures
of Samburu Life

"You have the power to harm someone you have stayed with together because they ate your food," explained Lopeulu Lekupano, an Lkiroro junior elder. "You have done good for him before God, so if he has wronged you it is not good before God. And so that anger will rise from your stomach, or be pronounced through your words, and will cause harm because that sweat of yours [they have consumed in your food] will inflict it."

Food is a potent gift. Anthropologists have long been aware, in light of Mauss's (1967) classic formulation, that sharing food creates powerful connections among individuals and social groups—not just mutual dependency and reciprocity but the exchange of substances intimately tied to the self. As Lekupano vividly explains, our food contains a vital part of us that we impart when we share food, either at a particular moment or in patterns over time. Individual relationships and broad patterns of relationship are constituted and performed in various ways through food, through what I will call the alimentary structures of society, much as Audrey Richards (1939) argued, in the first—and some would argue still best—ethnography of food, that social relations for the Bemba were most centrally constructed through experiences of hunger and food sharing.

If food plays a vital role in constituting relationships in all societies, there is considerable variation in its influence on the constitution of society, varying from quite diffuse in some contexts to more demarcated

in others. Samburu are among those for whom food plays a disproportionately significant role in shaping the social dynamic, most vividly
with the age-gender system and the institution of murranhood. For
Samburu, food constitutes dense webs of causation and meaning far
beyond the obvious material significance of daily sustenance. Ostensibly all cultural values and social relationships are constructed *through*
food, with varying, but always considerable, degrees of directness
and explicitness, and to a great extent they are *about* food: age and
gender relationships, masculinity and femininity, patterns of extrado-
mestic friendship and cooperation, and notions of moral personhood
and moral development, to name some of the most obvious examples.
Though perhaps in different ways, Stanley Walens's characterization of
the Kwakiutl worldview might also be applied to the Samburu: "Eating
is a universal property of the world, and thus it is the basis for morality" (1981, 6). Kahn's (1986) study among the Wamira (Papua New
Guinea) similarly finds food to be the central device for constructing
wide-ranging aspects of morality and proper social relations.

Thus, although Samburu may be on the farther end of the continuum in how important food is in constructing diffuse aspects of the
sociocultural dynamic, it is worth considering the extent to which they
are less an ethnographic peculiarity than an example that makes often
more hidden dynamics explicit. These dynamics may be less obvious in
other contexts but are also often masked by the analytical biases (particularly male-centered ones) of long-standing approaches to understanding society. Food is often given short shrift in understanding the
broad dynamics of society because it often belongs to a domestic sphere
encompassed within a political sphere dominated by men (Holtzman
2002).[1] Thus, although this chapter and the one that follows are both
predominantly ethnographic—focusing on a detailed explication of the
ways Samburu worlds are constituted through food and eating—my
aim is also to point to important dynamics that scholars might more
thoroughly explore in many other contexts.

Here I focus on Samburu social relationships as they are constituted
through food, focusing mainly on the "hows" of eating rather than the
"whats" of diet and cuisine, which will be the focus of the next chapter.
Looking principally at how food structures social relations, particularly
in the age-gender system, I consider the ways in which food is fundamental to the construction of both moral personhood and interpersonal
relations at the domestic level and in society at large. Chapter 4 extends
this discussion to a detailed examination of Samburu diet and cuisine,

explicating the cultural construction of foods, particularly their construction of a broad range of meanings in Samburu life. This explication
of the complex values, structures, dynamics, and beliefs that for Samburu constitute the world through eating is central to the book's broader
goal of understanding not only how food is a central arena through
which we may understand the dynamics of Samburu social transformations over the past seven or eight decades, but more significantly,
how and why food has become such a potent site for Samburu's own
memories of the past and readings of the present, laden with ambiguity
and affective ambivalence. The threads that connect through food are
dense and not simple. They are constituted at multiple levels—social,
symbolic, gendered, material, religious, ethnic, culinary, and others—
which, even as they gain significance in their relationship to these other
levels, function with some degree of independence. If one presumes a
likelihood of consonance among these threads, one must also reject a
necessary coherence in favor of a dynamic among these relatively independent domains that is not only complicated in itself but further com-
plexified by the shifting and contested terrain upon which each arena
rests—a fact of the past as much as of the present.

"FRIENDSHIP IS THROUGH THE STOMACH"

Food sharing, broadly conceived, forms the basis for a wide range—in
some sense virtually all—of Samburu social relationships. The view
that Janet Carsten (1997) takes regarding kinship in her analysis of
a Malay fishing community is useful in considering this assertion.
Carsten argues that kinship is not a static, predefined state but actively
constructed and cultivated through the ongoing process of food provisioning and other aspects of domestic care, in a manner not unlike
the ways Butler (1990; 1993) construes gender as being centrally constituted through its performance (see also Carsten 2000). Much the
same may be said of Samburu social relationships, though perhaps even
more diffusely. Though to a certain degree many Samburu relationships have what is, from a Samburu point of view, a highly juro-legal
component—there are sharply defined rights and expectations based
on age, gender, kinship, and the like—these are less prescriptions concerning how individuals must interact than socially recognized norms
that are employed discursively as arguments about obligations and
entitlements vis-à-vis other individuals (see chapter 5). That is, relationships are always constituted from an array of potentialities that

become actualized through their performance—which overwhelmingly involves, in one way or another, food.

The observation that food creates social relationships is an old one in anthropology, going back to Mauss (1967), and revisited in a wide range of contexts (e.g., Richards 1939; Strathern 1971; Rubel and Rosman 1978). What is notable among Samburu is not only the wide range of relationships that are constituted, directly or indirectly, through food but the extent to which these are understood explicitly through the idiom of food. These relationships are found in a diffuse set of contexts (the following examples are not exhaustive). Parents and children are defined, as in many societies, through the process of provisioning and the moral responsibilities of caring for children, and through the reciprocating respect that is expected to result. In marriage, the relationships between husband and wives are highly structured around food. Murran (the age grade of bachelor warriors) are in many senses the most highly regulated in regard to food. Their responsibilities to each other are embodied in strictures against consuming any food unless another age mate is present. Murran are defined by severing their ties to their mothers' food, symbolized by returning to her half a cow's femur when entering full murranhood. Murran are obligated to the elders, who provide them with slaughter stock. As elders, their relationships with peers are defined to a great extent by the ethos of food sharing—though not the same rules—inculcated during murranhood. Younger people display proper deference to elders, older women, and kin by giving them something to eat. Even the marriage ceremony is to a great extent organized around food. The formalizing moment of the marriage—the performative act when Samburu assert that a marriage has truly come into being—is the slaughter of the marriage ox *(rikoret)*, which provides food for those attending the wedding. Particular cuts of the meat are used ritually in the ceremony, and everyone at the wedding must eat something (whether parts of the *rikoret*, milk, or tea) to ensure that the marriage is blessed and not cursed. The affinal relationships created through marriage also themselves in many ways concern food, as they are forged through cattle and are to a great extent about cattle, which form the basis of subsistence.

In essence, then, food is at the core of Samburu social relationships; as the Samburu aphorism insists, "Friendship is through the stomach." Social relationships are constituted through food and, in the absence of food-sharing, are deemed to be in name only. The potency of food to forge ties is understood by Samburu not merely in the sense of goodwill enacted and performed through material give-and-take but also as creating a "supernatural" tie through the exchange of vital substances. In eating someone's food, you have partaken of and benefited from their sweat *(latakuny)*, creating a tangible bond that is strengthened through repetition (for an extensive discussion of *latakuny*, see Straight 2006). Consequently, sharing your food with others greatly augments your ability to curse them—a primary means employed to enforce social discipline—with the efficacy of a curse proportional to the significance of the food you have given them. Thus, you can readily curse someone who has served as a herder for you for many years because of the extent to which they have benefited from your food, even in the absence of a kinship or age relationship that might otherwise render a curse potent. At the same time, because their herding labor has contributed to your well-being, their curses may also be potent.

Even surreptitious sharing can create or restore a bond, since *latakuny* may be transmitted even without knowledge of it. One of the worst social states between individuals and groups is to be regarded as "someone you can't even share food with," because the ill will between you is so great as to negate the possibility of even basic commensality. One vivid example is the aftermath of a spear fight between murran of the Lorokushu and Ipisikishu sections in the late 1920s. A dispute arose between murran of the two sections, stemming from the ill treatment of a girlfriend of one of the murran. When this escalated into a pitched battle, several murran from Lorokushu were killed, and further violence was averted only through the intervention of the colonial authorities. For many years ostensibly all social relations were severed between the two groups. Eventually, however, elders from Ipisikishu became interested in restoring relations. When they consulted a *laibon* (seer) concerning the best way to do so, he advised that they first allow some of their cattle to wander freely in areas populated by Lorokushu. These cattle would be recovered as lost animals and held in Lorokushu herds, where they would be milked, bled, and their meat eaten. This veiled food sharing—the Lorokushu, at least at first, would not be aware that it was food sharing at all—was seen as a necessary first step in restoring open commensality between the two groups, eventually leading to a restoration of intermarriage.

Food, then, is a core component of ostensibly all relationships among Samburu. In some instances this is overt, for instance in regard to the constitution of murranhood and their relations with other sectors of Samburu society, which are explicitly understood through the idiom of food. In other contexts it is implicit, and food becomes one symbol and device—if one highly saturated with significance and meanings—within multiplex relationships constituted at a variety of levels. Yet food is always there and, indeed, is central to Samburu notions of morality and right action (see also chapter 5).

FOOD AND THE DEVELOPMENT OF MORAL PERSONHOOD

I gave a lift one day in 1993 to a man traveling with his little boy of four or five. In late afternoon we left my lowland field site of Lodungokwe, spending the night en route before proceeding to the town of Maralal in the morning. I was generally wary of giving too many people lifts in my Suzuki jeep, which was indispensable to conducting fieldwork in multiple sites but also highly vulnerable to Samburu District's rough roads—and the more weight in the car, the more the car suffered. At the same time, an abstract fear of wear and tear on the vehicle was difficult to explain and justify to people who wanted to save themselves a long walk and upon whose goodwill I depended (and after all, they invariably pointed out, God would help me, and the car would arrive safely regardless of the load). I therefore developed a strategy of making the car appear already overloaded by leaving the backseat constantly filled with haphazardly packed luggage. It might thus appear that with great effort and creativity a small spot could be carved out for a man and his child, but there would not be a wide open space for two adults, which then might be squeezed to fit three, or four, or five.

Though this system was fairly effective in discouraging excessive passengers, occasionally some items would get lost in the mess, reappearing much later. As I was reloading the car in the morning, a very old loaf of bread fell out into the dirt. While gathering my things, I left it there and returned to the car a few minutes later to find the little boy munching on the months-old, dry, dusty bread. Shocked, I told the father, "That bread is bad—it's very old. It's very bad!" He looked at me quizzically and in his disbelief sought clarification: "But . . . is it bad for *children?*"

Of course, he implied, an adult wouldn't eat something like that—you or I would know better—but children are inclined to eat all manner of odd things. Wild foods have long been a special province of Samburu children, and especially while herding, they find a wide range of sometimes peculiar berries, gums, tubers, and small animals to eat in the bush. Today, in the era of flashlights, a gum derived from used batteries is a favorite, with unknown health implications. Although children do not always eat foods that their parents view as necessary—"forced feeding" incidents (Batsell 2002) are commonly reported by Samburu with foods such as meat, fat, and even milk—Samburu view children as naturally gluttonous and undiscriminating. Consequently, one component of enculturation and maturation is teaching children restraint and discrimination in eating.

Not simply a matter of nutrition, the development of proper eating habits is fundamental to the development of moral personhood. Food is at the center of Samburu morality (see Spencer 1965; and chapter 5). *Nkanyit* (a sense of respect) is acknowledged as the fundamental Samburu value, and is defined most centrally through eating—eating the right foods in the right company, sharing properly, and not displaying greed. Someone with a well-developed *nkanyit* displays selflessness, thinks of others before self and self only in relation to others, and follows appropriate patterns of avoidance prescribed by the age-gender system. Individuals cultivate and develop *nkanyit* in the course of moral development in tandem with self-control and discrimination in eating habits.

Beyond the significance of how one eats, expectations concerning not eating in times of want similarly shift with moral development and vary across categories in the age-gender system. In a society where—historically and today—food shortages present a chronic threat, how one eats and is fed has a central role in right action and moral personhood. Thus the salient aspects of age-gender organization that structure virtually all aspects of Samburu life are expressed and reinforced in normative expectations concerning eating and hunger. Like patterns of food choice and eating avoidance, expectations and capacities concerning going without similarly shape moral personhood and right action.

Not surprisingly, Samburu maintain that children two to four years old should be most protected in times of want. In part, Samburu aim to shield their more fragile bodies, but this protection also reflects a belief that they are not yet socialized into a culture of hunger. Lacking the capacity to understand that there is not enough, small children cry helplessly if there is no food. The corollary is that an only slightly older child will be enculturated to tolerate hunger and sleep without eating.

Samburu construe major differences between boys and girls in relation to hunger, though there is little consensus on their overall physical and mental ability to withstand it. While many informants assert that boys are physically better able to go without food, others claim that

girls are naturally quieter and more respectful they are also
.eedy. However, it is perfectly acceptable for boys to sleep hun-
while for a girl to sleep without at least eating something small is
.ceptionally unpropitious. Samburu maintain that if a boy sleeps hungry, he will pray for the cows to multiply so that there will be enough
in the future. In contrast, girls who sleep without eating are reputed to
feel extreme bitterness and to curse their families for not providing for
them properly.

These differing beliefs reflect differences both in the structural
positions of boys and girls, and in attitudes concerning the short- and
long-term vision of males and females. First, because of patrilineality
and patrilocal marriage patterns, girls are temporary members of their
natal families. Thus they are like guests (a few informants stated simply that they were guests) and construe the failure to be fed properly
in terms of their temporary status. They are outsiders whose long-term
lot is distinct from the insiders who are failing to care for them. In
contrast, since boys will eventually inherit their family's cattle, it is in
their interests to wish for an improvement in the family's wealth. At
the same time, these attitudes concerning boys and girls broadly reflect
beliefs that men have long-term perspectives that look to the well-being
of the herds, and women have short-term perspectives that focus primarily on the food produced by the herds. It is impossible to determine
the extent to which this is a stereotype, as opposed to real attitudinal
and behavioral differences in men and women, but it is broadly maintained by both genders. Neither is it unambiguously favorable to men,
for some suggest that men may show greater concern for the well-being
of their calves than that of their children.

The transition to adulthood takes considerably different forms for
boys and girls. Common to their experience is that there is a distinct
cut (Straight 2005) separating them from childhood, understood both
metaphorically and as the literal cut of circumcision, which for both
genders decisively ends childhood. Yet the similarities end there. Among
girls, changes in behavior and expectations are small and incremental
following the rituals that commence womanhood. Although circumcision typically occurs on the morning of marriage, this is not necessarily
the case. Should she remain at her father's homestead following circumcision, relatively little may change. The shift is more pronounced when,
as is much more common, womanhood coincides with marriage, as she
relocates to her husband's homestead and is given a new name by her
new kin. Yet while many aspects of her identity are explicitly stripped

away, she remains in many senses a child, only gradually assuming the mantle of womanhood as she establishes her own house and, more important, has children of her own. In contrast, the transition to manhood is—ideally and for the most part in practice—abrupt and complete. Boys are transformed into murran, who are radically separated from the domestic sphere, with an abrupt commensurate shift in expectations of right action and moral personhood, exemplified, and indeed constituted, through changes in eating.

MURRANHOOD AS A WAY OF EATING

One Samburu story concerning the origins of the institution of murranhood involves two elders discussing the fate of their teenage sons during a severe drought. Each man had lost almost all his cattle, and their families were close to starvation. The first declared that they should kill their sons, so that there would be enough food for everyone. "No," replied the other "Let us instead circumcise them and send them to the bush, where they can find food for themselves."

Since Paul Spencer's (1965) now classic ethnography *The Samburu: Gerontocracy in a Nomadic Tribe,* the social dynamics of East African pastoralists have been understood principally through the age-set system, particularly its most striking feature—the institution of murranhood, a prolonged period of bachelor warriorhood. Sometime between the ages of fifteen and twenty, young men are initiated into manhood through circumcision and a variety of associated rituals, living as bachelor-warriors until the initiation of a new age set some fourteen years hence. Murran are expected to remain unmarried and distant from domestic life. Distinctively marked by their long, ochred braids *(lmasi),* murran spend their days in long-distance herding, raiding, and singing and dancing. Their distance from domestic life is most clearly expressed in the *lminong* (prohibitions) of murranhood. They may eat no food seen by women, with the exception of milk, which they may drink only in the company of at least one other age mate. Ideally they feed on slaughtered livestock at *loikar,* meat-eating camps in the bush.

Murranhood most saliently centers on how young men do and do not eat. Several features commonly regarded as defining features of murranhood are actually tangential to its defining food-centered features (Holtzman 1996; 2002). Spencer (1965), for instance, focuses on the prolonged bachelorhood of murranhood and its implications for what he termed a Samburu "gerontocracy." In popular accounts,

attention centers on their role as "warriors," as well as their distinctive hairstyles and adornment. Yet, although all these traits are closely
associated with murranhood, none are defining features. Murran are
discouraged from marrying until the next age set is initiated, but some
nevertheless do so. Many of the typical duties of murran may alternatively be carried out by young elders or uncircumcised youths. Murran
may shave their distinctive braids for ritual cleansing (or, in the contemporary context, personal choice). In contrast, to violate the eating
prescriptions contradicts their claim to murranhood.

Thus, in contrast to long-standing models of the age-set system,
murranhood may best be understood in reference to food (Holtzman
2002). Spencer (1965) drew on the models of structural functionalism that were then still vibrant, emphasizing the unmarried state of
murran and the resulting polygyny of elders, to argue that power was
invested disproportionately in old men. Leaving aside the question of
whether elders are actually better off than murran, not to mention
women (whose lower status was taken to be an obvious fact), Spencer's
analysis lacked deep consideration of the meanings of marriage and
other forms of gendered social relations created through the age-set
system. That is, the importance of elders' monopoly on marriage cannot be fully understood without considering the meanings and implications of marriage in Samburu life. These relationships are, in fact, less
about social structure per se—in the sense of the kinship systems that
create social order in a Durkheimian sense—than they are about the
alimentary structures regulating the nutritional realities of Samburu
life and explicitly shaping the ways in which persons and relationships
are constituted through food.

The *lminong* directly structures three distinct though interrelated
sets of relationships, based on avoiding, sharing, and providing food.
First, murran are defined as distant from the domestic sphere, based on
their prohibitions against eating food seen by women. Second, murran
are tied to one another, since *lminong* dictate that murran cannot consume any food—even milk—except in the company of another murran. Finally, murran are constructed as belonging to everyone. Murran
drink milk from many different families and eat slaughter stock provided by many different families. By eating the food of the community
at large, they are deemed to assume responsibility for the community
at large, participating in activities (such as warfare and long-distance
herding) for the common good and being ostensibly "on call" to any
elder who requires them.

FIGURE 6. Murran jump high while singing and dancing. Photo by the author.

From a material standpoint, there is good reason to associate the age-set system—particularly the institution of murranhood—with food in the most basic sense of caloric intake and expenditure. Without being overly teleological, murranhood presents one interesting solution to the widely recognized herd-management problem of balancing ratios of herders to consumers, by regulating the relationship of calorically expensive males to female-centered sites of food distribution (Holtzman 1996, 1999b). Due to their greater average body size, adult males are calorically less efficient workers for any task that can as effectively be undertaken by children or women—a description that characterizes most herding labor. It is consequently more efficient to be obligated to feed as few adult males as possible, which the age-set system and accompanying polygyny accomplish in two ways. First, polygyny reduces the numbers of elders fed by each productive unit—that is, a group of women and children responsible for herding livestock. Second, the *lminong* constitutes the murran as shared among all households but with inexorable rights in none, with the expectation that they fend for themselves in times of scarcity. The polygyny that accompanies the age-set system might be read as a function less of male dominance in the political system than men's relative marginality in the productive system.

The centrality of food to the constitution of murranhood is most vividly illustrated by the rituals that begin and end a man's status as a murran, which are specifically concerned with eating. These rituals are, of course, complex, operating at a variety of levels, which construct and communicate a broad range of meanings that may not be essentialized into a single message. Nonetheless, the key ritual act that instates a youth as a full murran is acceptance of the *lminong* (eating prohibitions) and dissolution of the mother's role as food provider.[2] Conversely, full elderhood is eventually attained through the re-creation of this role in the person of his new wife.

Circumcision—though the most dramatic aspect of male initiation—leaves a youth neither a boy nor a true murran. He spends a month in a liminal period between boyhood and murranhood, sleeping on a specially prepared bed in his mother's house and continuing to eat there, albeit special foods (particularly *saroi,* a mixture of milk and blood). He dresses in a black skin and spends his days hunting birds, which he wears on his head. Only at the end of this period of approximately a month is he inducted into full murranhood through *lmuget lekweeni,* in which the birds are thrown away and an ox slaughtered in the absence of women. Portions are left behind for the women to collect—particularly the initiate's mother, who brings back the head, comparing its heaviness to the many things her newly mature son will bring back to her house. Murran bring their share of the ox to the bush, where a fatty piece from the underside *(nkiyeu)* is rubbed on the initiate's body and fed to him by an elder murran sponsor. Following the roasting of the meat, the new murran breaks a bone with his *rungu* (club). He takes half of this broken bone back to his mother, telling her that he is now returning what she has given him and he wants nothing more from her. From this point on, his eating behavior is governed by the *lminong* of murranhood.

Samburu offer many explanations for the eating prohibitions encompassed in the *lminong.* Origin stories emphasize both nutritional and social elements, the latter organized around issues of *nkanyit* (respect), particularly between age groups. In the myth discussed above, *lminong*

FIGURE 7. Initiates in the liminal state before murranhood. Photo by the author.

was conceived during a catastrophic drought as a better solution to food competition than murdering one's teenage sons. Similarly, everyday Samburu explanations for the institution of murranhood frequently concern domestic organization and eating practices, particularly the need to reduce competition with children for food in the home. Samburu widely

FIGURE 8. An initiate eats *nkiyeu* (brisket) to be promoted to full murranhood. Photo by the author.

note that murran are stronger and require a large quantity of food, such that they might consume everything (even taking it from children by force) if they were allowed to eat at home.

In contrast, a more common myth concerning the origins of *lminong* involves two age sets, the Lwuantaro, who were murran, and the Lkipalash, who were junior elders. These age sets are not recorded in previously published chronologies but are said to have come just before the Meshopo, who Spencer estimates were circumcised in the 1740s. At that time, not only did everyone eat together but alcohol was drunk by all. In this story, the Lwuantaro murran fled a battle, but the enemy was defeated by the Lkipalash elders. Later the elders taunted the murran for their cowardice, and in an ensuing drunken quarrel many from each age set were killed. Subsequently, the senior and firestick elders met and decided to curse beer and prohibit murran from eating in the company of others. *Lminong* is thus linked to the necessity of separating age-gender categories to reduce friction and social competition.

Particularly significant in regard to *lminong* is the extent to which it constructs the masculinity and moral personhood of junior males. The

centrality of eating practices to understanding murranhood is evident
from the fact that few if any offences not concerning food can put a
murran's social status in grave doubt.[3] Being unusually rude or disrespectful, violent or ill-tempered in inappropriate ways, a notorious
thief, or even possessing some degree of cowardice will affect a murran's prestige but will not threaten his very status as a murran, but food
offenses will. When a murran becomes a *lanya ndaa*—by eating food
seen by women, or without his age mates—his claim to being a murran
is itself put into question.

The *lminong* instantiates values not only through its prohibitions
but also by the commensality it engenders. Samburu view the requirement that murran eat only in the company of others as forging solidarity among age-set members, instilling the value of thinking of others
before oneself and of oneself only in relation to others. Eating also
forges bonds to the community as a whole. Murran must help any family that calls upon them, and conversely all families are expected to
have a role in feeding them. Any home that has murran is expected
to have milk set aside for not only their own murran but also his age
mates. Murran may also drink milk in other homes, if there is a lot of
milk, and, more important, may feed on the products of livestock from
many families at cattle camps. Livestock that murran slaughter in the
bush come from many families—though typically a relative of some
murran. Murran may spend time in many different homes, while bringing age mates to eat in his own.

Eating practices centered on *lminong* create a specific form of Samburu moral personhood for murran. Someone who eats according to
these patterns, develops a sense of respect, but respect in which—to
some extent contradictorily—strength and beastlike ferocity are intrinsic elements of the social distance created through eating. Lemayon
Lekupano, a Kimaniki senior elder from the lowland area of Ndonyo
Nasipa, explains:

> When a lad is circumcised, he will not come back and eat among the
> children. And he will not be eating this gray food cooked using a pot. He
> goes and eats food in the bush. A murran who eats meat at home is not
> able to defend his animals against enemies. When the enemies strike, he
> is a coward. But a man who just eats food in the bush—he can com-
> pletely murder. He is just like a wild animal. He strikes wildly! Just like
> a wild beast—just like a wild beast. Now when you come and get him
> sleeping—when he wakes up abruptly—he strikes until he kills. But the
> one who eats at home, he has thrown away his respect. He can even take
> children's food by force. If these murran eat at home, can't they finish all

the food? Can any child get food, or any elder? Children and elders will be chased away.

Food thus creates intense, though contradictory, forms of moral personhood. They are expected to be restrained in how they eat, yet are also seen to have enormous appetites and to eat enormous quantities of food. It is a matter of pride to be able to eat huge quantities of food, and it is commonplace to discuss the vigor of murran in terms of how quickly they might eat a particular goat. Murran steal livestock for food, not only from neighboring ethnic groups but from neighbors, even, reputedly, from their own families. Murran are also the group (apart from the occasional child) most likely to steal milk in a home. If they enter a home and find no milk in the calabash for murran, they may occasionally take the elder's milk, marking it with red ochre to show that they took it—an act that is alternately interpreted as rightful, because of their role in defending the cattle, or simply a brazen announcement that they were the ones who took the man's milk. Yet, as Lekupano vividly explains, right behavior is a complex blend of deference and beastliness. Eating in the bush makes murran simultaneously fierce (mainly toward outsiders) and respectful (mainly toward insiders). To a great extent, the murran's respect is closer to beastlike ferocity, which is part and parcel of social and physical distance, than it is to behaving in a way that Samburu would regard as strictly appropriate for a good person in a normal sense.

In this regard, Samburu distinguish murran who frequently eat meat in the bush from those who mainly drink milk at home. While meat bolsters strength and ferocity, milk is seen as considerably more domesticating. While the vitality brought about by meat consumption is a common precursor to trances, milk is seen as a much weaker food and has no ability to bring on trancing. Each is viewed as excellent food, but meat is associated with the masculine atmosphere of *loikar* (meat camp), while milk is associated with the more feminine sphere of the homestead. Eating meat in the bush is closely associated with cattle raiding. Cattle roasted at *loikar* are frequently obtained through small-scale raids *(lwuamban)*, while the need to vent the excessive strength produced by large-scale meat consumption is thought to drive raiding. In contrast, murran who rarely go to *loikar* or on raids are disparagingly termed *naperto nanya malesin,* translated roughly as "pesty little calabash [milk] drinkers." They are sissies, drinking milk in settlements while chatting up girls and women, rather than in the bush engaging in manly pursuits.

EATING IN THE HOUSES OF WOMEN:
MARRIAGE AND THE MORALITY OF EATING

The marital relationship and the moral personhood of married men and women are also constructed largely through food, particularly regarding how their eating and provisioning habits affect those under their care. The ability to withstand hunger for the sake of others is an essential moral component for both elders and women, though with important permutations for each.[4] Both are constructed as responsible parties who should put the well-being of those under their care above their own stomachs. Yet each is in a sense the other's dependent. Women are, like children, called *nkerra,* though this designation is used principally to construct men's responsibilities in overseeing women's well-being as family members, rather than infantilizing women. Conversely, women are principally responsible for feeding men, insofar as they have responsibility for and control over the family larder. Men do not cook food or milk livestock under normal circumstances, and men should be largely oblivious to what food is in the home. From a woman's standpoint, then, a man is like one more child to be counted in the allocation of food. In most circumstances, men's food responsibilities only involve ensuring that nutritional resources are adequate through sound herd management practices, though this may extend to bleeding or slaughtering livestock to supplement the milk supply in time of want or, nowadays, to selling livestock to buy food.

The food-centered roles of elders and women are defined through the ritual reversal of the initiation rituals that sever a murran's nutritional reliance on women—particularly his mother. When he first marries, a man does not immediately assume the role of elder; rather he waits several months before he agrees to eat food prepared by his wife, not doing so until the ritual is undertaken that Spencer (1965) referred to as "the blessing of the elders," and that Samburu currently refer to typically as "killing" the *lminong.* This ritual involves a direct reversal of initiation into murranhood, employing the same *nkiyeu* cut of meat used in the first ritual. The ritual occurs in the home, and the wife actively participates. The meat is applied to the man's body by elders, preferably age mates who have already killed their *lminong.* His wife feeds him this meat, as well as milk and beer. He may then eat food in the presence of women, particularly his wife, who is now his primary food giver. He is now a true elder, not only in relation to eating but in wide-ranging ways. For instance, a widely circulated story concerned an elder who had inadvertently failed to kill

'aced with unexpected demise while traveling with an
evealed that he never performed this ritual and enlisted
ı to help him complete it—on the spot—to avoid unpro-
ations for his descendants.

en and men both are expected to exhibit a total but highly
ambiguous altruism in relation to food, which in the case of men results
in contradictions in the construction of their masculinity. Masculinity
is, on one hand, constructed to a great extent by how much one *can*
eat. Samburu brag about how two murran can finish an entire goat
in short order, and in men gluttony is the sort of vice that indexes
healthy manly vigor. Men should never say that they are full, which
would be an unmanly admission that the food had defeated them, and
they refuse food only to generously leave it for others. Yet masculinity
is also constructed by an ability to control one's appetite. An elder's
manhood is grounded in the discipline that his murranhood served to
inculcate in him, and it requires that he withstand suffering without
complaint, particularly for the sake of those under his care. Just as boys
are expected to sleep hungry, while girls must always be given at least a
taste, hunger should not prevent a man from sleeping, whereas women
are held to be unable to sleep without eating.

There are other important dynamics that affect both nutrition
and the gendered social dynamics surrounding food. Though women
lack visible political power—except in unusual ritual contexts (e.g.,
ndorosi, Llewelyn Davies 1981)—they are empowered in the home
to distribute food according to their own vision of fairness. Everyday
domestic food allocation—whether milk or cooked foods—is undertaken by women, and men should steer clear of this process. Cross-
culturally there is considerable debate concerning women's role as
"gatekeeper" of the family larder (Counihan 1999; McIntosh and Zey
1989), though both Samburu women and men view it as significant.
In principle, rules of food distribution suggest that the elders should
receive a privileged share as the "owner" *(lopeny)* of the family and all
the people and property that constitute it, but in practice women exercise considerable and culturally legitimate latitude in fulfilling this.
The assessment of Lanyaunga Letuaa, an Lkishilli elder, is telling in
this regard. His description of food allocation began with a glowing
description of the selflessness of Samburu wives, who think of their
children and husbands before themselves: "When things are scarce in
the land, a woman can count her husband together with the children.
It's like she counts the husband as her own child. She feels a lot of

sympathy. She is like a queen [*mfalme* (from Kiswahili)]. She is even all-caring." But after he completed this tribute to Samburu woman-hood, I inquired whether this was typical of Samburu wives or just the practices of a few. The caring and uncaring ones "are not equal," he replied. "It is just a very few ones that I see who are caring. You can't even compare them, those many bad ones and the few ones that are good, that nobody sees."

As Lanyaunga suggests, the extent to which actual food distribution conforms to ideal or idealized patterns is highly variable, in the case of both women and men (see chapter 5). Elders are frequently absent when food is prepared, and an elder has no way of knowing how much food was prepared in his absence. Because food preparation is the domain of their wives, Samburu men frequently display little knowledge about the food available in the home. Samburu women readily admit that wives generally (though they may be reticent to admit it personally) take advantage of this situation to give extra food to their children or themselves. Beyond possibly inequitable divisions of known meals, Samburu wives also engage in surreptitious self-provisioning and feed-ing of children without the knowledge of absent husbands.

Conversely, Samburu of both genders assert that "women have no share of food." Of course, this does not mean that women do not get food—their nutritional status is comparable or slightly better than men's. Rather their food is seen, for better or worse, as "not food." Women freely drink the buttermilk *(kamanang)* that remains after making ghee *(lkisich)*, a by-product that is considered unsuitable food for men because the fat has been removed. Regardless of how much women or children have drunk, they are not counted as having eaten. In the contemporary era of cooked foods, women are said to simply "lick the cooking pot," having no share of food set aside explicitly for them. Yet again, this is highly ambiguous. Although frequently expressed to indicate the low status of women—they are not even afforded a share of food!—a cooking pot may contain either minimal dregs or a tremen-dous amount, and whether or not a good deal of food remains in the pot is largely determined by the women themselves. Thus, while dis-cursively constituted norms appear to degrade women and erase their needs, in other senses they are central to the construction of culturally legitimate and illegitimate female agency in regard to food. Food is beyond both the view and the purview of men. Women are afforded considerable latitude in culturally sanctioned aspects of their largely invisible feeding, while the same expectations facilitate surreptitious

>reaching norms concerning the fair distribution of food and
s of elders to a sufficient share of the family food. This is par-
the case because men are often away when eating takes place.
_____s no food when a man returns home, the claim can always be
made that the children, rather than the woman herself, have finished
the food—she herself claiming (sometimes truthfully, sometimes not)
that even she has not eaten.

In contrast to women—whose status appears low but whose agency
is high in regard to food—men are regarded as deserving a privileged position in regard to food distribution, but are highly limited
in their means of exercising this privilege both for practical reasons
and for reasons related to contradictions in the construction of Samburu masculinity. As the "owner" *(lopeny)* of the family and all the
people and property that constitute it, elders have claim to a privileged
share of food. However, given the culturally legitimate female control
of domestic food allocation and men's lack of knowledge of the foods
available at home, men lack direct and culturally legitimate means to
control this process. How this plays out in actual food access is not
wholly straightforward. Nutritional data support the conclusion that
some men are underfed by their wives, though certainly not all. For
instance, a nutritional study conducted in 1994 indicates that elders
experience relatively higher rates of undernutrition (Kielmann et al.
1994). My own data, collected in 2002, similarly show women to be
better off nutritionally on average in comparison with men, a tendency
that generally increases with age.

Though far from the norm, women and men agree that wives sometimes starve their husbands. Reasons are various, none wholly legitimate but some more defensible. Sometimes it may be the result of ill
feelings, but the practice generally becomes more common as men age.
Not feeding a husband properly can be a result of the diminishment of
his sexual ability or of a wife's interest after completing childbearing.
Grown sons may conspire with their mother against their father. As
Lekadaa—a Mekuri elder whose distinct thinness was widely attributed to being starved by his young wives—remarked, "I am given food,
but it is not with any love. It is just the way you would throw a bone to
a hyena." Young wives married to an older man may want their husband to die. As Maria Lekilit, a woman in her fifties, explains:

There are many women who make their husband go without food. . . .
Like a young child who is forced to be married to an aged husband. For
instance, as I push my child now and give her to Lengiro [a man in his late

FIGURE 9. An old, thin man with a young, well-nourished wife. Photo by the author.

sixties], even her father is younger. And does the child want that old man? She doesn't. Isn't she saying that she wants him to die? She wants that, so she says, "It is better that he dies, that he dies faster, so that he goes." Then she can go look for a man who is young like herself.

These are largely illegitimate (though understandable) reasons to starve one's husband, but women see other rationales for why some deserve to be starved, such as excessive drunkenness or misusing family resources for themselves. Indeed, some women indicated that more men deserve to be starved than actually are. As Naise Lengerded, a young wife from Lodokejek, asserted, "There are so many reasons that you should

: husband, but you just feed him anyway for the sake of Nkai
your children."

perceptions that their share of food is unfair or inadequate
a tense but complex dynamic. A man often does not know
if the division was actually unjust or if his share simply reflected an
inadequate food supply. Men may quarrel with their wives over food,
even threatening to curse one of her children to death to ensure that
food will be left for his share. However, fighting over food in this way
is very unseemly, resulting in a loss of social capital and prestige in
the community—even if he is correct. Men maintain that it is their
right to speak up if they are not being provisioned properly, but the
community will perceive that he is more concerned with his stomach
than the well-being of those under his care. Thus, he is perceived to
be starting fights—perhaps with no basis—out of simple greed (lobu),
not unlike men who slaughter livestock irresponsibly or sell livestock
to buy alcohol.

"HAVING FINGERS": BOVINE AND HUMAN MORALITY

Gendered facets of food-centered morality are also exhibited in a fundamental competition for milk between humans and calves. The milk
humans consume is obtained only by refusing a calf some portion of
its mother's milk, making how much to take and how much to leave
for the calf both a practical and a moral question. From a practical
standpoint, Samburu maintain that the long-range vision of men differs from the short-term interests of women in balancing human and
bovine milk needs. Samburu recognize the necessity of leaving a sufficient quantity of milk for the calves, usually by milking only two teats
and leaving the others for the calf. Women, however, do not always
adhere to this standard, a defect attributed by members of both genders partially to practical incompetence, to being concerned only with
the milk entering their calabashes now and not with the danger to
future resources should their calves grow thin and die. This tendency
is by and large construed in moral terms. Overmilking is seen as a
horrible and universally female character defect, referred to simply as
"having fingers."

As Samburu describe it, women who "have fingers" are unable to
keep their hands from compulsively milking cattle, sometimes going
so far as to place manure-soiled fingers in calves' mouths to discourage
them from suckling. While many women are said to "have fingers,"

both genders agree that men universally despise it (as do those women who don't "have fingers"). As Namaikat Lekaram, a middle-aged woman from Ndonyo Nasipa, insisted, women with fingers "are bad, very bad because they just finish the calves. It is just her habit—she does so to increase the amount of milk, and she also *enjoys it*. No man could do that, [and if he sees it] he will just speak out. They will keep telling them to stop, even if it is in vain. The women who do this simply can't reason and think about tomorrow" (emphasis added).

Notably, very few informants of either gender interpreted this vice in relation to its obvious result—that overmilking allows one to have more milk for one's children in the short term, even if it may result in smaller herds in the long run. This interpretation might allow a more sympathetic and gender-neutral view of overmilking as a practice related to women's greater sympathy for their children, unlike men, who are often held to see cattle as more valuable and less easily replaced than their own offspring. Yet overmilking is broadly construed as akin to an illness, driven by an immorality somewhere between an innate inability to control one's fingers during milking and a desire to actually harm calves or wanting to have a lot of milk around the house for no logical reason. One of the very few rational reasons informants occasionally offered for overmilking was the immoral desire to have extra milk to hide as a gift for murran lovers. As the Kimaniki elder Lepanoi Lesuyai asserted:

> She keeps concentrating on the amount of milk that is entering the calabash, overmilking for her suitor. She fills the calabash with milk so that when the murran come, she tells them, "Sit down, this is your calabash." But meanwhile the calves are dying. You keep on saying to her, "Wife—how is it that the calves keep dying? Wife—what is happening with the health of the calves?" These days there are those who do this so that they can go sell milk in town. So she doesn't leave any milk for the calves. She finishes all the milk and she goes to sell it in town so that eventually she can buy her murran [boyfriend] ochre or snuff when she comes back.

Moreover, many saw this practice as evidence of a selfishness and coldness toward all under the woman's care—bovine and human alike. They held that—in contrast to the idea that they overmilk to feed their children at the calves' expense—women might be *more* likely to not feed their families properly, even as they were killing the calves through overmilking. That is, a woman who was predisposed to starve her calves might also be predisposed to starve her own family, since, as Namaikat Lekaram described it, women with fingers actually enjoy depriving the calves. Only a handful of informants allowed for the possibility that this was sometimes necessary to keep one's children alive, and that good husbands might look the other way. The tendency of some women to overmilk was additionally related to women's inability (generally, though not universally) to make long-term plans, while men's abhorrence of the practice was related to their role as managers, who should always be thinking ahead to plan for the next drought.

The notion that food plays a significant role in shaping social relationships—whether through food sharing, food production, patterns of cooking, or consumption—is in no sense a novel idea. Both recent and classic approaches have acknowledged the significance of food in a wide array of social processes. My aim here is somewhat more encompassing. In chapter 2, I argued that food has frequently been relegated to a supporting role in anthropological analysis: food becomes the medium through which we understand some "bigger issue," such as sociality, gender, or class. Taking this a step further, food does not simply play an important role in constituting such relationships—rather, these relationships often are centrally *about* food. I do not mean this in a reductionist sense, such as in cultural materialism, where the sociocultural becomes mere adornment to humans' fundamental search for protein and calories. Rather, I understand food as a complex composed of material, social, symbolic, and psychological facets, which are mutually reinforcing and thus not readily disentangled. Food is, therefore, a complex entity, which, both for us as analysts and for the people we study, may become the primary rather than the tertiary subject of focus.

In support of this view, I have considered Samburu social life through what I have term its alimentary structures: key relationships, based mainly on gender and age, which are central to the organization of Samburu life and are primarily constituted through and about food. This represents a considerable shift from the ways Samburu life has long been understood, as well as the ways we attach significance to food in anthropological analyses more generally. Thus, whereas the age-gender system, which is the central element in Samburu social organization, has long been understood mainly through the lens of its influence in structuring the system of polygynous marriage and the concomitant institution of murranhood, a fuller understanding of such institutions requires attending to their fundamental meanings and social dynamics. These quite squarely concern food. Central to the construction of marriage and bachelorhood is how these states create men's relationship to female-centered sites of food consumption. Across the life course, appropriate roles and central attributes of moral personhood are constituted through food. Thus—without a hint of reductionism—we may consider food to be the central player, rather than giving it a bit role in support of some more storied anthropological construct. Food is not a symbol for which, in our ethnographic imaginations, we could as well substitute shell valuables (Malinowski 1922) or grass skirts (Weiner 1983) or, as on Vanuatu, dried hermaphroditic pigs.[5] Yet neither is it mere fuel upon which the symbolic, social, and sensuous are overlaid. The fact that it is food—in all the ripe significance of its material and symbolic aspects, mental, sensuous, and corporeal—is neither accidental nor arbitrary.

CHAPTER 4

A Samburu Gastronomy

WORLDS OF FOOD

Samburu cuisine presents a seeming conundrum. On the one hand, what and how one eats is central to the complex construction of the most integral relationships and values in Samburu life. Food and eating practices are crucial to social action and the symbolic world, and the types of food one eats, the context for eating, and the company with whom one eats construct crucial aspects of individual and group identity across the lines of ethnicity, kinship, gender, and age. On the other hand, Samburu diet is sparse, ideally constituted of just three livestock products: milk, the daily staple; meat, a desirable supplement available mainly at ritual occasions or when an animal happens to die; and blood, a kind of quasi-milk, consumed as a boost to vitality or a supplement during times of scarcity. Granted, the real Samburu menu is rather more complex. Scarcity has always forced Samburu to frequently move beyond this pastoral triad, and even these three foods may be consumed in a number of ways (there are more than ten ways to take blood!), though these tend to be more practical responses to resource availability than epicurean creations of pastoral gourmands. Thus, even with these caveats, we remain with the enigma of a complex gastronomically centered worldview forged out of the simplest of ingredients.

Yet, if this may be surprising from a Euro-American standpoint in which cuisine and its social correlates are grounded in complex dishes created from a bounty of ingredients, cross-cultural precedents are more obvious. Weismantel (1988), for instance, has aptly demonstrated how a simple culinary vocabulary can create a symbolically rich worldview, though her simple Zimbaguan peasant cuisine (seventy-nine foods) is lavish compared with the traditional, or even contemporary, Samburu diet. From another perspective, it is worth considering how the very paucity of food can shape its meaning, as has been an important theme in analyses of food in Africa (e.g., De Boeck 1994; Shack 1971) since Richards's (1932, 1939) seminal studies of the Bemba. Indeed, the elaborately constructed role of food in Samburu life likely owes much to the emphasis on eating only particular foods, within a system of drylands pastoralism in which seasonal hunger is a common feature.

Core Samburu values are constituted at multiple levels through food. As will be explored with some intricacy in the next chapter, the fundamental Samburu value, *nkanyit*—meaning, roughly, a sense of respect—is most explicitly embodied by eating: eating the right foods in the right company, sharing properly, and not displaying greed. Relying solely on a diet of milk, meat, and blood is, as for other Maa-speaking pastoralists (Arhem 1987; Galaty 1982), central to ethnic self-definition, but it is also a goal that has never been wholly attainable. A family's ability to achieve this ideal reflects, by extension, their wealth, herd management skills, and the more nebulous virtue of living in accordance with supernatural forces.

Dietary restrictions also serve to construct ethnic boundaries. Samburu prohibit the consumption of a wide range of potentially edible items—for instance, fish, reptiles, birds, donkeys, and many game animals. By far the strongest prohibition is against eating elephants, which are considered to be similar to human beings. Such prohibitions help construct ethnic boundaries with Turkana pastoralists and Dorobo foragers. In criticizing their neighbors and frequent rivals, the Turkana, Samburu focus on two major traits: the Turkana's failure to circumcise—for which Samburu often mockingly refer to them as boys—and their eating habits. Turkana are well known to eat almost anything—birds, fish, reptiles, and all manner of game. They eat donkeys and drink donkey milk, and are reputed to actually sell donkey meat in Turkana butcheries. Worst of all, they eat elephants with zeal.

The eating of elephants is a characteristic that also sets Dorobo foragers apart from Samburu. This is particularly important because the foraging lifestyle in Samburu District was largely extinguished in the 1930s through forced relocation by the colonial authorities. As such, most Dorobo may best be characterized as either Samburu-ized Dorobo or Samburu who are known or reputed to have Dorobo ancestry. These Dorobo are generally not considered to be true Samburu, and "pure" Samburu sometimes disparage the status of those descended from Dorobo with the innuendo that, in secret, they still eat elephants. Other distinctions in the segmentary structure may be marked through food or feeding practices, though these are less significant. Some Ltoijo—a major subsection of the Lmasula—are not supposed to eat from the cooking pot. *Laisi*[1] of the Lukumae section are not supposed to eat certain types of game eaten by other Samburu, including waterbuck and dik-dik.

Perhaps most important, food and eating practices serve to construct and represent the age-gender system. In the case of meat, the age-gender system is mapped onto the culinary system, with every part of the slaughtered animal "belonging" to a particular age-gender sector of Samburu society. Consumption of certain foods is passed through the family over time. For instance, blood from slaughtered animals—which conveys strength and vitality—is usually drunk by younger fathers but is relinquished to their sons as they become older youths. Milk—which is considered the most perfect food—is collected by women, who allocate shares in different calabashes for children and general household use, for their husbands, and for murran. Women's identity is constructed around the provisioning of food, and in most contexts, women both cook the food and allocate it according to their perceptions of the needs of various household members. Central to the construction of masculinity is discipline and restraint in eating, particularly in domestic contexts, so that the desires of men's stomachs do not interfere with their responsibility to safeguard the well-being of women and children.

This chapter builds on the previous chapter's concern with the ways in which Samburu social structures and social relationships are constructed through food, through a shift of focus to the foods themselves. I present here a kind of menu outlining in detail Samburu diet and cuisine. Yet this is intrinsically a sociocultural menu, envisaging the ways Samburu worlds are forged through food. I am concerned not merely with the foods themselves, but with the cultural logic that orders this culinary system and how it coalesces with other meanings central to Samburu life.

THE PASTORAL TRIAD

Samburu diet is ideally composed exclusively of the pastoral triad of milk, meat, and blood. Although likely not sustainable for prolonged

periods—even during times of relative plenty—as for other N
speaking pastoralists (Arhem 1987), this diet forms a core compo
of Samburu cultural identity. Not only are these foods significan in
constructing identity vis-à-vis other ethnic groups, but each is encoded
with specific attributes in regard to the construction of social relationships and Samburu personhood.

Meat

Meat *(nkiri)* is the culinary center of the Samburu social universe. In a
pastoral diet, meat takes a nutritional role secondary to milk, which is
the mundane staple food of everyday pastoral existence. A diet based
on meat is simply not sustainable, as it is not possible to maintain livestock numbers adequate to pursue such a nutritional strategy. Meat,
consequently, is a highly marked introduction into the routine diet
of milk—or, nowadays, purchased foods—that is consumed at ritual
occasions, to fete visitors or cure the sick, and only occasionally out
of a desire for meat or when an animal happens to die. The occasional
and special circumstances that surround meat eating make it the most
highly desired food.

As in many societies, meat is disproportionately masculine for
Samburu. Meat is the ideal food for murran, consumed in the bush
(loikar) to build strength and ferocity. Those who do not feast on meat
at *loikar* have traditionally been disparaged as *naperto nanya malesin,*
"pesky little calabash drinkers," loitering around the settlements and
disturbing people like flies. Today the perceived degradation of murran's behavior is attributed to their failure to eat enough meat. Elders
are also far more closely associated with meat than are women. Even
in elderhood, men's meat consumption takes place disproportionately
away from the gaze of women in the company of their age mates at the
lpul (roasting fire), either when eating the *rikoret* (marriage ox) at weddings or when cattle die out grazing.[2] Although all age-gender sectors
have their share of slaughtered livestock, the biggest, meatiest portions
are mostly eaten by men. Men make most decisions about slaughtering livestock and do the work of butchering. Thus, meat always passes
through male hands before reaching women and children.

Cows have the most desirable meat, with goats a close competitor.
Goat meat is, however, far more common, since small stock can be
slaughtered more frequently. Cows are usually eaten only if one happens to die or at important *lmuget* (rituals or ritual celebrations) in the

age-set cycle or at marriages. Goats are the principal mundane meat. They are eaten to provide strength, and the hardness of their bodies is seen to foster similar qualities in the humans who consume them. Goats are usually the slaughter stock of choice for treating illness. Goat meat is the unmarked category of small stock, with few exceptional negative or positive features. In contrast, sheep meat is more unusual, particularly suitable for certain circumstances but less broadly appealing. On the positive side, the high fat content of sheep meat is desirable during recovery from childbirth, and eating sheep is viewed as a way of putting on fat rapidly. Sheep are used exclusively in rituals where small stock are slaughtered, partially because rituals typically require large amounts of fat and because sheep are construed as pure, innocent, unblemished animals in a way that goats are not. However, the high fat content of sheep meat renders it less palatable to some and, in the Samburu view, dangerous to others. Samburu believe that sheep meat can trigger malaria, hepatitis, and *suul*, a disease characterized by swelling. Sheep are believed to cause asthma; asthmatic children should not even go near sheep to milk them. The negative characteristics associated with sheep meat are also associated with camel meat, though the slaughter of camels is extremely rare, even in the lowland areas, where the animals are relatively common.

Slaughtered livestock are butchered into closely prescribed cuts of meat, and careful and effective butchering is essential to the supernatural well-being of the herd and social relations. Dismembering an animal in the wrong place or breaking the wrong bones "kills the house" of the animal, leading its kin in your herds to soon die. In areas where camels are rare, owners may seek an expert to make sure that the carcass is divided correctly. Because particular cuts of meat belong to specific age-gender sectors of Samburu society, errors in butchering can be an affront to the "owners" of that meat, sometimes actually forcing one to slaughter another animal. For instance, if you break the back (belonging to girls) when slaughtering a goat, you must slaughter another to provide them with a perfect, unbroken cut of meat.

The marked desirability of meat helps construct it as a common good in which everyone has a designated share, the age-gender system ostensibly mapped onto the carcass. This is particularly true of cows, since the quantity of meat is much larger, and cattle are viewed largely as a shared community resource. The much smaller amount of meat from a sheep or goat restricts meat distribution to an inner circle—a family, a group of visitors, or a patient for whom an animal is slaughtered. Though one hind leg *(lwuantan)* from a sheep or goat must be designated *muro* and gifted to a friend or neighbor, other cuts typically leave this inner circle only if the appropriate age-gender category cannot be found within it.

In rituals, specific cuts of meat create and iconify key relationships. For instance, in the promotion of new initiates to murranhood, a salient bond is formed between the new murran and the man who in the context of the ceremony slides a piece of brisket *(nkiyeu)* from the slaughtered ox from the initiate's chest to each arm. The individual who does this is a special friend, your sponsor into murranhood; like the meat, he is referred to as *nkiyeu*. Swearing upon your *nkiyeu* is a particularly strong oath, while others might take your *nkiyeu* in vain, like one's mother in a Euro-American context (also with potentially violent results). In marriage ceremonies, two cuts of meat are brought into the house of the bride's mother, as the ritually significant parts of the *rikoret* (marriage ox) whose slaughter legally consummates the marriage.[3] These include the *nkiyeu* and one *lngeilat* (a boneless cut between the ribs and the foreleg). Fat from the *nkiyeu* fills the rounded calabash *(mbolbol)* that the bride carries on her back when walking to the groom's settlement, while the remainder of the *nkiyeu* is used to make the *lmutuchu* (a soup, described below) given to the elders who bless the couple as they depart. The *lngeilat* is given to the father's brother of the bride.

Factors specific to a particular occasion can influence actual meat distribution, though not negating everyone's ideal entitlement to a share. For instance, murran cannot share in any animal that catches women's gaze, and they will take meat from one slaughtered at home only if the owner specifically wants them to share it. In such cases, he will send the murran to slaughter it outside the settlement, roasting and eating their own share and returning the other parts to the home. Conversely, when murran eat livestock in the bush—acquired through theft, as gifts, or simply from their own herds—they need not bring the parts back home to be eaten by the appropriate age-gender sectors. Patterns of meat sharing can also differ considerably depending on whether a sheep or goat is given to a visitor to eat, slaughtered for a sick person, or simply killed for meat.

Not surprisingly, meat distribution from cows is much more diffuse than that from small stock. The need to share with all age-gender groups is far more imperative, and (unlike small stock) cows are under normal circumstances always shared with large numbers of people beyond the domestic group. Everyone in principal has a share of beef, though in practice the true requirements are that no one is denied a share and that the appropriate parts of the cow go to representatives of the appropriate age-gender sector. As with small stock, murran are sometimes an exception to this pattern. When murran eat cows far from settlements, they may consume the whole animal themselves. They cannot eat meat that has been seen by women, though efforts are typically made to slaughter cows away from the eyes of women. Murran are principally excluded from eating meat from animals slaughtered for rituals in which they have no part and animals that die in the settlement or are too sick to be moved. If possible, however, debilitated cows are carried into the bush before they are slaughtered.

Samburu offer a variety of reasons for their patterns of sharing. They recognize that they have an insatiable desire for meat, which the relatively small amount that is typically available cannot satisfy, a fact canonized in the proverb *Mebaki nkiri tungana* ("Meat can never be enough for the people"). Some suggest that prescriptions for meat distribution simply reflect that Samburu "love one another," and the rules ensure that "everyone gets something." Others suggest that people can fight over meat, and determining its distribution beforehand allows meat to be given out in a peaceable and orderly manner. Underlying this is a strong belief in the danger of being cursed—intentionally or subconsciously —if people are denied their fair share of meat. Indeed, while denying a person food can always result in a curse, that from not sharing meat is especially potent. Since meat consumption occurs infrequently, cheating someone of their rightful share might mean that they will not taste meat again for months.

Meat is usually either roasted or boiled. In Samburu this cross-culturally significant distinction (Levi-Strauss 1969) maps onto other crucial dichotomies, specifically bush/home, masculine/feminine, and hot/cold. The last of these is notable in regard to Samburu understandings of the humoral qualities of food, since a human's moral center is the stomach. Foods may make someone's stomach hot or cold, which is central to their moral personhood.

The archetypal food of the bush is roasted meat, consumed by murran at *loikar* (meat-eating camps). Even the commonplace *lpul*—the ordinary meat-roasting site—is gender-segregated and almost exclusively male. The sole exceptions are cow organ meats that are normally eaten roasted (liver, spleen, and kidneys), which women may cook near the slaughter site *(mpereto e nkiteng)*. Other parts for women's or general family consumption are brought back to the homestead. Elders and murran roast the portions allocated to them in the bush. Murran and male visitors to a homestead may roast an entire goat outside the settl. ment, while the hind legs and ribs of a cow are roasted in the bush, the right side of the cow for murran and the other for elders. The stomach and other internal organs are returned to the settlement, as are other parts used either for general family consumption (e.g., forelegs) or for particular family members (e.g., the back for girls, neck for women, heart for boys, etc.). Though some parts may be roasted over the house fire, the bulk of this meat is boiled as soup. Whereas roasted meat is associated with and produces hot, masculine vitality, boiled meat is by and large cool, feminine food, prepared in the cooking pots of women. Similarly, when livestock are slaughtered to treat sick people, the meat is boiled, often with medicinal herbs, to cool the body and aid in recovery. The association of boiled meat with the homestead is not, however, absolute, as murran also boil particular cuts of meat with herbs to make soup at *loikar*. Some herbs (esp. *seketet;* see Spencer 1965) are added to increase the ferocity of murran, but most are simply intended to cool the stomach and speed digestion, thereby allowing more gorging on meat.

Frying is the least common means of cooking, and lacks strongly masculine or feminine associations. Apart from *kunuru* (described below), frying is traditionally a method of preservation. Meat preserved through frying is allocated in different ways than dried meat *(sirikan)*. *Sirikan* is made by cutting meat into thin strips, which are dried by hanging in the ever-smoky house. This method is mainly used by women as a supplement to foods cooked for general family consumption. Fried meats are generally the domain of elders, though they may share them with other family members or visitors. Two of these are *lakulii* and *mununa,* both made from finely chopped pieces of meat that are stewed until the fat has been rendered out of them and they become dry. They differ in that additional fat is added to *lakulii* during cooking, while *mununa* is mixed with additional fat before being put in its storage calabash. An additional type of preserved fried meat is *ngauwa,* made by frying very fatty meat, such as sheep tails or other body fat *(sunya)*. This is also mostly eaten by elders but may be shared with women and children. Children's first meat is *ngauwa,* which they begin to eat at around eighteen months.

Milk

Milk *(kule)* is the traditional staple food. Under ideal conditions, Samburu diet is composed almost exclusively of milk supplemented with blood and meat. Milk is taken in two main forms, fresh (*kule nairewa,* hot milk) and curdled (*kule naoto,* ripened milk). Curdled milk sits anywhere from a few days to a few weeks and should be allowed to fully ripen. Curdled milk is considered superior, having ripened into a tastier and more satisfying state. Fresh milk that has begun to sour *(keisukut)* but has not yet curdled is drinkable but undesirable.

In contrast to meat, milk is a highly feminine resource and a moderately feminizing food. Possible associations with human breast milk, and that it comes from lactating animals seem obvious, but Samburu instead highlight the fact that milk is collected by women, who control its distribution as the main source of daily sustenance. Whereas meat and its consumers are quintessentially of the bush *(soro),* milk is the centerpiece of women's houses. Whereas meat breeds hotness, strength, and ferocity, driving men into trances or off to cattle raids, milk makes stomachs cool, inducing people to repose in gentle satisfaction.

Alongside the two main types of milk, Samburu also drink *kamanang* (buttermilk) and *manang* (colostrum). *Kamanang* is the soured milk remaining after the removal of butterfat for the production of ghee *(lkisich).* It is highly gendered. Because the fat has been removed, men consider it to not be real food, and only recently have some men in highland areas begun to consume it. It is typically left for women and children but, being essentially a consumable residue, is not considered part of their daily food allotment. *Manang* (colostrum) is available whenever livestock—particularly cows—give birth. Anyone may drink it, though Samburu usually don't give it to children because the high fat content renders it dangerous if eaten with other foods, and children lack the restraint to limit their eating. If consumed with water, it can cause severe diarrhea, while in conjunction with other foods it can cause severe malaise, bloating, and flatulence. One informant claimed (perhaps dubiously) to know of an older boy who died after he drank *manang* and then ate wild tubers.

Milk from various types of livestock is perceived to differ in a range of characteristics, partially reflecting actual differences in the composition of the milk of cows, goats, sheep, and camels, though other factors also are involved.[4] Cow's milk is usually considered to be the best, and its texture is described as light or fine *(kebebek).* Occasionally people, particularly elders, will drink only cow's milk, holding other types of milk to be inferior and beneath their tastes. Sheep's milk is also considered good for drinking but is described as sticky *(kemaga),* perhaps because it has far more protein and fat than that of other livestock.

Goat's milk is deemed thick *(keirosha)* and is believed to contain a lot of bile, such that it is best to dilute it for drinking. Camel's milk is considered dilute *(nkarar),* but many believe that it can give the drinker considerable endurance in walking. However, some, especially in areas where camels are not common, refuse to drink camel milk. Today, many Samburu believe that the best use of goat or camel milk is to drink it in tea.

Milk is typically collected twice a day, although in some areas small stock are also milked in the afternoon. Women are principally responsible for milking, although children of both sexes do much of this work. Since women are absent from cattle camps, milking may be done by anyone present, although it is typically done by boys or girls if they are present. Milk may go directly into the calabashes *(lmalesin)* for each person, or into a milking cup from which the calabashes are then filled. There is a wide variety of calabashes, made from wood or gourds *(nkirau),* and different types are used for different classes of people. The elder's calabash *(naitu)* is a slender wooden calabash with a skin lid. The calabash for murran *(lmala lo lmurran)* is a black wooden calabash with a wooden cup top, and is decorated with green beads on its neck. Each child has a calabash, with boys typically having *nkoting*—similar to the elder's *naitu* but shorter and stouter—and girls having a slender, decorated calabash called *nkilip.* Women do not have a calabash specifically for their own consumption, but control the remaining supply of milk. Women may drink from this supply, dispense it to visitors, or store it to later make *lkisich* (ghee). Women also drink milk intentionally left for them *(lmonge*—literally "the bull") in the calabashes of elders and murran, in reciprocity and gratitude for the cleaning and care of the calabash.

Blood

At least for contemporary Samburu, the least common of the pastoral triad is blood. There is some scholarly disagreement concerning the importance of blood consumption among Maa-speaking pastoralists (Johnsen 1997), some emphasizing its dietary significance (Merker 1910; Kipury 1983), while others suggest it is a relatively infrequent foodstuff (Grandin 1988; Nestel 1989). In my own observations, blood did not constitute a significant part of the diet but also was not rare. Moreover, blood is consumed disproportionately at *lale* (cattle camps), such that it would be less common around homesteads. The Samburu in highland areas note a clear decline in their drinking of blood. Many forms of blood are undesirable famine foods, for which purchased foods may be substituted. Livestock holdings are typically lower in highland areas, so a significant supply of blood often is not available.

The unmodified blood *(loodo)* may be drunk by anyone if the milk supply is inadequate, but is more often consumed in one of a surprising array of forms, many of which are marked by gender and age. Blood is something of a categorical oddity between meat and milk. It is red like meat, has a taste closer to meat, dribbles from undercooked meat, and sometimes is a byproduct of slaughtering. Its associations and uses are, however, closer to milk, and some, such as Lentiwas, a Kileku elder, go so far as to assert that "it is just another kind of milk." Moreover, by coagulating, it can actually change from milk to meat. In its liquid form it is considered milk, and murran can drink it in the sight of women, but in its solid form it is meat and prohibited by the *lminong.* Blood is generally associated more with males, partially because it is more frequently consumed in cattle camps, which are mostly male contexts. Women also tend to be repulsed by the deep redness of fresh, uncooked blood and prefer it in one of its cooked forms, if at all. Blood's desirable forms tend to be associated with masculine vitality, and it is mainly young men who consume it enthusiastically.

The most masculine form of blood is *nchopet,* drunk directly from a slaughtered sheep or goat. These are killed through suffocation, with one man holding its mouth shut, and another kneeling on its chest. When it passes out, its throat is slit and the blood pools within a flap of skin pulled out from the neck, from which it is slurped up. Consuming blood in this way is exclusively male, practiced especially by murran, but also by older boys and young, active elders. Young married men may drink *nchopet* from livestock slaughtered at home but tend to relinquish this as they and their sons age. Drinking *nchopet* typically takes on the air of a drinking contest, with men sucking up as much blood as the can before rising up with a smile of satisfaction across their blood-stained faces. In the bush the *nchopet* is normally drunk in its entirety—failure is a black mark on the virility of those present—but in domestic contexts, some of the blood may be added to soup or meat, or even used to decoratively stain calabashes.

Apart from *nchopet,* blood is taken from livestock (usually cattle, though sometimes large goats) by tying a tourniquet around the neck, and shooting a specially made arrow into the resulting bulging jugular. Blood flows out in a steady stream, and is collected in a calabash or other container. When enough has been taken, the tourniquet is released and the bleeding stops. This blood may then be used in a wide variety of ways. *Lood'orok* ("black blood") is consumed in its unadulterated form. It can be a famine food or given to the sick or badly injured as a direct replacement for lost blood. *Lood'orok* was until recently the principal food for postpartum women.

The two most common forms of blood are mixtures with milk, and they tend to have associations that are mostly, though not exclusively, masculine. *Saroi* ("pink") is made by stirring the blood to remove the coagulant (which is given to dogs) and then mixing it with curdled milk. It is considered to be highly nutritious, and is normally given to newly circumcised boys and girls to replenish lost blood. *Njuloti* ("mixture") is the same as *saroi*, except that it is made with fresh milk. It is considered even more nutritious and blood-restoring, though some informants indicated that it was too filling to drink very much. It can be drunk by anyone, but especially murran, who may drink it at home.

Less common mixtures or means of consuming blood are associated principally with murran and herd boys. *Nchakule*—blood mixed with animal fat and milk—may be consumed by murran arriving home from eating meat at *loikar*, using fat from the animal they ate in the bush. *Lukuworie* ("warmup") is made by mixing quickly collected milk and blood from the first few animals that return home from grazing. It is consumed immediately, while the milk and blood are still warm, and the coagulant is not removed. It serves as an appetizer before the main meal or an energy boost before milking and bleeding the other animals or other activities. If it is not consumed immediately, the mixture may be allowed to sit and coagulate. This gelled milk-blood mixture is typically cut into chunks with sticks, and is called *ncharligi* (chunks) or *ntananga*, referring to how the chunks slap against your mouth as you eat them.

Some other blood preparations are odd and unusual, prepared mainly out of boredom by boys in cattle camps. These include *nchorde*, which is like *njuloti* (fresh milk and blood) but cooked until it is curdled. More unusual is *ntis*, which is made by removing the coagulant from *njuloti* only after the milk and blood have been mixed together. This is roasted on a stick, and its name comes from the hissing sound it makes as the steam escapes in the fire. It is made only by children and is foreign to the world of adults. On one occasion, a woman of around forty burst out laughing when I mentioned *ntis* while we bled a cow— she had completely forgotten its existence and was shocked to hear a white person mention it.

FIGURE 10. Milk mixed with uncoagulated blood makes a kind of jelly. Photo by the author.

A final traditional form of blood is *mpupoi,* boiled blood with added fat, which is consumed during drought or famine. It is highly caloric but not very palatable and very dehydrating. It is uncommon now with the greater availability of purchased foods. New forms of blood continue to develop. For instance, murran in the summer of 2004 discussed novel preparations involving the mixture of blood, and sometimes milk—or even meat—with maize meal. These new concoctions had (for no apparent reason) been given exotic names that the young men had apparently heard on the radio, such as "Egypt" and "Libya."

FAT (PASTORAL TRIAD + 1)

Fat *(lata)* is a highly desired food. It is collected and stored from slaughtered animals or obtained from curdled milk that is agitated in a large calabash. Fat in its various forms is stored in a woman's calabashes, and she retains principal control over it. It is not allocated to specific individuals (like milk), nor does any individual have specific rights over it (like meat). To a great extent, women are empowered to dispense or use it as they wish, although husbands may make attempt to make demands for it if they know that their wife has some.

Ngorngo (butter) is removed from milk that has curdled for one to three days. Babies are fed *ngorgno* at a very early age, and pregnant women experiencing stomach problems may be given it as a first treatment, before slaughtering a goat if problems persist. Usually, however, *ngorngo* is cooked to make *lkisich* (ghee). Cooking removes the remaining milk solids *(raganyia)*, which may be eaten by children or women, leaving a very pure fat. This greatly enhances preservation, since the remaining milk and milk solids make *ngorngo* highly prone to spoilage. Since *lkisich* is made from a woman's milk supply and she does the work of preparation, it is regarded as hers. She may eat it, give it away to friends, or nowadays, sell it. She may add it to food she is preparing for the family, spoon it into individual food dishes for family members, or add it to their tea. If men know it is present, they may also directly ask for some to be added to their food or tea. Obtaining *lkisich* is particularly desirable for pregnant women, who eat it to soothe their stomach during pregnancy or store it to make sure they have enough food after they have given birth.

Other fats are obtained from slaughtered livestock and stored. Although these are also generally controlled by women, men decide when to slaughter (sometimes out of a desire for fat) and undertake slaughtering, so their knowledge of what fat exists in the home and their legitimacy in determining its allocation is greater than with dairy fats. Animal fats include *lata oriong* ("back fat") obtained from the exterior of a slaughtered animal, which is liquid or nearly so and often given to sick people to drink to aid in their recovery. *Siret* is fat from the inside of the stomach and intestines, which is typically hard at room temperature and is considered most palatable when added to warm food. Some, however, simply cut off a piece and eat it whole in its solid form.

Today Samburu also buy fat from shops, mainly vegetable shortening, under such popular Kenyan brands as *Kimbo* and *Kasuku*. Samburu like these *lata e lduka* ("shop fats") but consider them markedly inferior to animal fat. Not only is the taste inferior, but they are uneasy about not knowing the fat's origins. To improve flavor, people may mix purchased fat with animal fat.

MIXED FOODS

As noted in chapter 2, Samburu principally eat food in its unadorned
form. No spices or other flavorings are used, apart from salt. It is
unclear even whether salt has long been used on food, although rock
salt *(magad)* is used with chewing tobacco. A variety of herbs are added
to soup for medicinal purposes, though not to enhance flavor. Indeed,
these herbs tend to be bitter *(kedua)*, and the harshness of their taste
is taken as evidence of the efficacy of an herb. Samburu do not have a
strongly developed taste vocabulary, with only five terms to describe
flavors: *kemelok* (sweet, but also generally tasty or good); *kesiisho*
(salty, like curdled milk); *kesukut* (sour, as in partially fermented milk);
kesagamaka (partially putrid meat); and *ketuka* (tasteless). Only two of
these are favorable, and only one refers concretely to a specific flavor.

Desirable foods are seen as intrinsically desirable and do not require
special preparation to make them tastier. There are very few dishes, in
the sense of mixing foods to enhance flavors. Mixing foods is generally
viewed with disfavor, in fact, although this specifically concerns only
eating meat in conjunction with milk. Mixing milk and meat leads to
the development of *lkuposhoi,* a condition that advances from general
laziness to parasitic worms. *Lkuposhoi* is associated disproportionately
with women, who (according to men) may lack both the discipline to
avoid eating milk and meat too close together and the resolve to consume the strong herbs required for treatment.

Apart from the previously described milk and blood mixtures, few
dishes involve mixing foods. One is *kunuru,* a type of fried meat, made
from a variety of meats and significant fat and blood, that is occasionally prepared by murran especially. Some suggest it was borrowed from
the neighboring Mukogodo Maasai. A second mixed food is a thick
soup called *lmutuchu* ("Last as long as life"), which is drunk by elders
who provide the blessings for the departing bride at marriage, or at
other ceremonies, such as *nkaji naibor.* Meat from the chest *(nkiyeu)* is
boiled overnight, and blood is mixed with the soup, along with curdled
and fresh milk, and honey or (more commonly nowadays) sugar, and
hand-blended to frothiness. This is the only dish in which disparate
foods are mixed to produce something intended to be especially tasty.
Informants could not fully explicate the significance of this mixture,
but it is notable that *lmutuchu* is given to elders in the context of a particularly significant blessing. Moreover, there is some suggestion that
its reference to the life course signifies that all manner of things should

be included, as they are in life (although no bad things are added to the soup).

The remaining "dishes" are relatively undesirable mixtures taken traditionally as famine foods, like *mpupoi,* the previously described mixture of boiled blood and fat. A number of plant foods are similarly cooked with blood and fat, such as *loordo* (a type of wild green), the seeds of various species of acacia, and *lpaas,* a soup made from the fruits of various plants. These dishes are prepared and eaten out of necessity rather than to create particularly tasty dishes. All of them are now uncommon with the wider availability of purchased foods, and their consumption has disappeared from the highlands in the past decade.

SPECIAL FOODS

Samburu cuisine is not characterized by a wide array of specially prepared dishes. Apart from *lmutuchu,* the only special foods mixed for ritual consumption are unusual items taken in small quantities at large-scale age-set rituals, particularly at the *Lmuget Le'Nkarna,* which promotes an age set to senior murranhood. The age-set leader *(launoni)* is made to drink a mixture containing odd things—such as date palm leaves and flies—as a form of oath ensuring his dedication to the age set. Later a sweetened mixture, made of blood from a cow slaughtered by the *launoni,* fresh and sour milk, and honey (but absent any flies) is drunk first by the *launoni* and then by all murran. After taking a sip, they spit it on their stomachs four times before drinking it freely.

More significant are particular ways of eating associated with particular occasions or marked statuses. Ritual occasions are, for instance, always associated with meat. The central component of all rituals *(lmuget)* is the slaughter of a cow or sheep, and the meat is consumed by those attending the ritual. The other essential food for contemporary Samburu rituals is tea (see chapter 7). Although tea has no ritual significance, it has become the quintessential food of hospitality and must be given to welcome all attending the ritual.

Pregnant and postpartum women also follow particular ways of eating, as do newly initiated boys and girls. Counterintuitively from a Euro-American standpoint, pregnant women strive to limit their caloric consumption. If they cannot control their appetites they must be forced by their husbands, who are in turn severely chastised by older women if they fail to do so effectively (see also Johnsen 1997). The goal is to limit the size of the infant, out of fear that a woman will be unable to deliver successfully if it grows too large. Pregnant women also frequently develop *ngaman,* a condition characterized by cravings for particular types of food or, alternatively, disgust for not only particular foods but also particular people or animals. Pregnant women cannot eat meat or drink the milk of any animal suffering from foot-and-mouth disease, out of concern that it may cause an abortion, scars, or birth defects. Pregnant women also refrain from drinking water collected from a place where elephants drink, as it may cause a funny shaped nose, extra fingers, or strangely shaped hands.

Traditionally, several animals are slaughtered after a baby is delivered, though this has been drastically reduced in an era of pastoral poverty. The first animal slaughtered is a sheep *(moor)* that is not eaten by the woman herself but ritually given to all community women. A woman nursing a boy cannot, however, eat *moor,* since this exclusively female meat would reach him via the breast milk, nor may pregnant women, since they do not know if their fetus is a boy. *Moor* may not come from the husband's herd but is taken from a neighbor's herd without asking. Today in areas where few people are wealthy in livestock, a few people may have animals taken frequently, leading to some grumbling about this practice.

The first food a postpartum woman takes should be pure blood to replace what has been lost. In highland areas, Guinness is also given to cleanse her stomach. In the past, blood would be her only food for several days, though now after the first day it is replaced with light porridge. On the fourth day, a cow or (more typically now) a sheep is slaughtered as *lbutan,* which is eaten by her and the men. In the past, numerous animals would be slaughtered, but now it is usually just one. She eats fat but is also forced to vomit, using the partially digested grass from the *lbutan*'s stomach, to cleanse her system. Women normally do not take pure water or milk for about a month, which is also the case for people who have suffered injuries.

Particular diets and styles of eating are also associated with male and female initiation. After circumcision, both male *(laibartak)* and female initiates *(nkaibartak)* feed on *saroi,* meat, fat, and sour milk. The meat is cut into small pieces that they eat with sticks without touching it with their hands. New initiates are not allowed to wash, so eating with their hands would result in the extremely unpropitious act of auto-cannibalism by eating their own *latakuny,* sweat and body dirt (see also Straight 2006).

WILD FOODS: EDIBLES AND INEDIBLES

In Samburu, as in other dialects of Maa, the word for a forager is *Ltorrobo*. Commonly Anglicized as Dorobo throughout East Africa, its essential meaning is "a poor person." *Dorobo* is, in fact, a polythetic category, applied by various Maa-speaking peoples to groups of neighbors bearing little resemblance to each other. While some of these groups may be remaining pockets of previously widespread foraging groups, they also include impoverished pastoralists, such as the Mukogodo Maasai, who are believed to contain remnants of the Laikipiak, who were vanquished in the mid- to late nineteenth century (Herren 1991). Central to the notion of *Dorobo* is its contrast to a superior, pastoral way of life. Foragers are essentially defined by an absence of livestock, and in widespread myths Dorobo are held to have severed the leather strap that previously allowed livestock to pass freely between the place of humans on earth and the place of Nkai in the heavens (Kipury 1983; Straight 2006).

Despite this negative attitude toward foraging, Samburu at least periodically eat a wide range of wild foods. Pastoralism is characterized by seasonal scarcity and not infrequent droughts and famines. Consequently, the ideal diet of milk, meat, and blood has of necessity always been supplemented with selected nonpastoral foods that could be eaten without strong stigma during times of want. One option was to acquire grain from neighboring agriculturalists, such as the Meru and the Dassanetch (Sobania 1980). The second option was to consume wild foods, either acquired in trade from Dorobo or collected themselves.

Wild foods vary tremendously in their acceptability. Many are prohibited, while others are basically acceptable, especially in times of want. The only wild food with unambiguously positive implications is honey *(naisho)* perhaps not surprising in light of the arguments of Mintz (1985) and others (Jerome 1977) concerning the natural desirability of sweet things. Honey is acquired from Dorobo foragers specializing in bee husbandry, or acquired from wild bees found in the forest.[5] Although bees are more commonly associated with Dorobo, there is no stigma associated with either eating honey or gathering it. Indeed, finding honey is considered to be good luck—when bees occupied our house in 2003, some neighbors questioned the virtue of driving away the "lucky bees" who had chosen our home. Elsewhere "finding honey" or "finding bees" is used metaphorically to describe unexpected good fortune. For instance, if a man easily receives permission to marry a highly sought after bride, people may explain it simply as *letorro lenyanna*—"his bees," which he was destined to stumble upon. Honey is highly prized; if you see honey you should taste it lest you deny yourself good fortune. Honey is either eaten as a raw comb or brewed into beer. Indeed, the word for honey *(naisho)* is the same as for beer (see chapter 8). Bee larvae *(lchangaro)* are both included in the beer and eaten with the raw comb. This is surprising, since eating insects in other contexts is wholly repugnant to Samburu. However, some Samburu not only eat the larvae but prefer them to the honey. As Lekeren, our host in Loltulelei, explained at the late-night honey feed after driving bees from his own house—when the annoyance of the infestation finally outweighed its luck—"I prefer the white part. The oil [honey] is overly sweet."

A variety of largely undesirable wild plants is also eaten. These are eaten mainly as famine foods, though children also eat various tubers and berries while herding. Some plant foods continue to be used today, although the increased availability of purchased agricultural products limits their necessity. The most commonly eaten wild plant is *loordo,* a green cooked into porridge with blood. The seeds of some acacia species are also used as famine foods, including *sagaram* from the *ltepes* tree *(Acacia tortillas)* or *ldalam* from the *lkiloriti* tree *(Acacia nilotica),* both of which are boiled and drunk like tea. Berries of various plants are boiled to make *lpaas,* a hot fruit soup to which fat, blood, honey, or sugar may be added for taste or caloric value. All these are regarded as normal famine foods, and no particular stigma is attached to their consumption, nor any virtue beyond their ability to keep one alive.

Game meat, however, is considerably more complex. Hunting is closely associated with Dorobo, and ideally Samburu do not eat game. In practice, however, some species are prohibited, whereas the consumption of others can be read as a sign of poverty rather than depravity (see also Evans-Pritchard 1940 on the Nuer). In the context of contemporary pastoral scarcity, most Samburu will eat permissible game animals with relish and often downplay any negative associations with their consumption. This contrasts with earlier accounts (Spencer 1965) and wider attitudes about other Maa-speaking pastoralists. The impetus to eat game in the context of contemporary scarcity has likely encouraged a re-reading by Samburu of their past attitudes toward game meat, but it is also possible that past attitudes were in some senses peculiar to the colonial period. The colonial period was a time of unusual pastoral plenty—including, for murran, fat cows easily stolen from European ranches—and many informants indicate that this marked a low ebb in the consumption of game meat. At the same time, the colonial government was particularly keen on enforcing antipoaching regulations and highly admired Maa-speakers' prohibitions against eating game, perhaps leading to stronger (real or perceived) prohibitions against eating game at that time.

The truth may lie between present renderings of the past and images formed in the colonial context. There may be reasons for Samburu to develop more permissive attitudes toward game owing to contemporary poverty, but it is also clear that precolonial Samburu ate some game. One interesting piece of evidence is the original Samburu word for *shop*. Today the common term is *ldukai* (Kiswahili *duka*), but the older term, *lkerinket,* is derived from a type of trap used to catch large game animals, such as giraffe. Informants suggest that the two were associated metaphorically because large quantities of food were found at each, but also because in preparing donkeys to go to distant shops, neighbors might surmise that they were going to *lkerinket* to load up large quantities of meat.

While the general acceptability of eating of game animals is ambiguous, Samburu have well-defined ideas about the edibility of specific ones. While some are regarded as basically edible, many others are strictly prohibited. The only acceptable game meats are those bearing a close resemblance to domestic livestock: Large ungulates such as eland and buffalo are seen as being "close" to cattle and regarded as having very good meat. Antelope are close to goats and may be eaten during famines without strong stigma. Nonmammals—reptiles, birds, and fish—are not regarded as food and not normally eaten. Attitudes concerning large mammals vary. These range from Thomson's gazelle, which members of some kinship groups will eat and others will not, to warthogs, which are generally held to be repugnant, to elephants, which there are strong, supernatural strictures against eating, owing to their perceived similarity to human beings. In historically remembered times of severe famine, however, all restrictions could be set aside. During the infamous *mutai* of the 1890s—the triple disaster characterized by the livestock epidemics of rinderpest and pleuropneumonia, drought, and human smallpox—not only were elephants eaten but there are well-known accounts of cannibalism.

Game meats are not a communal resource in the way livestock are. Slaughtered livestock are divided into specific pieces, each belonging to specific people or categories of persons. Dividing the carcass correctly is essential to preserving your herds, since breaking a bone in the wrong place is seen as "breaking your herd." Conversely, allocating these very specific cuts correctly is essential to social well-being. Game animals belong to no one, nor does the meat. Consequently, the sharing of game meats follows no prescribed pattern. Indeed, the carcass of a game animal is neither conceptually nor literally cut into the same pieces as a domesticated animal. This is highlighted by a popular humorous story concerning an elder named Lenasolu during *mutai*. He was said to have in desperation killed an elephant, and when others came to request meat, he greedily feigned a reluctant refusal. He sadly explained that it was a female elephant, so the amount of meat was very small—it didn't even have *lwuantan*, the lower part of the hind leg, one of which must always be given out to friends or neighbors.

DIETARY RESTRICTIONS AS A POLYTHETIC CATEGORY

Dietary restrictions, at least since Frazer (1922), have been a favorite subject of anthropological analysis (e.g., Levi-Strauss 1969; Douglas 1966; Harris 1966). Whereas many of these analyses focus on a particular strand of causation—such as Douglas's famous symbolic-structural analysis or Harris's cultural materialist ones—Samburu food restrictions defy a single seamless explanation. Indeed, closer inspection of some Euro-American practices highlight a similar lack of coherence. The reason Americans do not eat dog meat, for instance, is very different from why they do not drink dog milk (or, for that matter, commonly eat dog food). Although Samburu are keenly aware of the importance of their food restrictions, they do not attribute them to a single cause or place them in a single category. Indeed, restrictions seemingly emanate from a diverse set of sources, ranging from grave supernatural danger to general sense of unsuitability to mundane disgust.

By far the strongest prohibition is against eating elephants, which are regarded as similar to human beings, with explanations for this similarity typically focusing on a comparison of human and elephantine breasts. Eating elephants puts one in grave supernatural danger and extends far beyond literally eating elephant meat to the metaphorical eating involved in any benefits derived from killing an elephant—for instance, participating in the ivory trade, especially if you were the one to split the elephant's skull to remove the tusks. A somewhat different example involved a man killed by an elephant. Though compensation was due from the Kenya Wildlife Service for the death, no one was interested in claiming it because of its association with elephants. When one man finally stepped forward to claim the compensation, he deliberately frittered the money away in town; if he had purchased livestock with the money, for instance, it would have been as if he were adding elephants to his herd. Indeed, if a person or cow is killed by an elephant, no Samburu will even go near the body.

Other animals are somewhat more ambiguous. Thomson's gazelle, for instance, is eaten by some Samburu but not others. Samburu from the Black Cattle moiety *(Nkishu Narok)* eat it, but the White Cattle moiety *(Nkishu Naibor)* does not, arguing that the Thomson's gazelle is not historically justified, insofar as it was not present when Samburu were living at Oto in southern Ethiopia. It is also undesirable because it has a "black stomach," a term used to describe a person who is selfish, ruthless, and self-centered.

Other nonedible game animals are in a category deemed *nguesi ngiro*—brown or gray animals. This is a polythetic category, including warthogs, gerenuk, and rhinos. Most of these animals are never eaten, although some Samburu clans will eat rhinos, although they are *nguesi ngiro,* as well as an animal that kills human beings. Some suggest that gray and brown animals are avoided because the color acts as a *suget,* a charm made by *laibonok* to hide things, such that eating the animal could hide luck and bring decline to herds. Prohibitions against eating warthogs are interesting in the array of black marks perceived to taint their edibility: their brown color renders them *nguesi ngiro,* they are ugly, their omnivorous diet resembles that of humans, they eat many dirty things, their tusks can be used by *laibonok* to conduct sorcery, and they have many teats, like a dog, which extend all the way up the chest, as on a woman.

These examples illustrate the complex range of factors that inform Samburu eating restrictions. Unlike Douglas's argument concerning the Abominations of Leviticus, it is not inconsistency that is problematic. Rather, diverse individual factors can render something questionable—having breasts like a person, having breasts like a dog, being ugly, harming humans, eating humans, eating dirty things, being brown, not being a historically validated food, having a black stomach—but the presence of any single individual trait is sufficient to render it inedible. These varying factors are to some extent discrete, in the sense that they are informed by different kinds of motivations and experienced at levels that are potentially divisible. Consequently, even if one facet

FIGURE 11. The Samburu's most forbidden food: elephant. Photo by the author.

of a restriction might to some extent be overcome, other facets may nonetheless remain.

Chickens, which some Samburu have recently started eating, provide an intriguing example. Many Samburu offer the somewhat perplexing perspective that "I like the meat but I don't like the bones." I quizzed our neighbor Lepariyo on this one day, and he agreed that it was the bones he didn't like. When I pressed him on why he didn't like the bones, he pinched his face, half as if to mine a thought from his inner psyche, half at squeamishness at the thought it revealed. "When I see the bones," he explained slowly, "I don't know—it just somehow looks like all those other birds and other small things."

In some ways this explanation is less than sensible. His explanation for distaste at the sight of chicken bones is that it looks like you are eating a bird—which of course you are. Traditionally, birds were not eaten for various reasons. Samburu divide birds into two main categories: small birds *(nkweni)* and large birds *(motonyi),* of which raptors and scavenger birds (especially vultures) are prototypical. The *motonyi* are the principal focus of bird-disgust, *nkweni* perhaps being too small to even be thought of as an edible. A principal concern with *motonyi* is what they eat, particularly in the case of vultures. Consider, for instance, a stock line in the *lbaringon* that murran sing to boast of their accomplishments in raiding:

The birds *[motonyi]* are descending on [the name of the place raided]
To feed on the meat of our spears
It is not the meat of a cow
It is the meat of a human being

Since some within the category of birds (i.e., vultures) eat human beings, all birds are to some extent seen as being bad in this way. Even those *motonyi* that don't scavenge human flesh similarly eat "dirty things," such as bugs and feces.

Chickens, then, provide an intriguing example. Many Samburu, particularly in highland areas, have begun to accept chicken—owing largely to exposure in the context of wage labor or because they are forcefully promoted by missionaries and development groups—but they have done so ambivalently. Eating chicken is closely associated with a worldview that embraces modernity, at least a willingness to discard those customs and beliefs that are perceived to conflict with contemporary practical reason. Yet some still mock chicken-eaters as "eating *motonyi*," and others, although they eat chicken, *feel* at some level like they are eating *motonyi*. This is not wholly unfamiliar—consider how different a chicken looks on a farm than it does in a package of boneless chicken breasts in a grocery store; a disconnect between animals and their flesh is a central aspect of Euro-American attitudes toward meat (Fiddes 1991). To draw on a personal example, one of the few Samburu foods that I avoid is roasted goat or sheep face, which I dislike to a great extent because it involves staring into the face of the goat or sheep that you are chewing on. Similarly, at one level Samburu like Lepariyo have overcome their bird disgust concerning chicken. The social construction of its grossness has to a great extent been supplanted by the notion that it is like an aspect of development. Yet this does not automatically vitiate repulsion at all levels, as the small bones still produce some disgust from an internalized sense of grossness.

In this sense, much like taste itself, distastes and taboos are constituted at multiple levels.[6] Certainly, some eating prohibitions are governed by rules, and violating them is simply bad, like the eating of elephants. Whether elephant meat makes an appealing dish has nothing to do with whether or not you would eat it. By contrast, some foods are avoided for no good reason—even in the eyes of informants—except that they are "not-food." However, psychologically sedimented associations of disgust with aspects of those things that are "not-food" may exist independently from conscious rules or beliefs concerning foods, and consequently may persist even after those beliefs diminish in conscious significance.

NEW FOODS

Many introduced foods have gained prominence in the context of pastoral scarcity. Some of the more important ones will be discussed in detail in coming chapters, but I will briefly outline of some of the key foods here.

The two most significant introduced foods are tea (the subject of chapter 7) and maize meal. Tea, introduced in the 1930s or 1940s, is the only introduced food that is valued as highly (if not more so) than historically validated foods, and—drunk with large quantities of milk and sugar—is a centerpiece of both daily eating and ritual occasions. Its dietary significance is surpassed among introduced foods only by maize meal *(ngurama)*, which is the principal food consumed on a daily basis in the absence of sufficient pastoral products. Apart from tea, introduced foods are viewed, with various degrees of disfavor, as poor substitutes for the bountiful livestock products of the past, dismissed by a variety of terms, including *gray or brown foods, poverty foods,* or *government foods*. Although these are welcomed for their ease of acquisition and as an alternative to starvation or even less palatable autochthonous famine foods (such as *mpupoi,* or boiled skins), they are regarded as grossly nutritionally inferior to livestock products, while also being the source of a variety of social and cultural maladies.

The archetypal gray food, maize meal, is typically consumed in a thick porridge or gruel *(loshorro)*. *Loshorro* differs from the typical means of consuming maize meal elsewhere in Kenya and in eastern and southern Africa, where it is boiled to a much stiffer consistency, as in *ugali,* the Kenyan national dish, or *ubwali,* about which Richards (1932) wrote at length in her nutritional ethnography of the Bemba. *Loshorro* may be the entire meal, with additions like salt, milk, or fat added for flavor and nutrition if available. As is the case elsewhere in Kenya, white maize is the norm. Yellow maize normally comes only as famine relief from abroad, and its lack of popularity is ensured by rumors that yellow maize is only used as livestock feed in the United States.

Grains are not entirely new to Samburu. They have long played a role as a famine food acquired in trade with agriculturalists, such as Meru to the southeast and Dassanetch to the north. The twentieth century, however, witnessed major transformations in the use of grains. Informants regard changes in the variety of grains utilized—from indigenous ones such as millet and sorghum to the introduced maize—as unimportant, but they found changes in the flour initially disconcerting. Informants who are old enough to remember the transition from hand-ground indigenous grains to finely milled European ones recall disgust and confusion as to whether it was really food rather than ash or dust.

Beyond the changes in grains, the entire framework for eating grain has changed markedly. Grain has changed from a rarely eaten famine food to a staple of daily diet. The previous infrequency of grain consumption is evidenced in the name—Lanyaunga Letuaa—of an Lkishilli elder I met in Lesidai, a highland community. His first name is an amalgamation of Samburu and Kiswahili: *lanya*, "one who eats," and *unga*, the Kiswahili word for "flour." *Lanyaunga* is, therefore, "he who eats flour," a peculiar name in an era when essentially everyone does—as nonsensical as naming someone "He who drinks water," "He who sleeps on a bed," or "He who defecates in the bush." Yet the difference here is one of history—for if eating flour is now as commonplace as these other everyday activities, when Lanyaunga Letuaa was young they were not. His name was derived from the particular circumstances surrounding his birth, around 1940. In the midst of a major drought, his family took donkeys down to Rumuruti, some sixty miles to the south, to purchase maize meal. The fact that Lanyaunga was born at a time when his mother was depending on grain—and European-style flour at that—was of sufficient note to result in his name.

Today, maize meal is a mainstay of Samburu diet in all parts of the district, though there is considerable variation. In highland areas it has become the centerpiece of Samburu diet, under normal circumstances providing the bulk of the daily fare. While use decreases under some circumstances—for instance, when pastoral products or other nonpastoral foods are plentiful—the normative diet for all household members increasingly centers on *loshorro*. This is less the case in lowland areas, where livestock holdings are generally higher. There maize meal is used by most families on a daily basis throughout the year, but it continues to be viewed primarily as a supplement to ensure that children have enough to eat. Another important variant concerns how maize meal is acquired. Overwhelmingly, maize meal is purchased from shops and is typically available in all trading centers. Where cultivation is at least plausible—if not always possible—Samburu increasingly have attempted to grow their own maize, along with other crops. In lowland areas, cultivation is not possible, and many areas of the highlands are also marginal for agriculture. However, in the highest areas of the Leroghi Plateau (6,500–8,000 feet), cultivation is possible, and in some small areas cultivation has, in fact, become more important than pastoralism.

Maize meal remains problematic for murran. According to most informants, murran did not begin to consume maize meal until at least the late 1970s or 1980s, and then only in great secrecy. Thus informants related an account of a murran coming to a shop that our host, Lekeren, formerly ran at his settlement. The murran refused to ask Lekeren's wife for maize meal directly, instead euphemistically requesting "two kilos of my grandfather's white beard." The ability to maintain a pastoral diet is most important symbolically for murran, and maize meal is not considered a suitable part of murran diet. In Leroghi, maize meal has now been accepted as a staple for murran, though not consumed in the sight of women. In lowland areas, however, murran continue to avoid *loshorro* when at all possible.

Maize *(lpayek)* is also eaten as whole grain, acquired as famine relief or occasionally from an individual's agricultural plot. Fresh maize can be roasted or boiled on the cob, but typically it comes as dried grain, which must be boiled for hours to be chewable. It is typically eaten plain, with salt and fat added if available. Plain maize is undesirable, not only because of its absence of flavor—the prototypical *nchata natotoyo*, or dry stick—but also because it can be difficult to cook it sufficiently to make it chewable for those too old or young to have sufficient strength of tooth. Many elderly people and young children are simply unable to eat it.

Maize is far more desirable when it is mixed with beans (*maharagwe*, as in Kiswahili), as is common in the widespread Kenyan dish of *githeri*. Bean consumption is relatively new—they were fairly uncommon during my 1992–94 research but were eaten much more frequently by 2001. Although they are not nearly as desirable as animal products, they are considered to be tasty and nutritious. In some highland areas that are marginal for maize cultivation, beans can be grown more reliably, contributing to their acceptance.

A handful of other introduced foods are far less common. Eggs are now consumed by some people, especially in highland areas. Like chickens, eggs have been promoted by missions and development agencies as a good source of calories and protein, especially for children. Some people also drink raw eggs as a treatment for chest ailments. Chapatis—a common Kenyan version of the Indian flat bread—are regarded as tasty by Samburu in all areas but are rarely prepared at home, owing to the low availability of wheat flour and a general lack of knowledge concerning preparation. Rice (*musheli,* from the Kiswahili *mcheli*) is neither widespread nor highly valued. It is considered to be an effete food and not very satisfying. Although there is nothing especially bad about rice per se, it is principally associated with town life and not seen as a useful staple. It is, however, commonly eaten when available by pregnant or postpartum women, because it is a light food that does not stress delicate stomachs.

In all societies, the foods one eats and shares play a significant role in constituting both the person and the interpersonal. Among Samburu despite—but also because of—the relative paucity of diet, this dynamic is particularly marked. Through food, Samburu mark and *live* who they are relative to a plethora of core signifiers: ethnicity, age, masculinity and femininity, respect, sharing, morality and immorality, modernity and tradition. Food constitutes a complexly ordered domain of interconnected meanings, meanings that are thought, lived, felt, and experienced.

CHAPTER 5

The Calabash behind the Calabash behind the Calabash

A sense of respect *[nkanyit]* is an attitude which is inculcated into persons of both sexes from a fairly early age. It is a virtue which is constantly referred to by elders in many contexts and it is the keystone of Samburu morality.

Paul Spencer, *The Samburu*

A wife who is clever will have a second calabash hidden with her husband's milk when he is away on a journey, or even a third one that no one will ever find.

Mamai Lekanapan, Samburu elder, Ndonyo Nasipa, 2002

Nkanyit (a sense of respect) is, as Paul Spencer rightly explicates in his now classic monograph, perhaps the most fundamental Samburu value. Nkanyit dictates a certain selflessness, evenhandedness, and cool-head-edness, giving everyone their due even if it is at your expense. It is fundamental to the ethos of Samburu life, and to the bearing with which Samburu carry out their daily affairs and daily interactions. Nkanyit is a value that fundamentally ties the most trivial of everyday actions to religious mystery, as well as to blessings and curses and pollution—for Samburu continue to hold today, in the words of Spencer's informant in the 1950s, that "*nkanyit* is a wonderful thing. . . . Nkai [God] likes *nkanyit*" (Spencer 1965, 135).

Yet there is another side to nkanyit, one that Spencer was no doubt aware of but did not explicate. As with the Euro-American notion of respect, nkanyit does not strongly differentiate between an internalized reverence and an externally expressed deference. Like respect, nkanyit may reflect honor or fear, and it may be the product of either virtue or duplicity. A display of respect may represent genuine affect, or it may be the product of a strategic, two-faced diplomacy. In the Euro-American concept, these varying facets are to an extent intertwined. Deference commensurate with a person's social position must be properly displayed, yet it should also not appear to hinge entirely on social obligation or a too obvious extrinsic interest, lest the respect appear to be manipulative or disingenuous. Like the *méconnaisance,* or misrecognition, that Bourdieu (1998) emphasized was fundamental to gift-giving, the precise balance of obligatory deference and internalized regard can never be known, lest the respect itself dissolve into air. Nor is it necessarily the case that actors themselves typically make in their own minds a distinction between the often ambiguous blend of genuine and instrumental respect.

In some ways, these two facets of respect are even more inexorably entwined in Samburu nkanyit. Samburu also recognize that nkanyit may be based in affect and goodwill, convention, instrumental interest, or fear, but the condensation of these varying loci/motivations of respect is far more central to the power of nkanyit, which makes it misleading to attempt to disentangle the "genuine" and less genuine aspects. For while there is a strong belief that nkanyit emanates from an internalized feeling of respect, it is in actions—not thought—that the test of nkanyit lies. Nkanyit is fundamentally defined through the practice of maintaining a bearing, a plausible visage—whether artifice or actual—of evenhandedness, and giving everyone their due. Indeed, what is most essential in living through nkanyit, by living a life of respect, is not being *truly virtuous,* not of never *really* doing anything wrong or *really* being evenhanded and selfless. Rather, the essence of nkanyit is to not clearly and visibly wrong someone—that is, to not breach respect. Understanding the complexities, contradictions, and ambiguities that make nkanyit such a complex concept, an amalgamation of internalized morality and strategic duplicity, is fundamental to an analysis of Samburu eating, because—although notions of right action centered around nkanyit are fundamental to virtually all interactions in everyday Samburu life—nkanyit is most fundamentally, directly, and poignantly embodied through eating.

Understanding a Samburu view of morality and right action is central to understanding how they valuate change, in that present behavior is understood in reference to deviations from historically validated right action. It should be noted that, through attention to transformations, this analysis dances at the edges of widespread scholarly and popular notions of a "rupture of modernity," both engaging with this trope and problematizing the moral underpinnings of the "moral economy," which is now experiencing major shifts. Long-standing patterns of Samburu eating in essence constitute a system in which right action, social relations, and moral personhood are fundamentally defined through food. Thus an analysis focusing on change implies a kind of "Things Fall Apart" *geist,* in which a traditional system focused on sharing and interpersonal relations is replaced by a modernity that can consume humanity itself. This motif is a staple of Euro-American popular culture representations both of our own past and of Primitive cultures that are held to at least partially represent ourselves in simpler times. Such a view also permeates countless anthropological analyses of change brought about by capitalism, modernity, globalization, and the state.

One might easily read such convenient tropes of a shift from gemeinschaft to gesellschaft into statements such as those of Noldirikany, a woman from Ndonyo Nasipa who asserts that "Samburu no longer love each other, and they used to love each other very much. . . . That's what we see these [new] foods are bringing to Samburu nowadays." Yet we would be wrong to assume that our informants' seeming romanticizations of the past are isomorphic with our own romantic nostalgia for the past and the Primitive peoples who represent it. What an idyllic past means to Samburu readings of the present may differ from our own, because what they read as important about both past and present may be very different from what is imagined in Western images of idyllicism and dystopia. A specifically Samburu morality informs their readings of the past and present. The key questions then become: What kinds of relationships or behaviors have actually changed, or are seen to have changed,[1] and how do these relationships or behaviors affect facets of moral behavior that are central to how Samburu understand the present? How do cultural constructions of the past become an integral part of how actors understand the present? To answer such questions requires a close exegesis of the "moral" in the Samburu "moral economy," in order to understand the implications—material, social, and symbolic—of the food-centered transformations in patterns of social relations that have led in some instances to new tensions, real or potential inequalities, and new interpretations of interpersonal relationships.

THE PRACTICE OF NORMS: STRATEGY, MORALITY, AMBIGUITY

Bourdieu's approach to practice, which has remained an important strain in anthropological theory since it gained prominence in the

1970s and '80s, argued for a fundamental shift in social analysis from norm to strategy. Focusing, for instance, on marriage patterns among French peasants, Bourdieu (1976) argued that analyses focusing on normative behavior failed to account for how and why peasants forged the marriage alliances they did. An emphasis on normative rules suggested, in an overly legalistic sense, that peasants were fulfilling some abstract set of rules about whom they (or their children) should or should not marry, when, in fact, they were pursuing strategies aimed at enhancing their social and economic capital. "Norms" were not rules that governed behavior but post hoc explanations of behavior (by actors or outside observers). Though his argument for the importance of strategy has rightfully been highly influential to understanding of social practice, it has also been subject to many critiques.[2] Most significant here is that there is a flatness to his actors, with an overemphasis on the strategic maximization of social or economic capital—ostensibly on the exercise of power (Brown 1996; Ortner 1989)—that deemphasizes culturally constructed values and motivations that run counter to simple maximization (Holtzman 2001). It is also useful to compare Bourdieu's explication of strategy with that of Erving Goffman (e.g., 1969). Goffman's hypnotizing explications of strategy and counterstrategy paint an unparalleled picture of the complex blend of argument, ruse, and deception that form the basis of strategic behavior. An approach to strategy that speaks to the intricacies of strategy so deftly chronicled by Goffman serves not only to explicate the kinds of strategic behavior undertaken by Samburu in regard to food, but complexifies the relationship of norm and strategy problematized by Bourdieu.

Analyzing strategy requires greater attention to ambiguity, which is relatively underdeveloped in anthropology specifically and the social sciences generally. While social science tends to avoid the ambiguous, in the humanities there is a long tradition of embracing ambiguity as a central facet of textual interpretation, anchored in William Empson's classic work *Seven Types of Ambiguity* (1930). Where anthropologists have engaged with notions of ambiguity, it is often in ethnopoetical analysis of spoken or written texts. One approach that does acknowledge the role of ambiguity is Roy Rappaport's (1979, 1999) analysis of the functions of ritual, though his conclusions are largely counter to my own. Rappaport seeks to explain ritual in evolutionary terms, focusing on its potential to canonize and make true things that might otherwise be ambiguous or subject to mendacity. The need to reduce ambiguity through ritual is driven to a great extent by the evolution of the capacity to lie that accompanied speech, and also by the cultural need to "digitalize analog information" by transforming continuous states (e.g., age) into discontinuous ones (e.g., age sets). Rappaport emphasizes that rituals reduce ambiguity by serving as performative acts: having participated in a particular ritual creates a particular, unambiguous state. Thus, a marriage ceremony, for instance, reduces ambiguity by creating a relationship defined by participation in the ritual. Rappaport and others (e.g., Erikson 1966; Jackson 1982) have looked at ambiguity as a problem that must be minimized for effective social functioning. Drawing on the varying functionalist paradigms of the times at which they were writing, there is a clear assumption that ambiguity is socially undesirable and social transparency desirable. This elides the fact that ambiguity can itself be useful, both at an individual and a social level. It can be individually useful for one's motives to remain ambiguous,[3] while in social contexts ambiguity can play a positive role in substituting a space of acceptable uncertainty for undesirable certainty. For instance, at the forefront of the U.S. military's recent "Don't ask, don't tell" policy is the notion that homosexuality is not problematic per se but overt, unambiguous knowledge of homosexuality is—and creating an official statement means that something must be dealt with officially.

Moreover, reducing one kind of ambiguity can give rise to another, perhaps even more potent form. By creating an official, unambiguous status, one opens the door to other forms of ambiguity. For instance, while, in Rappaport's view, performing a marriage ceremony serves an important function in reducing ambiguity—when the preacher *says* you are husband and wife, *you are* husband and wife *because he says so*—this status may create more questions than it answers. Creating an official, publicly sanctioned state, imbued with tremendous social and cultural weight, raises the standard at which behavior would apparently contravene the state that has been ritually created. Thus, for instance, while lovers would be likely to terminate their relationship should they feel that love no longer exists, the fact that spouses are tied together by a *pledge* of love ironically reduces the need for the *actual* love implied by the pledge. Thus, the reduction of status ambiguity created by the marriage ritual is accompanied by a burgeoning of practical ambiguity in the sense that the unambiguous status obviates the need for many of the features of the actual relationship upon which the status is predicated.

This observation is central to understanding the dynamics of food sharing, since Samburu society is characterized by a high degree of status awareness. Status awareness is central to the age-gender system and is exercised to a lesser degree in regard to kinship. Males are members of age sets, which move through a series of formalized statuses defined by age grades. Since they don't have age sets, age is less formally structured for women, but their social age is nonetheless sharply defined in relation to the age of their fathers, husbands, and children. The age-gender status of both women and men is instantly visible in clothing and ornamentation. It is an integral component of any face-to-face interaction, with greetings involving the acknowledgment of both absolute age-gender status and the other person's age-gender status in relation to the speaker. The only exception to this involves individuals with whom one is very familiar, where an acknowledged kinship relationship may be substituted.

Yet this low level of status ambiguity gives rise to higher levels of practical ambiguity. The exercise of nkanyit mandates that you behave in accordance with the official status, following normative patterns spelled out by your relationship and relative status. This is, of course, never complete, and many complexities of strategy serve to elude the potentially odious implications of nkanyit, as the need for selflessness clashes with the necessity of self-interest. Detailing these strategies, however, pushes us to rethink Bourdieu's norm-strategy dichotomy. To a great extent, Samburu strategy is about norms—playing with them, arguing about them, seeking to elude or extend them. Norms are not, as Bourdieu concludes, part of a post hoc analysis of behavior. Rather, as Comaroff and Roberts (1981) point out in regard to Tswana disputes, norms are part of the terrain upon which debate takes place and are subject to considerable manipulation by actors, particularly because there may be substantive contradictions in the courses of action they prescribe. Samburu are similarly aware of their norms *as rules*—rules to which you must conform or which you may conform to your needs, or to which you may creatively aim to conform others. Thus Bourdieu is right that practice is not simply the realization in behavior of legalistic norms. Yet norms are part of the shared space of social relationships; they are used discursively as arguments to promote one's interests and as rationalizations for defending actions taken in one's interest. Nkanyit does not dictate that everyone give (or receive) their normatively defined due (particularly because what is due to one person may conflict with what is due to another person). Rather, it dictates that one not breach respect, either discursively or by actions that cannot be defended discursively as being in line with nkanyit.

Brief examples will illustrate these points. First, nkanyit mandates that one display total respect for one's father; openly disagreeing with one's father is almost unthinkable. Only rarely do sons directly contradict their father's wishes, and even more rarely is the contradiction total. For instance, in 1994, Lesengei, a senior elder from the Mekuri age set (circumcised in 1936) announced to his family that they would be moving from a seemingly desirable spot near Lodokejek, where the sons had begun cultivating a six-acre agricultural plot, to a more remote area ten or so kilometers away. His junior elder sons—one of whom was married, the other marrying soon—did not want to abandon the plot, so Lesengei ended the debate by declaring that whoever stayed behind in the same settlement would be cursed to death. One of the sons was nonetheless determined not to go. Rather than outwardly defying his father, however, he sought to escape on a technicality: he built a new settlement just outside the existing one, thus staying more or less in the same place without remaining in exactly the same settlement. Not long afterward, however, he succumbed to his father's will and rejoined the family. But if openly defying one's father is a breach of respect nearly inconceivable to Samburu, seriously harming him is far less problematic, provided it is not done openly. For instance, covertly starving one's elderly father to death by passively or actively diverting food away from him and toward others (though certainly in some senses reviled) occurs with some frequency. Certainly, he may fail to get the food he is due—but no one, including him, may know how or why it happened in a particular instance. There is a material absence but not a social breach.

In more mundane instances, one's obligations may be highly debatable. For instance, it is common for an old person (especially a man) to demand a small amount of money for alcohol or some other minor purchase based on the fact that he is owed it because he is old and should be respected, often emphasized by removing his hat to show his white hair. Such assertions are both true and not true. They should be respected, but it is impossible to fulfill such a request for every old person. The essence of maintaining nkanyit in such an instance is to agree to the principle but not necessarily always to the outcome—to demonstrate that it is impossible to give him something in that particular instance, even though he is correct that he deserves what he seeks. Fundamental to success in this, therefore, is duplicity, artfully and regularly employed.

THE MORALITY OF DUPLICITY

In eliciting Samburu proverbs about food, I was struck one day by an example that on the surface seemed to have no relation to food. The proverb is given voice by a hyena, who asserts, "It is not that I am strong—it is only that my legs cannot know to feel tired." On the surface, the proverb praises perseverance and determination: your abilities and physical strength are less important than the mental strength and discipline you apply to the pursuit of your goals. Yet the proverb's relation to food was not at all apparent. How, I asked a group of informants, was this a proverb about food? They chuckled, and then Barnabas offered his explanation. "After all," he volunteered, "to Samburu the greatest pursuit is the pursuit of food." The image evoked in this proverb was not simply a resolute hyena running through the night in pursuit of some abstract goal. It was a resolutely gluttonous hyena, running through the night with its ungainly gait, its mouth agape, hoping to sweep into its maws whatever edible thing was unlucky enough to cross its path.

There are contradictions in this proverb that beg to be resolved. Food is perhaps the arena in which nkanyit is most centrally embodied. Extreme care is taken to be fair, respectful, and on the surface at least, honest in regard to food. Gluttony *(lobu)* and stinginess *(laroi)* are perhaps the two greatest character faults a Samburu can exhibit, exposing the person not only to social shame but to mortal danger from the "bad eyes" and fatal curses of your fellows. Yet, in this proverb the shamelessly ravenous hyena is upheld as a role model for pursuing your nutritional needs.[4]

This contradiction may be resolved by engaging with notions of duplicity and ambiguity, both among Samburu and as a general dimension of social life. Many scholars, starting with Simmel (1950), have noted the extent to which *too* much information can be disruptive to social life. Insofar as no social group is a cohesive, peaceful, unified whole, only by keeping unpleasant truths under the table can a semblance of peace and unity be maintained. That is, social contradictions cannot be resolved, but their consequences can be suspended by keeping them in a state in which they perpetually elide resolution. Thus Robert Murphy, commenting on Gregor's (1970)[5] analysis of lying among Mehinacu Indians, concludes:

Mehinacu are as good at lying as they are at gossip and adultery. Nobody really knows, then, what is true and what is false; they are given ample doubts and few convictions. Everything is both true and false, and all information is diluted and adulterated. . . . And perhaps this can be said of all social life and all normative systems, for man lives with this curious mixture of both hard perception and collective delusion; the cultural images of social life are not all clear reflection nor absolute refraction, but a mixture of the two that reduces it all to shadow. (1971, 228)

Like the Mehinacu and others (e.g., Gilsenan 1976 on the Lebanese; Siskind 1973 on the Sharanahua), Samburu themselves, explicitly recognize the importance of duplicity. A variety of key cultural values—for instance, bravery, fidelity, and generosity—are central to the construction of moral personhood yet also seen as either unattainable or sometimes undesirable. Consequently, Samburu recognize the necessity of effectively crafting an outward persona that conforms to an acceptable degree to these values, while deftly skirting the potentially odious consequences of too rigid adherence to them. Effective duplicity thus becomes a covert cultural value, a symptom less of morally problematic mendacity than of strategic intelligence.

Consider, for instance, attitudes toward bravery. While bravery is a central cultural value, with young men embarking on sometimes fatal cattle raids to earn a reputation for valor, cowardice is, conversely—if not totally openly—applauded as a sign of intelligence. While extreme cowardice is highly denigrated, extreme bravery can also be viewed as unmitigated idiocy—epitomized by warriors known as "shitting bulls" (laingoni lomodio), whose extreme animal urge to enter battle leads to a loss of control in their bodily functions.[6] It is notable that alongside the commonplace stories of particularly courageous heroes, there are also stories of famous cowards. These stories are ostensibly humorous but also laudatory of the cleverness cowards employ to avoid battle. Some male informants also note how fathers encourage their sons to avoid dangerous or difficult tasks, to be a bull but a "clever bull" or "a bull who hides." One man, for instance, noted the contrasting advice offered by his father and his mother concerning what he should do while herding. His mother told him that he should stand alert among the herds, so that he would be ready to defend the animals if enemies came. In contrast, his father told him that he should rest while herding—this way he would remain fresh, so that if enemies came he would have the energy to run away. A song commonly sung by elders while playing the board game ntotoi similarly hails the virtues of cowardice over bravery. Songs sung in this context often describe famous cattle raids and the brave murran who undertook them. Another common song offers commentary on the famous deeds of brave warriors: "These are our heroes, but we are better than them." Sung with almost smug, knowing humor, the crux of this assertion is that, although these murran became famous for their courageous exploits in war, they were eventually killed by enemies. Thus they never married and never had children, but wasted their lives by dying young in the pursuit of martial glory. In essence, then, the public emphasis on bravery encourages a private emphasis on employing the measured cowardice necessary for a long and successful life.

Issues of adultery provide a different illustration of ambiguity and duplicity. Female adultery is universally despised by Samburu elders but also condoned by them (and practiced with others' wives). Adultery archetypically occurs between married women and murran (e.g., Llewelyn Davies 1981), though elders also have affairs with each others' wives. Mothers often tell their daughters before marriage about the virtue of "mixed herds," in which calves are sired by a variety of bulls. Adultery is essentially universal and regarded as unpreventable. Individually, husbands may, however, aim to interfere, and anger and violence commonly arise from its discovery. Conversely, however, there is a collective acceptance of adultery's inevitability and an emphasis on minimizing the conflict that ensues. For example, Lenyuki, an Lkiroro junior elder, began to suspect that his wife was secretly meeting a murran on trips to fetch firewood in the forest. He followed her one day and caught her with a murran of his own subclan. The confrontation that ensued ended in violence, as Lenyuki speared the offending murran in the buttocks. As a consequence of this incident, the Lmooli murran held a meeting, resolving to beat up any Lkiroro they found alone. To avert violence, the elders of more senior age sets met. They decreed that any Lmooli who organized to beat up the Lkiroro would be cursed. In addition, however, they decreed that anyone who followed his wife to uncover adultery would also be cursed.

Thus, despite the profoundly negative views of Samburu elders toward female adultery, the collective emphasis is not on preventing it. Certainly adultery is seen as bad, and individually men act to prevent it. Yet at the collective level, the emphasis is on avoiding the disruption portended by the discovery of adultery. Stories are common concerning unnecessary violence perpetrated by men who foolishly returned home at an hour past the time when they might reasonably be expected to be spending the night elsewhere. Men who seem overly concerned with monitoring their wives' activities are viewed as unreasonably controlling, suspicious, and small-minded., Indeed, activities that have a likelihood of uncovering adultery—such as following wives or returning unexpectedly at night—are openly discouraged.

Duplicity is perhaps most significant in regard to food. Eating is to a great extent the most important seat of nkanyit, yet it is also the site of both the venal desires of the greedy and the deep play for daily sustenance in a society where famine has never been far away. Thus, if in principle a deeply internalized sense of nkanyit should negate natural tendencies toward greed and stinginess, in practice the art of remaining alive while living through nkanyit necessitates a delicate dance of vigorously seeking resources while avoiding the appearance of doing so greedily, and denying resources to others while never appearing to do so stingily.

DYING OF YOUR OWN FOOD

Lemantile, a senior elder, mused one day on the importance of sharing food and the consequences of not doing so: "There is no age set without [greedy people], not one single age set that can pass without them. You know there are always those greedy people who find it very painful to give food to people. And so, such a person just dies of his own food." The danger of greediness and not sharing properly goes beyond a simple a matter of etiquette, involving questions of life and death. Indeed, "May you die of your own food" *(Mikiwa ndaa ino)* is the archetypical Samburu curse. The wages of retaining something that is rightfully someone else's or of valuing your stomach over your fellows' are inevitably death. The food that you value so much you cannot bear to share it does not benefit your stomach but rather makes it swell unnaturally in an inevitably fatal illness. Thus this curse asserts that it is neither want of resources nor the evil machinations of others that will bring your demise; rather it is the very thing you hold too dear.

Commensality provides the basis for the strength and quality of Samburu social relations. Samburu maintain that "friendship is through the stomach," and the most important way to create and cement social relationship is through reciprocal sharing of food, slaughtering small stock for one another, and giving friends milk and tea. Men are closest with their age mates, with whom they are bonded through the communal eating and meat feasts in the forest characteristic of murranhood.

Yet the inverse is that an absence of commensality is the dark shadow of friendship, of jealousy and covetous eyes that inevitably lead to death.

One important way to avoid the profound jealousy surrounding food is to never eat in front of others without offering them some and, further, to never even let your eating be known. Elders are expected to follow a range of normatively defined strategies with their age mates to avoid revealing that they have eaten or are going to eat. For instance, if you are relaxing under a shade tree with other men and then go home to eat, you should not return to the same shade tree. Samburu suggest that if you returned to the same tree after eating—particularly because traditionally this would involve drinking milk—you would later have to urinate. Needing to urinate would demonstrate to your fellows that you had gone off to eat without offering them anything, an act seen as no different from actually eating in front of them. Similarly, if you decide to go eat when you are with a group of age mates, resting or playing *ntotoi,* you should never announce why you are leaving or even that you are leaving. You may simply suggest that you are going to the bush to urinate or defecate, and only later will your friends realize that you never returned.

There are many Samburu stories that emphasize the jealousy surrounding eating, the related necessity of hiding eating, and the consequences of not doing so.[7] One notable example tells of a man who was relaxing with his age mates beneath a shade tree when he complained about heartburn he had been getting after drinking his curdled milk. He maintained that this malady had to do with the milk produced by cattle that ate a kind of grass found in the area where they were living. This was an inappropriate complaint, displaying not only that he had eaten his fill without his age mates but even finding fault with the bounty he had failed to share, and his age mates responded in kind. "I know a place," one of his age mates volunteered, "where the curdled milk will not give you heartburn" and pointed to an area beyond some distant hills. On his friend's advice, he migrated to that area, only to find that it was close to enemies, who stole all his cattle. Destitute, he returned to his original area. "You see," his friend pointed out, "now that curdled milk does not give you heartburn."

Beyond avoiding revealing to others that you have eaten without them, Samburu maintain tight prescriptions on patterns of food sharing at and beyond the household level. In the home, food division is carefully structured for fairness. Food division—whether milk or cooked food—is undertaken exclusively by women, and men are expected to not interfere, although some suggest that it is acceptable to make a helpful inquiry to ensure that a particular child has received enough food, particularly if the child might be sick. Women (ideally) determine the exact quantity that their husbands and each child can eat, adjusting the amount upward each day until they no longer finish the food. The goal is to provide a share of food for each family member that is commensurate with their needs, while showing favoritism only by giving small children a disproportionately large share if food is not adequate for everyone's needs.

This food division transforms food from a shared resource to individually allocated portions, the full ownership of which is invested in particular household members. This transformation takes place as food is put in individual containers belonging to household members. In the case of milk, the husband and each child has his or her own calabash, into which a share is poured at milking time. There are many shapes and types of calabashes, which are used by different age-gender sectors, such that it is not possible for a child, for instance, to accidentally drink from the father's calabash, or vice versa. Similarly, everyone has his or her own bowl for cooked food, into which the food is served at the time of cooking. Even if an individual is not there, his or her food is put in a bowl and thus earmarked for that person to eat later. Stealing someone else's food or milk is extremely unseemly. It is least serious among children, who are naturally greedy. They can, however, be severely beaten to inculcate the importance of controlling their greed. For an elder to steal food is shameful and extremely uncommon, since it casts him as equivalent to a small child pilfering a sibling's food, when he is supposed to be a pinnacle of respect who is primarily concerned with caring for the well-being of his family. Only murran may rightfully transgress this allocation, by taking an elder's milk if they find it unattended in a house when they are hungry. Doing so is not a casual, everyday act, but if necessary, it is considered their right to take milk allocated to others as recompense for their role in defending the cattle (see also Spencer 1988). In such cases, murran mark the calabash with red ochre to show that they have taken the milk, in a mixture of defiance to the owner of the milk, assertion of their right to the milk, and to absolve other possible thieves (e.g., children) of responsibility.[8]

Distribution of meat is more closely prescribed and typically involves sharing beyond the household, and with a particularly broad group of community members when cows are slaughtered. Samburu offer a variety of reasons for their highly regimented patterns of meat sharing. They recognize that they have an insatiable desire for meat, so the relatively small amount available in all but the most unusual circumstances cannot satisfy everyone. This is notable enough to be canonized in a proverb: *Mebaki nkiri tungana* ("Meat can never be enough for the people"). Some informants suggest that the closely prescribed patterns of meat distribution simply reflect the fact that Samburu "love one another" and that having a fixed share norma- tively allocated for everyone ensures that "everyone gets something." However, many suggest that people might fight over meat, such that determining its distribution beforehand allows meat to be given out in a peaceable and orderly manner.

In general, Samburu emphasize avoiding social disruption from food sharing, holding that food is not something that should be fought over. One common proverb concerning food states, *Ndaa naidaiya* ("Food gets finished"). This proverb contrasts the transitory nature of food, which is eaten and is gone, to the ongoing importance of social rela- tions. Some informants even suggest that the word *ndaa* comes from the verb *to get finished*. Some add to this proverb the conclusion "So it is better to share with your brothers." If you quarrel about food with your brother, or wife or age mate, you are harming a relationship that is of lasting importance to your survival and well-being over a piece of meat or bowl of food that will be quickly gone. Thus Samburu broadly maintain that underlying the tendency to delineate exactly what each person's share of food is—whether in the household or outside of it—is a belief that this clarity mitigates the tendency to fight over food.

A powerful undercurrent to food sharing is the fear of being cursed— intentionally or subconsciously—if someone is denied their fair share of meat. The curse from not sharing meat is seen as especially potent, and many informants went so far as to assert that "meat has a curse, but milk has no curse." This is somewhat of an overstatement—whenever one denies a hungry person food, there is serious potential for a curse, and in particular circumstances, such as the *mbaran* (described below) stored by wives when a husband is away, milk can carry an extremely potent curse. This points, however, to an intensity surrounding meat that is typically absent regarding milk. Whereas milk is principally a domestic resource, meat is to a great extent a community resource. Milk is a fungible resource *until* it is distributed to individuals, but meat *always* belongs to someone and must be properly distributed. Whereas milk is a daily staple, renewable and replaceable at the morning and eve- ning milkings, meat is a rare treat eaten only at rituals, when an animal happens to die, or on the rare occasions when an animal is slaughtered for food. Therefore, cheating someone of their rightful share of meat could mean that person will not taste meat again for months.

Consequently, examples abound of the curses and related unpropitiousness arising from failing to share meat according to the prescribed patterns.[9] Lesiisho, for instance, went for a very long time without producing a son—his wives usually gave birth to daughters, and his few male offspring died before getting big. Later it was learned that he was eating the hearts of slaughtered small stock, which would rightfully belong to boys. By refusing to give the hearts to their rightful owners, he had acquired a type of misfortune (ngoki) that prevented him from having boys himself—he had in a sense eaten the boys he should have sired. Similar cases involve women giving birth to children with misshapen heads after having wrongfully eaten the heads of goats (which belong to elders), and a dead crippled man coming back in the shape of a tortoise to haunt a brother who had not offered him the hip meat that was his rightful share of a marriage ox.

Samburu hold that for particularly egregious offenses these curses could be fatal in short order. One widely cited example is from Lanyasunya, who worked away from home in the General Service Unit (GSU) of the Kenya police. One day a large bull of his died just as Lanyasunya was returning home on leave. When he arrived home, he discovered that elders from the neighboring settlements had come to butcher the animal and had nearly completed the job. They fully expected to roast the animal and divide it among the neighbors, according to normative patterns of meat distribution. Lanyasunya, however—a salaried man, with regular involvement in the money economy—had other ideas. He preferred to sell the meat in the butchery, where he expected to make a substantial profit. The elders asserted that, even so, he would certainly still give them one hind leg (lwuantan), which must always be given out and is the due of elders. He refused. Finally, they implored him to at least give them a small share of meat in payment for the work they had done for him.

Once again Lanyasunya resisted. Exasperated, the elders left, refusing to even wash their hands, the bull's blood remaining as a mark of the iniquity wrought against them. Lanyasunya then took the meat to a nearby butchery but soon became seriously ill. His stomach became bloated (illnesses caused by curses, and particularly those involving food, typically are manifested in the stomach). He was rushed to the hospital but died before nightfall, the meat of his bull still hanging unbought in the butchery.

These examples illustrate that in food sharing there is more at play than either an internalized sense of nkanyit or the necessity of ensuring that everyone gets along, owing to the social and economic interdependence integral to a life of subsistence pastoralism. These are both true, but they do not encompass the whole of the truth, either from an analytical perspective or in terms of how they are experienced by Samburu actors. Food sharing is serious business, for failing to adhere to prescribed patterns of food sharing is arguably the most common source of curses and misfortune.

Supernatural misfortune takes a variety of forms (see Straight 2006) and typically emanates from the ill feeling of an aggrieved party. The curse begins in the stomach, usually emerging in words or expectorated saliva. Curses are typically made intentionally, but a curse can also come out as an (often even more potent) unvoiced curse without the knowledge of the one who is aggrieved. Thus, a central goal of nkanyit and related forms of food sharing is avoiding the potentially catastrophic consequences of curses and unpropitiousness.

WHERE'S THE BEEF?

Tricking and refusing are not equivalent, even if the outcome is similar. If someone doesn't know that food exists, they cannot experience the aggrievement that presages a curse. People can be given all the respect due to them without giving them food, if—to all reasonable appearances—there is no food to give.

The virtue of duplicity, or the artifice of respect, is vividly exhibited in a widespread proverb that calls you to "cheat the eye"—that is, to present food to guests in a way that makes it appear to be a substantial quantity, even if it is relatively little. By "cheating the eye," you present an appearance of generosity commensurate with the level of respect your guest deserves, but do not do so at the expense of what you and your family need to eat. It is, in essence, a sort of how-to guide to having your cake and eating it too. How often Samburu actually follow this in practice is difficult to assess—I saw no evidence of it (but, if done properly, I wouldn't). What is key here, however, is the extent to which it heralds the importance of duplicity—that what is important is not so much *being* generous or fair but *appearing* generous and fair.

Similarly, the tightly prescribed rules concerning the sharing of meat are not evidence that everyone endeavors to be completely fair and equitable in the division of meat. Indeed, if everyone wanted to be fair, there would be no need to have rules about it. Again, what is crucial is not being *truly fair* but creating the *premise of fairness*. Anyone who comes to get meat must be given it, but there is no need to advertise that a cow is dead or dying, for instance, and even some amount of deception is acceptable.

Consider, for instance, an incident that occurred in April 2002, when a bull belonging to Letoole suddenly fell ill and died in the bush. When the bull collapsed, a number of neighbors were called to assist with the butchering, and they divided it into the three main requisite shares: one for the elders, one for murran, and one for women and children, with each group then responsible for cooking and dividing the meat among themselves. Elders and murran took their shares to separate roasting sites, while the women divided their share near the place where the cow was butchered.

Disinformation quickly spread, however, concerning the location where murran had taken their share of the meat. Some murran were directed to the wrong spot, and there were rumors that the owner had sold the meat to a group of murran from a distant settlement and they had carried it away, when in fact, the local murran were roasting and eating the meat nearby. This misinformation reduced the number of murran who successfully found the place where the meat was being eaten, and thus the number of people among whom it had to be shared.

If the effect of such deception is similar to denying someone food, it is nonetheless considered to be perfectly fair, whereas denying someone food is not. Despite an emphasis on fair division of food, people are also encouraged to eat quickly to avoid having to share. Thus, a common proverb urges, *Mepuonu enapita maitesioi* ("Let us hurry up, for those who come shall not come carrying"). In other words, eat what you have now, so that you will not need to divide your food among a larger group of people who will not come bearing their own. In the case described above, the misinformation could, after all, simply be bad information rather than an intentional attempt to cheat. Even if, as in this case, the deception is thinly veiled, the fact that someone could arguably have been acting in good faith means that no breach of social etiquette has occurred.

FEEDING GUESTS

Feeding guests is a key means of exercising proper forms of nkanyit and forging and maintaining social relationships. Ideally, visitors should be offered something to eat, though this can vary according to the circum-stances of their visits—it is, for instance, less crucial if it is a frequent visitor or if the person is simply passing by on a brief visit. Moreover, there are some visitors whom it is more important to feed than others, such as an old person who deserves particular respect or a person who is demonstrably hungry. However, from a Samburu perspective, true friendship does not exist—and friendship in any form could not exist for long—in the absence of giving a person something to eat at least on occasion when he or she visits your home.

Consequently, willingness to share food is fundamental to the con-struction of prestige and moral personhood. Someone who is very gen-erous is typically viewed as fundamentally good, while an unwillingness to share may cast one as guilty of the two most significant Samburu character defects: being greedy *(lobu)* and stingy *(laroi)*. These two defects can but do not necessarily overlap. A person who is *lobu* will feel driven to consume excessively, while a *laroi* will simply avoid shar-ing out of a miserly nature. A person who is *lobu* may or may not share, and if they do not share, it is not out of stinginess per se but because of excessive gluttony, which does not allow them to leave anything for others. In contrast, a *laroi* may not necessarily be gluttonous at all; they may, rather, be as miserly to themselves as they are to others.

These two characteristics are not valued/devalued equally. While being a *laroi* is universally reviled, being *lobu* is far more ambiguous. *Laroi* is, in fact, a derogatory term, which derives from the word for a junior murran who accompanied more senior murran on cattle raids. A *laroi* acts as a servant for the older murran—like a page to a knight—carrying his spears, perhaps cooking for him, and the like. Because the *laroi* acts only as an assistant rather than taking part in the raid, he is provided with no share of cattle—and hence has nothing to give away to anyone. Thus, calling someone *laroi* is a sarcastic and some-what emasculating slight, suggesting that he or she has nothing to give away—even though the person might, in fact, be quite wealthy.

Whereas a *laroi* is cold and antisocial, someone who is *lobu* may have quite favorable social qualities. *Lobu* people may be very friendly, even gregarious, as they make the rounds trying to drum up something to eat. At home, *lobu* people are frequently held to be as generous as they are gluttonous, while someone who is *laroi* may even starve his or her own family out of a refusal to expend resources. Being *lobu* becomes a problem when they are so consumed by gluttony that it is painful to give others something that they themselves could eat. Alternatively, *lobu* people can be so obsessed with their stomachs that their resources are quickly finished, leaving their families destitute. Thus Samburu advise their children to be "in between"—displaying reasonable generosity, while also guarding their own resources.

There is something of a gendered component to greed and stinginess. There is no clear consensus on whether men or women display these vices to a greater or lesser extent; some attribute them more to one gender or the other, while others suggest that it is "just in someone's nature" and can be found with equal frequency in men and women. Informants are quite clear, however, that greed is expressed in different contexts and with different implications in men and women. Broadly speaking, women's greed is mostly at the expense of their own family. Greedy women may eat food secretly when their husbands, or even their children, are not present to gain a bigger share for themselves. In a well-known example, a woman was even reputed to wake up late at night to cook food that she would greedily consume by herself, a habit that earned her the nickname "Eats at night." Alongside the possibility of withholding food for her own use is the possibility of keeping a secret supply of milk to share with lovers.

In contrast, male greed normally is seen as being exercised outward, beyond the family, by not fulfilling largely male expectations of sharing with one's age mates or other visitors to the home. Women have some expectation for sharing beyond the home—some women keep a small amount of sugar or tobacco hidden in reserve to avoid the curse of an elderly or other potent visitor who really needs it—but outward commensality (and the sin of its absence) is disproportionately the domain of men. Among men there can be a complex battle of strategy and wills centered on feeding or not feeding a visitor to the home. This should not be taken to suggest that Samburu do not wish to feed visitors, nor that every visitor is greedily angling to be fed. Hosts often genuinely desire to feed visitors, either for diffuse reasons of friendship and reciprocity or for short-term tactical goals of softening up the person for a future request. And not all guests are particularly interested in being fed or are motivated enough to devote energy to seek out an offer of tea, or milk, or cooked food when it is not immediately forthcoming. Yet, not infrequently, the ideas of hosts and guests on these matters do not fully correspond, creating the potential for machinations on one or both sides of the interaction.

Visitors may intentionally employ strategies in attempts to be fed, while hosts may employ countermeasures. On a routine basis, the most important strategy is to employ a waiting game of never asking for food but just not leaving until they have been given something. No adult—particularly a man—can eat while the visitor is present, unless they are willing to offer them something to eat. Thus a visitor (male or female) can try to force hosts to give them something to eat simply by not leaving until they are fed.[10] While they cannot compel someone to feed them, they can, in essence, starve them out by denying their hosts the privacy to eat without sharing. It should not, however, appear that this is what the guest is doing; rather they are just being friendly and have no particular place to go. To be too obvious in this tactic will have deleterious affects on the person's reputation, reflecting profound greed. Informants in Ndonyo Nasipa were shocked to hear that a particular old woman regularly made a point of giving us and our children milk, noting that, despite being quite wealthy, with a large herd of livestock that included several lactating camels, "you would think she was very poor. She will just come into your house and refuse to leave until she has been given something." By employing this tactic too often and with little guile, she had earned a reputation for unseemly greediness.

In response to such a strategies, hosts can simply refuse to eat. This is particularly the case for men. Women are also constrained by a need to share, though this is not quite as stringent for a variety of reasons. Visitors tend to be disproportionately male, and men's reputation and prestige rest to a greater extent on sharing what they have, owing to patterns of communal eating inculcated during murranhood. Consequently, to thwart a guest who is trying to force a host to feed him by waiting, some men will simply not get around to eating while the other person is present. This may be done to preserve the general food supply for the home. Often, however, there is a direct competition between the man's stomach and his guest, since often a visitor is fed from the man's own share of food or milk rather than shared family resources. As with guests, however, a host should not play a waiting game too often or too obviously. Saying that someone "never eats when someone else is present" is, in fact, a deliberately insulting insinuation that he is stingy or greedy.

The processes are different in regard to larger gifts of food, particularly slaughtering small stock, which is the most important form of hospitality offered to special guests. Here the issue can be the earnestness of a particular offer. Someone may say that they will slaughter a goat or sheep for you or that they want to slaughter, without necessarily being willing or able to do so. Thus receiving such a magnanimous offer and having it come to fruition can be two totally different propositions, since gaining the social capital of offering to slaughter for someone is intrinsically desirable, whereas carrying it out can be odiously expensive. If the person making the offer does not act quickly, visitors may then seek to close the deal or at least test the host's earnestness.

Take, for example, an incident that occurred while I was doing some short-term data collection in the lowland site of Ngutuk Lmuget in 1994. A junior elder from the Lesuuda family realized that my research assistant was a relative of his, and told us that if we came to his settlement sometime—even right now, if we wanted—he would slaughter a goat for us. He left, and we discussed the situation. We were hungry and thought a goat sounded good, so we headed out to his settlement. When we entered the settlement, we found him moving about excitedly and collecting his spear. He explained that he had just heard that there was a big raid being organized against the Somali, and he was running off to join it. He quickly left the settlement, apologizing and telling us that he would slaughter another time. After a few quick inquiries, however, we found that no one else knew anything about an impending raid. He had simply seen or heard us coming and quickly came up with the first excuse that sprang to mind for why now was not the time for the goat he had promised.

This example is extreme and unusual, and a deception carried out with such clumsiness would not deflect the ill will of someone denied a meal. It is, however, illustrative of a common dynamic. Offers are frequently framed with caveats concerning how someone would like to slaughter a goat now but can't because of some extenuating circumstances, or can't until some specified or unspecified time in the future. An offer can be implied or suggested, without it being clear how serious the offer is, or if it is really for the present or for some hazy time in the future. Most guests are reticent to press a host too hard, which could itself be a sign of unseemly greed. Rare individuals may, however, feel free to do so. Thus, in 2002, while staying with a small group of Samburu junior elders at a remote lowland settlement, the host, Lesirayon, vaguely alluded to a goat he was going to give us. He was, however, a bit drunk when we arrived, and continued to drink as we relaxed outside his wife's house, such that we were unsure both about how serious he was about the initial offer and whether he would get around to giving us the goat before he passed out. I exchanged surreptitious comments in Kiswahili (which Lesirayon does not speak) with one of the members of our group, Lekupano, concerning the outcome of the goat. He concluded, as Lesirayon's wife cooked tea with the sugar we had brought them, "We will wait until they have hold of their tea cups and then we will enter the wealth [flock of goats]." He was proposing that a drunken man holding a boiling hot beverage would be ill positioned to prevent us from going to the goat pen and selecting whichever one we wanted to fulfill our host's promise. As it turned out, Lesirayon directed us to a sheep before it came to that. However, Lekupano's suggestion represented the extreme end of normal brazenness in pressing a host's offer. Friends of his from the community suggested that his boldness resulted from the fact that he was Lkunono—a member of a blacksmith clan, which has the reputation of lacking manners—and he acted as if he was entitled to make demands upon people because of his special position in the community. A junior elder, he was the only community resident who had finished primary school, and consequently acted as a kind of unofficial chief—he was the only person who was literate, and the government-appointed chief rarely deigned to visit this remote, desolate area.

A further aspect of host-guest relations concerns the typical dependence of hosts on their wives for providing hospitality. Though not an issue in slaughtering small stock, everyday hospitality in the forms of milk, tea, and cooked food depends on a man's wife providing the food to be eaten. It is broadly within a husband's rights to tell a wife to provide food, but he typically does not (or should not) know what food is available, since the family larder is his wife's domain. Yet the wife may or may not wish to feed the guest. If it is not her guest, her friend or relative, she may have no reason to want to feed the person, hence expending resources without gaining social capital. She may have very good reasons to not want to feed a guest—such as needing the food for her children—or she may simply feel ungenerous or wish to preserve whatever extra she has for a friend or a secret lover. Thus, in everyday hospitality, strategic maneuvering is not simply between host and guest, but also between male hosts and their wives.

LEMPIRIKANY AND HIS THREE CUPS OF TEA

Over the course of about a decade, I received three offers of tea from a Samburu elder, Lmomonyot Lempirikany—the first of these in 1993 and the most recent in 2002.[11] Having met him shortly after my first fieldwork in Lodokejek began in 1992, we quickly came to be on good terms, despite his reputation in the community for being something of a warlike loner. He was a Kimaniki senior elder (probably somewhere in his early sixties), and people joked at what they saw as a refusal to leave behind the warriorhood of his youth: he went everywhere with a spear (some joked two) and always had a *rungu* (club) close at hand. Despite his reputation in the community for being asocial or outright bellicose, he was a very cooperative informant. Any possible self-interest at work in his uncharacteristic friendliness was not readily apparent, since (unlike many in the community) he asked for little beyond seemingly pointless rides when I was going to Maralal and, on one occasion, a hat.

These three cups of tea illustrate the varied facets of the social complexity entailed in sharing, and the ambiguity (strategic or otherwise) through which it is constituted. Not all the cups went smoothly. The first of the tea incidents occurred in late 1993. I had been at his settlement doing an interview and was about to leave, when he commented that I had come to his home many times but had never drunk tea. He told me and my assistant, Benson, to sit and called to his wife—a large woman not much younger than Lempirikany—to make the visitors tea. From the doorway of her house, she called out to him, "We have no milk!" Without a pause he replied, "What about *turunge* [tea without milk]?" "We have no sugar!" Lempirikany apologized that he didn't have anything this time, and we went on our way.

Fast-forward to 2001. I met him again in October, shortly after having returned for another period of fieldwork. Making the rounds of the settlements in my Lodokejek field site, I came upon him beneath a tree near his settlement, resting, watching the sky for signs of the rains that were anticipated in the coming weeks. He showed distinct pleasure at my arrival and immediately sent a child to the house of his younger wife to instruct her to make me tea. The child returned immediately. There was no milk. What about *turunge*? There was no sugar. The déjà vu was broken, however, when Lempirikany produced a few coins and sent the child off to a nearby settlement where a small shop had recently been set up, where he bought a small amount of sugar and tea leaves for *turunge*.

The final cup of tea came some months later, in 2002. When I had visited his settlement some weeks before, he told me he was going to come to my house for *paran*—to visit for the purpose of requesting some type of assistance—because his younger wife had recently given birth. When he came, I gave him a kilo of sugar and some rice, along with two hundred shillings to buy a few additional treats typically given to postpartum women, such as soda and Guinness. When I visited a couple of weeks afterward, he called the wife out of the house and told her, "This is the man who gave the things when you gave birth." He wanted to give me tea. This time we went into the house (we usually just stayed outside under the tree), where we sat and drank tea prepared with the heretofore elusive milk and sugar.

The seeming simplicity of these acts of actual or aborted hospitality belies a complex social dynamic between host and guest, and host and wife. Each of these two dyads is masked in considerable ambiguity. Consequently, while I can portray the strategic landscape, I can only speculate about the truth. Consider the first cup. As part of the general framework for all these interactions, Lempirikany is dependent upon his wives for the production of hospitality. To offer tea to his guests, he needs to direct—or attempt to direct—a wife to do so. Because the milk and sugar are under the stewardship of his wives, the actualization of his offer of hospitality is contingent upon his wives bringing forth sugar and milk, though Lempirikany may have no idea whether or not it exists. This is constraining in some ways at the same time as it is liberating in others. On one hand, it restricts Lempirikany's ability to provide *actual* hospitality. But it also frees him from the stricture of offering hospitality only when the resources are available to actually provide it. He can, in essence, be a good host without reference to the actual resources he is able to provide his guests, since his hospitality can be offered without knowing whether there is or is not tea.

His lack of knowledge (or purported lack of knowledge) is also fundamental to the other dyad. Is there or is there not milk and sugar to make tea? Practically speaking, if a man's wife says that there is no milk and sugar, there is no milk and sugar. Yet whether there actually is or isn't can rarely be known. Since men are not supposed to know what food is in the home, women can deny the presence of tea and sugar to avoid sharing[12]—indeed, if it is the husband's guest she may have no incentive to tell the truth and thus give up her resources. This may particularly be the case in polygynous households, where a wife might prefer that, if you are going to drink tea, you drink her co-wife's tea instead. And insofar as men are not *supposed* to know what food is in the home, it is rare for a husband to call his wife out on this even if he strongly suspects that she is lying, since it will appear that he is interfering in her business and quarreling senselessly with her over food. Occasionally men press their wives. In another incident, Lengiro, another Kimaniki elder, tried to offer me tea, and when his wife denied that they had milk he good-naturedly called her a liar and sent her to make the tea. When she left to cook it, we asked him how he knew, and he whispered conspiratorially, "I feel her calabashes. You can't just put your trust in women." Yet such incidents are rare. Moreover, it is not necessarily in the husband's interest to call his wife out on this, unless he has a strong and genuine desire for you to drink tea. For even if there is milk and sugar, he has still offered you hospitality, even if a lack of resources or perhaps a stingy wife has prevented you from receiving it. Thus, a false denial on the part of his wife allows him to offer his tea and drink it too—he, as well as his wife, may very well later drink the tea that his wife now denies exists.

A few particulars bear noting in relation to these incidents. In the second incident, Lempirikany was able to circumvent his dependency on his wives for hospitality because he happened to have a small amount of cash, and a small shop had opened nearby where he could buy tea leaves and sugar. However, it is also plausible that his wife knew he had these coins—thus she could deny that she had anything for his guests, letting him use his own resources rather than hers. It is also notable (though its precise significance unknowable) that on the third occasion, when I finally received a proper cup of tea, I had recently given him the postpartum gifts for his wife's benefit. It is thus likely that she felt more obligated or desirous of reciprocating (as opposed to the earlier incident, when she was asked to expend her resources for her husband's friend), while he may have also felt more entitled to press her on the matter because of my recent gift.

THE CALABASH(ES) OF MBARAN

Mbaran, the milk a wife reserves for her husband while he is away on travel, is an archetypal example that simultaneously encompasses the visible aspects of nkanyit, the fear of malice that lies just below the surface of selfless generosity, and the strategies employed to avoid ill will and supernatural harm. On the surface, *mbaran* appears to epitomize duty, selflessness, commensality, and good will. Elders are entitled to their daily share of milk, even if they are not able to drink it because they are not home. Consequently, a wife should dutifully ensure that his share of milk remains intact, putting it aside in a special calabash to await his return. His wife ensures that he is not denied his due share simply because he is absent, while he ends up with a large quantity of curdled milk, which he may generously share with his friends and neighbors when they come to hear the news he has collected on his journey.

Yet—although the sharing of this milk is generous, and is construed as generosity—the fact that men share this milk with others cannot be understood merely in reference to the value of altruism and sharing. Most men genuinely fear this milk. They are very reticent to drink it, such that only rare loners drink *mbaran* alone, and many do not drink it at all. If no friends or neighbors come to see him shortly after his arrival, he may give some or all of the milk to his children, and if neighbors do come, he may simply give it to them to drink without partaking of it himself.

Men's concerns center on the fear that the milk is not safe for them to drink. It may become harmful in several ways. Rarely, a man may fear that his wife has somehow poisoned it in his absence. More commonly, however, the fear centers on the possibility that a hungry person has been denied food while *mbaran* was sitting in the house. An age mate might have, for instance, slept in the house while they were away and, touching the calabash, found that there was milk that he was denied. By touching the calabash under these circumstances, the milk could become cursed to its owner. As Leyopoko, a Kimaniki senior elder, notes, "You know, an elder cannot put that milk in his mouth . . . because there is one problem. Maybe there are men who came, and they saw that calabash with milk. Then they whispered to themselves, 'This elder's calabash is ours, and she has not given it to us.' So the elder won't drink it when he comes. He just waits for the cows to return in the evening and drinks fresh milk." Similarly, Lekupano, a junior elder, explains:

> It might be that while you were away a visitor came and slept here. Maybe he was given just a little food, that wasn't enough for him. He is hungry, and he touches that *mbaran,* and just leaves it the way it was. When the owner comes back and drinks that milk alone it will cause a disease in the stomach. So what is good to do is that when you come back you give this milk to others, because you are not sure whether someone has touched it. But when they [your guests] give you some [of your] milk back to drink, it can no longer harm you, even if it has been touched.

Even if no one has specifically touched the *mbaran,* additional danger lies in the fact that all of a man's neighbors know it is there, and that it rightfully should be shared with other men. No person or group of men specifically have rights in the milk, but all are aware that the milk is there to be shared with someone. Should a man return from a journey and no one comes to share the *mbaran,* the resentful eyes of his neighbors may result in a curse being placed upon him. As Lengiro, a senior elder, maintains, "It's very bad. It's very bad. It puts a disease in your stomach, then people will say 'Oh! He has taken his *mbaran* alone.' It can kill—there is no man who can survive if he drinks milk of his cows that has been kept as *mbaran*. If you come home and drink that *mbaran* alone, it will just kill you. Because people see you coming home and say with hope, 'Later he will call us [to drink it].'"

Thus seeing a man arrive from a journey in essence promises not only news from afar but partaking the food that has accumulated in his absence. By not being called, someone may feel individual resentment, which can then coalesce into collective resentment when the neighbors realize that no one has been called at all. The curse resulting from the *mbaran* is a horrible, and subsequently fatal, stomach ailment. Informants disagree whether sharing the *mbaran* defuses its danger or whether the *mbaran* should simply be avoided entirely by its owner. A man who admits to this transgression may seek a blessing of the elders to cure him of the illness, which, barring treatment, is inevitably fatal.

Yet sharing is not the only means by which the potential curse associated with *mbaran* can be averted—at least not sharing everything. As Lengiro explained further, "A clever wife hides the milk of her husband. She hides some milk, she hides his milk in a smaller calabash. Then when the husband comes with men who were following him home, those men drink the *mbaran* and they go home. Then she hands you your calabash. *Yours*—which was hidden there, which was just put separate. So you are given milk."

The first calabash, the true *mbaran,* is stored in an obvious place. This calabash then becomes the target for any ill will from hungry visitors potentially denied milk in the home. This obvious *mbaran* is, in essence, a decoy, with milk actually intended for the husband stored in a second, hidden calabash. Yet the process of decoy, ruse, and counter-ruse need not end there—for visitors know that clever wives may hide a second calabash and can seek it out. Thus a wife may keep a third, more artfully hidden calabash—the calabash behind the calabash behind the calabash—rendering even the second calabash essentially a decoy, hiding the milk truly designated for her husband.

Morality is the companion of memory. It is the lens through which our subjects assess the transformations they have experienced, and through which they understand their present. If this morality and its meanings are constituted in very different ways from Euro-American notions of a rupture of modernity or a transition from gemeinschaft to gesellschaft, the mythic tropes through which Samburu fuse the present and the past are nonetheless fundamentally concerned with deeply held notions of right action and moral personhood constructed in everyday transactions of meaning and resources.

To understand Samburu memory—as well as the actual material and social transformations with which it is concerned—one must direct attention to the ways in which morality is constituted in belief, word, and practice, primarily through nkanyit, the core value through which all things Samburu are ultimately judged. Nkanyit is not a simple morality, providing transparent prescriptions for evenhandedness, respect, and giving everyone their due. Rather, nkanyit, this "keystone of Samburu morality" (Spencer 1965, 135), may more closely resemble the multiple hidden calabashes of *mbaran*. On the surface, *mbaran* typifies the selfless evenhandedness of giving everyone their due—a wife selflessly saving milk for her absent husband, only for him to turn around and selflessly share it with others. Yet this is a selflessness born in no small part of a fear of malice that must, at times, be thwarted by duplicity.

But nkanyit is not the simple deception of the second calabash, an ulterior motive behind artless, visible respect. Where a second calabash might be read as a simple lie that disrupts truth, the third calabash in a sense restores Truth by contending that truth is ultimately unknowable, by suspending notions of truth and falsehood entirely. It suggests that we are all in a game of truth and fiction, where whether you are good or bad depends not on whether you are good or bad but on how you play the game, where the morality becomes some odd balance between the vulgarly material consequences of sharing or not sharing and how artfully you have masked the steps that led to those results. In such a game you judge morality not by what is in someone else's head, which Samburu maintain is unknowable, but rather by what ultimately ends up in your stomach. You cannot truly know motives or truth but can only judge them within carefully crafted representations of plausibility, often tested through multiple encounters over time.

Nkanyit is not a false morality, but it is at times a morality resting on falsehood. It is not a disinterest that falsely hides true interest, but rather a disinterest that denies the question of interest entirely. If it may sometimes be a façade, it is never merely a façade—it does not hide immorality but makes morality possible. Nkanyit is neither genuine nor false, but simultaneously both and neither, a morality that lies in neither truth nor deception but in the shadows of ambiguity.

PART THREE

Histories of Eating

CHAPTER 6

Mixed Like a Pot of Gray Food

"Children never used to stay around old people," said my cantankerous old friend Lmomonyot Lempirikany contemptuously, as we rested under his shade tree. The new ways of eating, he explained, had mixed everyone together—old and young, men and women. Everyone just sits huddled around the same cooking fire, and respect has been lost, even to the point that "these days, if you tell a child to go look after the goats, they will refuse if the tea pot is on the fire."

Cooking, Mintz (2003) has argued, is an underexplored area of the anthropology of food. While food choice, food production, food sharing, the act of eating, and other dimensions of the social life of food have enjoyed considerably greater attention, the quotidian transformation of the raw into the cooked has remained largely hidden in the shadowy confines enclosed by kitchen walls. Yet food preparation can be a profoundly meaningful act to key social domains. Gender is an obvious example. Cooking is often principally the domain of women (perhaps contributing to its long-standing anthropological neglect) and serves as a major locus for constructing family and kinship relations between men and women, or old and young. Thus, it is often around the cooking pot that some of a society's most significant relationships, values, and meanings are cast.

Samburu offer something of a twist on this dynamic. Cooking is largely seen as a new thing—at least as a commonplace part of daily life—since cooking is not an everyday affair in the diet and cuisine of

,istence pastoralism. Milk, the staple food, is drunk fresh or fer-
,nted but uncooked. Cooking is mainly confined to relatively infre-
,uent roasting or boiling of meat. This is often part of ritual occasions
and always governed by strict rules of division, such that it is not a simple
dimension of everyday provisioning. Yet, as Samburu become increasingly dependent on purchased foods, cooking is ever more central to
how Samburu eat every day, with profound implications for the constitution of social relationships, values, and meanings through the mundane, everyday experience of the cooking pot. These "foods of the pot,"
as purchased foods are often referred to, are also called "gray foods,"
an indistinct blend—neither as light as milk nor as dark as meat, but a
vague, mixed-up color somewhere between the two. And just as the food
itself is an unappetizing color, like a muddied admixture of pure forms,
the preparation and consumption of these gray foods mixes up types of
people, disrupts boundaries, and problematizes values and relationships.
As Lemantile, a Kimaniki elder, puts it, women and elders and murran
"are all mixed together now, and that is why we say this world is dead.[1]
We say that the world is dead, and old men are no longer respected. It is
these foods that have brought such a change."

Thus, in Lemantile's view, the world is dead, and it is by and large
cooking that has killed it. If there are troublesome properties inhering
in qualities of the foods themselves (or stemming from the absence of
pastoral foods), they are less important than *how* the foods are eaten,
seeing as they are prepared around a single cooking fire. Cooking disrupts a host of meanings and practices central to the age-gender system
and the construction of respect and shame. These transgressions are
particularly salient in regard to murran, with particular implications
for shaping the gender of memory. Specifically, transformations associated with cooking are emasculating for murran, which is significant
not only for murran but for all Samburu who are invested in the historically validated prestige of the murran.

In this chapter, then, I explore the significance of cooking or, more
directly, the implications of a shift to cooked foods. Food and eating
practices are a crucial site where Samburu experience and shape aspects
of change and an important indigenous historical idiom through which
they understand their own social transformations. A model of Samburu history centered upon food effectively situates Samburu within
broader political-economic forces without subjugating the agency
and the meanings of Samburu actors to concerns raised by Western
notions of modernity and global processes. In addition, focusing on

the mundane, lived-in realities of everyday life is valuable in forging a unique and meaningful alternative to Western models of change, without Otherizing our subjects in the process.

ANALYZING CHANGE: GLOBAL AND LOCAL, MAGICAL AND MUNDANE

Social change, globalization, and modernity have become a pervasive focus in recent anthropology. The spread of global processes to even the most remote areas of the globe has presented challenges to a discipline founded on the study of culturally distinct, non-Western peoples, heralding to some a crisis in anthropology and to others novel research opportunities. Many have reacted to these developments by retaining a largely traditional anthropological field site but using these as arenas for understanding global political, economic, and cultural forces through particular local forms of modernity—in short to look at the global in the local (e.g., Ferguson 1999; Miller 1995a; Piot 1999).

Dominant features of global capitalism provide tempting lenses to analyze even the most remote areas of the globe in an era when the unique qualities of the local community have frequently ruptured (Appadurai 1996).[2] There is something almost intoxicating to anthropologists about finding Samoan gangsta rappers in Los Angeles (Swedenburg and Lavie 1996) or, as I have noted elsewhere, about the unusual attachment of certain Nuer in Minnesota to Barney, the beloved purple dinosaur of American children's television (Holtzman 2000). It invokes a world of dizzying time-space compression, where anything is possible and nothing is as it seems. Yet, however alluring such images may be to the irony-conscious anthropologist, they often elide the overriding realities of the lives of our informants, particularly in remote parts of the developing world. Moreover, in an excessive concern with "the global," we risk underemphasizing indigenous understandings of change, as well as processes that have little or nothing to do with "the global" (Holtzman 2004). While *the global* or *modernity* can be useful analytical tools, they are, after all, no less Western constructs than *love* or *the family* or *the supernatural,* and can be burdened by similar ethnocentric limitations (see also Donham 2001; Englund and Leach 2000; Tsing 2000). Moreover, focusing on global-local interactions creates a largely Western-centered worldview in explicating how processes from the center—our processes, even as they have become part and parcel of cosmopolitan locations around the world—affect the lives of non-Western others throughout the globe.

One avenue through which anthropologists have sought to preserve
the uniqueness of the local in the context of global modernity is local
cosmologies surrounding capitalism, invoking reimagined indigenous
understandings of the supernatural. While there have been many
important studies on this subject, they suffer to varying degrees from
the famous caveat described in Evans-Pritchard's (1937) "Witchcraft
Explains Unfortunate Events": that we know, of course, that witches
do not exist. This is perhaps most clearly expressed in Luise White's
fascinating study of colonial eastern and central Africa, in which she
argues that what she calls "vampire stories" are a particularly good
means of exploring colonial history not because of their accuracy—
White seems convinced that the rumors do not depict actual events—
but rather because "confusions and misunderstandings show what is
important. . . . Their very falseness gives them meaning" (2000, 43).
The same is implied—if not explicitly argued—in similar studies of
change. In Taussig's (1980) classic study of indigenous South American understandings of capitalism, he does not ask us to believe that
the devil *really* is in Bolivian silver mines. Nor does Shipton (1994)
insist that Luo who become wealthy from the "bitter money" gained
in gold or the bhang trade *really* fall quickly into ruin. Although
these studies are notable for their importance, lucidity, and analytical power, the genre as a whole risks replaying "the old opposition
between secular mundanity and spectral mystery, between European
modernism and African primitivism" (Comaroff and Comaroff 1992,
4). Their subjects remain the inhabitants of a magical Other world of
anthropologies past (albeit now with sunglasses and digital watches),
richly portraying indigenous metaphors of change but not proposing an alternative but equally valid understanding of change—unless
we are willing to accept that emerging elites really gain their wealth
through the work of armies of zombies moving with their unseen hand
(Geschiere 1997).[3] Instead of indigenous understandings of change,
they offer—more or less in White's (2000) words—indigenous *mis*understandings of change. As such, they reinforce, albeit inadvertently,
the global validity, centrality, and reality of the processes—capitalism, modernity, and the like—underlying the metaphors created by
our subjects.

A fuller riposte to hegemonic, homogenizing global visions may
be found in processes that are quintessentially mundane, the quotidian yet profound minutiae of everyday experience—here, changing
processes and meanings concerning food. A domain like food gains

equal validity not through suspended disbelief concerning a Samburu metaphysics but rather through Samburu meanings and social relations as they are entwined, historically and today, with pastoral praxis and processes of change. Its explanatory power rests neither in Western taken-for-granted assumptions about capitalism and modernity nor in indigenous models of change that are, from an outside perspective, ostensibly metaphorical in nature. A food-centered model of Samburu history—like similar histories of mundane, everyday processes—gains power from its primacy in how actors forge and give meaning to their everyday lives. Consequently, food provides a rich site for engaging with both externally driven aspects of change and the agency of local actors in structuring and bringing meaning to processes of change that are simultaneously both of and not of their own making.

MORALITY IN A COOKING POT

If, to paraphrase Lemantile's earlier statement, the world is dead and cooking has killed it, the complex and intense moral valuations Samburu attach to cooking in no sense reflect complexity in the act of cooking itself. Indigenous Samburu diet and cuisine are marked by great simplicity in preparation (see chapter 2) and near-total lack of epicurean sensibility in consumption. Samburu cannot be characterized as either gourmands or gourmet cooks. Foods are consumed largely in their unmixed, unadulterated form; enhancing the flavor is not central to food preparation; and the highly limited Samburu taste vocabulary reflects little interest in the sensuousness of food. The recent widespread adoption of purchased foods has not changed that. The most common food, *loshorro,* is a thick maize meal porridge, prepared by stirring maize meal into boiling water and adding fat and salt, if available, before eating. Less common foods, such as beans and dry maize, are prepared similarly—left to boil for hours on a cooking fire, with salt or fat possibly added at the end. With tea, milk and water are boiled together and sugar added when it has finished cooking.

There is, then, nothing in these mundane acts that hints at the profundity Samburu attribute to a mode of subsistence dependent on cooking. Yet this mode of eating is deeply problematic for most Samburu. This is attributed less to the additional labor and complexities that go into cooked food than the ways these foods threaten or diminish key cultural values. Cooking is not part of the daily pattern under the Samburu pastoral dietary regime. Women collect milk into separate

ir each family member, who may drink it whenever they
lk-based diet, there is no mealtime. An individual is more
shortly after milkings, but this is in no sense obligatory.
ink hours later, or even days later in the case of fermented
iver, excepting murran's obligation to eat with an age-
mate, there is no requirement to take one's food in a group, family or
otherwise. Each—child, murran, elder, woman—eats at a distinct time
of his or her choosing.

Thus milk-based meals facilitate the maintenance of social distance
that is intrinsic to Samburu notions of respect *(nkanyit)* and shame
(lkiti). The same may be said—perhaps even more strongly—for the
cooking of meat. Not only do family members eat different parts of
the animals (see chapter 4), but they eat them at different times, in different places, and cooked over different fires. Murran may eat separate
animals entirely, which they have slaughtered in the bush. The parts
designated for children, such as kidneys and heart, may be summarily
roasted at home or at the slaughtering site. The head, belonging to the
elder, is slowly boiled as soup and eaten at a time of his liking. Thus
the cooking of meat reinforces the distinctness of age-gender sectors
and the social distance and physical separation intrinsic to appropriate interactions.

In contrast, cooking purchased food often brings tends to bring
everyone—including to a lesser extent murran—together around the
same cooking fire and the same cooking pot. Cooking occurs at particular times—morning, afternoon, and evening. Food is set aside if
someone is absent, but there is a strong preference for getting food
while it is hot, and people tend to wait nearby during food preparation.
Consequently, rather than creating physical and temporal distance in
the act of eating, thereby reinforcing the social distance and distinctive-
ness between age-gender categories, cooking blurs differences. A variety of age-gender groups eat more or less from the same pot, breeding
familiarity and lack of respect.

"THAT ONE IS NO LONGER A MURRAN"

"Someone who eats with everyone," asserts Lopelu Lekupano, an
Lkiroro junior elder, "that one is no longer a murran." Lekupano considers ongoing transformations in how murran eat, linking them to a
general deterioration in the respect displayed by and afforded to the
age-set of bachelor warriors. He continues:

You just find them eating together with women, you meet them eating together with children. Now should you mention a murran, nobody has the fear of respect for them. So if a murran is walking and a child is walking and they meet, the child will not bow. They meet and just pass each other. In the past, like in our time [1980s], if murran came home the women inside the settlement wouldn't look in that direction. They would look in the opposite direction, they fear looking in that direction. And if you meet her on a path she will keep on going, and look down until you pass each other, then she will steal a glance after you are gone. In the highlands they no longer have that respect, although here [in the lowlands] they are still mostly behaving like that, they still have a little respect.

As Lekupano explains, how you eat and who you eat with are more than simple, mundane facts of subsistence; rather they fundamentally symbolize and structure who you are and your relationships with others. This is most highly charged in regard to murranhood, both as a long-standing cultural practice and as an aspect of contemporary transformations. Eating practices have long defined murranhood, as murran identity and practice are constituted by the *lminong,* which requires them to eat no food seen by women and to eat only in the company of other murran (see chapter 3). Not only have murran eating practices always been afforded much greater scrutiny, but contemporary scarcity has also posed great challenges to their attempt to eat in a morally upright way. Murran now rely heavily on agricultural products, which only recently were deemed unbefitting. Even more significant is the increasing tendency for murran to eat in ways much more closely linked to the domestic group—even eating in the houses of women—and thereby eroding the social distance that is a fundamental manifestation of discipline and respect.

The precise form this has taken is highly variable. A few students—particularly close to town—have essentially abandoned the *lminong,* positioning themselves as enlightened outsiders in relation to an antiquated tradition. They are only vaguely recognized as murran and are similarly vague in their self-definition. These young men are mostly seen as a peculiar anomaly, but at the same time ever fewer murran adhere to the strict letter of historical forms of *lminong,* continuing to honor its significance but in diluted forms. Most dramatically, in the highlands, murran frequently eat in the houses of women, though not in their presence. Murran may loiter around for their mother to leave the house so they can cook with their age mates. Sometimes they may even ask the women to leave. In response, by 2001 some mothers of murran had built multiroomed houses, which did not exist during my

1992–94 fieldwork. Thus they provided separate spaces for murran, where they could cook around their own cooking fires just out of the sight of women without chasing away their mothers.

   This shift to cooking at home is seen largely as a matter of convenience, since it is easier to cook there than to bring a separate cooking pot to some secluded location, and reflects the shift from milk to maize meal. The *lminong* traditionally prohibited porridge consumption at home, but the staple food—milk—was regularly consumed there with other murran. These changes are widely criticized and have been completely rejected in lowland areas, where the pastoral economy is stronger and exposure to Development is less intense. Here historically validated forms of *lminong* continue to be stridently emphasized. Thus Nosoruai Lekupano, a woman in her forties with murran sons, expressed shock and disgust when asked about highland murran eating in the houses of women. "Oh! That is not heard of here. We say that is sheer madness. . . . Imagine the kind of thing [person or murran] that comes and chases away his mother so that he can cook! Another women might see and ask herself, 'Whatever bad thing could be in the house that has made you to run away?'"

   In the lowlands, Samburu of all age-gender sectors reject the transformations in *lminong* that have occurred in the highlands, viewing them as a shameless and emasculating breach of both self-respect and respect for others. Yet even there one finds important changes that, if less brazen, nonetheless problematize murranhood. Murran there also do not subsist exclusively on the historically validated diet of milk, meat, and blood. Some may come close while herding in cattle camps where milk can be quite abundant, yet all murran depend to some extent on purchased foods, and many consume them regularly. And when eating purchased foods, they are far more open and shameless than they were even during my research in the 1990s, when just the acquisition of "gray foods" was marked by secrecy. Thus Meruni, a woman of about thirty who worked at her husband's shop during the early days of Lmooli murranhood in the 1990s, noted that some lowland murran were ashamed to ask her directly for maize meal, asking euphemistically to purchase "two kilos of my grandfather's white beard." Both cooked and uncooked food was largely acquired outside of the view of women. Today, however, even in the lowlands it is largely acceptable to get uncooked maize meal or other foods from one's mother, sister, or other women, as long as one then cooks it in the bush. Tea—the rival of maize meal as the most important introduced food (see chapter 7)—has been largely accepted as a food that murran can consume at home.

Though the change is most dramatic in highland areas, all murran are seen as being to some extent degraded by the loosening of *lminong*. Murran have moved closer to domestic consumption—whether by receiving maize meal at home, drinking tea at home, or loitering around settlements and chasing women away so they can cook. Though murran do not eat the same food as other family members, many perceive them to be following the *lminong* that are central to their murranhood only in the most technical sense, rarely eating in the bush. The consequence is that social distance and respect are seen to have radically diminished. As Letoronkos, an Lkishilli elder, reflected: "We never used to eat these foods people eat today. We only ate meat away from home. . . . The murran these days just stay at home." Lmomonyot Lempirikany, a Kimaniki elder, states the same sentiments even more strongly: "We say that these ones have become worse, because they aren't listening, because there is no order that is followed. . . . Those before did everything they were told and did not eat food in the house. Now they eat everything at home. . . . These foods eaten with women are bad because we used to drink herbed soups in the forest and we would know a sense of shame."

Food is not simply something one eats; rather it creates proper behavior at many levels. In talking about food, these elders paint a time when pastoral foods were plenty and those who deserved respect received respect—in marked contrast to an impoverished present, when food is lacking and behavior has degenerated. In a society disproportionately constituted through alimentary structures that shape facets of right action and moral personhood, a disruption of proper eating is a broad and potent threat to morality.

TO EAT IN NAIROBI

Barnabas told a story, perhaps apocryphal, of a transport lorry that overturned downcountry as it descended the Rift Valley escarpment between Nyahururu and Nakuru. It was filled with hundreds of sheep and goats on their way to market, and when the lorry rolled they escaped unharmed into the dense surrounding thicket. Retrieving the lost animals proved difficult, and large numbers of small stock were left wandering freely in the bush. When news of this oddity spread to the Samburu working as watchmen in the nearby towns, they flocked

ea, abandoning their jobs in favor of a boundless supply of
atton. There they stayed for several months, living in the forest
ing goat after goat after goat, until the last had finally disap-
l into the now fat, healthy stomachs of the erstwhile watchmen.

Could those watchmen really have abandoned their jobs in this way?
I asked Barnabas. Could enough meat really lure a man away from a
job, losing the earnings that he has traveled far to acquire, losing a job
that might be replaced only with great difficulty? I could see that it was
a tall tale, but it was hard to know just how tall. Barnabas laughed.
"Building your body," he replied sagely, was, after all, one of a man's
most important life works. Of course it made sense, even if the story
was funny (and maybe not all that true)—these Samburu watchmen
descending hungrily on a forest of lonely goats like Hansel and Gretel
upon a gingerbread house replete with gumdrops and a sugar glaze. It
was more than sensible; it was, he implied, a shrewd career move for
someone working, as much as anything, as a means of putting on some
extra pounds.

Migratory wage labor has become a key economic activity to supplement the declining livestock economy. It has become an important
pursuit for murran especially—who work most commonly as watchmen (usually in Nairobi), though also in the army, police, and other
jobs[4]—raising issues that have implications for memory and subjectivity. The narratives around which Samburu construct wage labor are
framed with a historical consciousness of poverty following plenty and
are scripted in response to the "food problems" that abound in an era
of pastoral poverty, with young men embarking on journeys to seek
menial work, thus earning their daily sustenance and perhaps remitting
wages home to help their families or at least relieve their families of
the burden of one more mouth to feed. In this context, the *lashumeni*
(watchmen, from English) has become a largely virtuous, though still
ambivalent, subjectivity for young Samburu men. While it is typically
viewed as a positive response to contemporary conditions of poverty,
it is nonetheless part and parcel of the endemic social and moral decay
bred by an era of pastoral poverty.

Older Samburu men typically deny having ever had an interest in
wage work, stating simply, "We had a lot of cows at that time." Through
the 1920s and into the 1930s, virtually all the "native" employees
in Samburu District were Turkana, who showed an interest in work
that was missing in Samburu. Through the 1930s, Samburu "employment" consisted mainly of forced labor, often as a punishment for

cattle raiding. In contrast, colonial authorities claimed that Turkana would attempt to sneak onto Samburu road gangs in hopes of gaining future employment (Colony and Protectorate of Kenya 1934). Widespread Samburu employment began with recruitment into the King's African Rifles during World War II, though archival and oral accounts differ markedly on whether enlistment was voluntary, at least until the 1950s. Colonial reports of having to turn away scores of eager recruits are directly contradicted by widespread Samburu accounts of being captured by European policemen and led off—perhaps with a chain through their bored-out earlobes—to unwillingly fight for the king. There may be reason to doubt both extremes.[5] Occasional chinks in the colonial accounts provide a less sanguine view of recruitment. In one instance, when authorities found it difficult to get murran to participate in a track and field competition, they attributed the murran's reticence to a rumor that "it was merely another method of recruiting for the K.A.R., and the competitors would never return" (Colony and Protectorate of Kenya 1948, 31). Conversely, stylized Samburu stories of forced recruitment are sometimes tempered by admissions of volunteering.

Yet the key issue concerns less history than memory—how Samburu accounts of the past frame the present. One telling point is that the few Samburu who admit to having willingly enlisted typically frame this in terms of a problem they had at home: they were very poor, they had no mother, or they were in some other way outcasts. In contrast, narratives of forced conscription into wage employment construct a collective view of the past in marked contrast to the present. If the obvious message is the brutality of colonialism, an equally significant subtext concerns transformations in the Samburu economy and values. Since they "had a lot of cows at that time," wage work was a pointless undertaking. The claim of eschewing wage work juxtaposes past times of pastoral prosperity and moral uprightness with the poverty and errant youth of today—a critique both of contemporary Samburu life generally and of younger generations specifically. The need for British soldiers to forcibly seize murran for military service—today the most desirable, indeed coveted, form of employment—highlights the inseparable divide between that epoch and today.

Wage labor is common among murran and fits squarely with their cultural construction as outsiders to domestic consumption, as well as their special difficulties in following the *lminong* in the context of pastoral poverty. Though overtly self-pitying, Lentito Lengosek, a Mooli murran, asserted, "There is only one group that has food problems today. It is us [murran] who have problems, because it is us who aren't given anything." Migratory wage labor is consonant with a masculine identity defined by eschewing food of the house and fending for themselves in times of need. In the past, murran excused themselves from a home where food was scarce by going to the cattle camps of wealthier age mates or eating livestock stolen on cattle raids, but these are less viable options today. Consequently, going to eat in Nairobi serves to redefine their identity in a context not only of profound economic change but also of an acutely felt awareness of profound change.

Yet, although being a watchman meshes with this historically validated subjectivity, it is not inherently virtuous. Food problems are universally blamed for the prevalence of wage labor, though many also note that this virtuous explanation can mask other, less virtuous motives. As Lesurmoile, a Kileku elder, asserted: "Some go out of food problems, others go out of *purda*." *Purda* is a term used to describe a type of foolish recklessness. Born of pride or hubris, *purda* drives you to uselessly cast aside something valuable, such as throwing away perfectly good milk because you feel you have a limitless bounty of it. Lesurmoile was therefore not asserting that food problems were the only reason for seeking work but rather that it was the only *good* reason to seek work—and therefore the explanation almost universally offered to explain seeking work, irrespective of true motives.[6] Others might go for less socially acceptable reasons such as to buy beads for their girlfriends, hang out with age mates, or seek the excitement of life down-country. The latter is particularly associated with the dubious morality of going to tourist resorts on the Kenyan coast, ostensibly to sell beads and spears. There drinking is chronic and the ultimate goal for many is to acquire a "Mzungu wife"—a white girlfriend to buy them cars, alcohol, or whatever they desire.

THE GENDER OF MEMORY

Lenaipashipash, a murran who prided himself on his adherence to Samburu traditions, laughed and poked my research assistant Sammy in the ribs. "Samburu culture is very good," he asserted. "But these ones just want to join the majority [tribes]—these women!"

Memory is not gender-neutral. If memory is morality's twin, integrally tied to the valuation of right action and virtuous personhood through reference to a real or imagined past, memory and morality are inexorable from the gender roles and gender identities that constitute the subjects of these valuations. In practice, a transformation such as the widespread adoption of cooking does not have equal impact on the lives of elders, children, women, or murran, who ate in ways that were different from one another under a more purely pastoral dietary regime, and whose eating practices are transformed in varying ways and degrees in the age of gray food. The meanings incumbent in these transformations differ according to the significance embedded in eating for particular actors, which is problematized in differing ways. Moreover, elders, murran, women, and children are in a Samburu view not equally constructed as moral beings, but vary in the behaviors that constitute right action, in perceptions of their ability to be moral, and in the implications if they transgress. Nor are moral valuations the product of a seamless set of shared attitudes and beliefs, invariable across lines of gender and age. How Samburu judge others—whether elders, murran, women, or children—reflects the position of the judge vis-à-vis the one(s) they stand in judgment of, despite significant degrees of commonality in the problems attributed to the reliance on "foods of the pot."

Leniapashipash's good-natured ribbing of Sammy—a high-school-educated murran with no place for *lminong* in his aspirations to modernity—casts these issues in sharp relief.[7] As with other Maa-speaking peoples (e.g., Hodgson 2001), abandoning one's self-defined "tradition" is seen in highly emasculating terms, and desiring to abandon Samburu culture for mainstream Kenyan culture is decidedly associated with a feminizing of masculine agents. Notably here, it is difficult to pinpoint the exact meaning when Lenaipashipash sums up a desire for modernity with the epithet "these women." Did he mean that the "majority tribes" were more or less just women? Were people like Sammy women? Or did he refer to concrete settings, like Christian churches, which are attended disproportionately by women? Yet the exact meaning of his offhand (and unexplained) comment is less important than recognizing that it resonated with all these possibilities, the multiple levels that problematize someone's masculine identity through failures in key facets of murranhood. The converse of this is that since abandoning tradition is understood largely in emasculating terms, key facets of memory and tradition are also disproportionately—though not exclusively—masculinized.

This raises two related questions. First, why for Samburu do memory and tradition, particularly regarding food, have these masculinized components? Second, to what extent do discourses concerning food cross from the murran they concern directly to Samburu memory generally? Moreover, how do similar or different processes, discourses, and valuations implicate changing eating habits of other age-gender sectors? How do these relate to other discourses concerning gender and memory, for instance in clothing, ornaments, and religion (Straight 2005), which are skewed disproportionately toward women?

While food-centered discourses are more masculinized, as bearing most directly on murran, they are also not *just* about murran for two reasons. First, if themes of transgression bear most frequently and potently on the misbehavior of murran, they have serious implications for all age-gender sectors. Second, masculinity—particularly the carefully constructed aspects of murran prestige—concerns not just men but a kind of public good. That is, masculinity is a set of practices and symbols that, in varying ways and degrees, is significant to all Samburu. Thus critiques centering on gray foods pay disproportionate attention to murran, not only because these transformations affect murran more significantly but because the effects on murran carry disproportionately greater meaning for all Samburu.

FOOD, MEMORY, AND MURRAN

It is unsurprising that the most vehement critics of the new ways of eating are elders directing their criticisms at the current murran. The criticism of murran by elders is an institutionalized facet of Samburu age organization, aimed at inculcating proper forms of behavior in the murran. Spencer (1965) highlights the significance of haranguing to the enculturation of murran, with elders accusing them of being rude, weak, disrespectful, and generally useless in order to breed respect and shame. Consider, for instance, a harangue vividly recalled by Lelenguya, an Lkishilli elder, which took place following a major raid by Somalis in 1965, in which many Samburu were killed and thousands of livestock stolen: "It was the Kileku [age set] who were young elders then, and the Merisho. So the world was blessed with a sweet smell at that time, even if it was then during the fights. And so it was that those elders harangued us, saying, 'Piu! You are just shit-eating dogs. It wouldn't have been like this if it had been us [who were the murran].'"

The other side of these ostensibly well-meaning, institutionalized harangues, designed to aid murran's moral development, is a genuine competition between age sets, particularly adjacent ones. An obvious dimension is sexual, since elders marry the girlfriends of murran, while the young wives of elders are the targets of murran's sexual adventures. Competition asserting the superiority of different age sets is most intense between junior elders and murran, and competition between adjacent age sets continues long after murranhood. Mekuri (initiated 1936) were, for instance, in intense competition with the Kileku (1923), who accused them of being poor, weak murran who never raided anyone, owing to the colonial ban on carrying spears following a number of murders or suspected murders by Kileku—discourses that remain salient even though only dwindling numbers of Mekuri and but a handful of Kileku remain. The Kimaniki (1948), the subsequent age set, took up the same criticisms of the Mekuri as did the Kileku, who were the Kimaniki's firestick elders (the age set that mentors the murran). For their part, the Mekuri effectively branded both the Kileku and the Kimaniki as warlike and stupid, and were joined by the Lkishilli (1961) in fixing this reputation to the Kimaniki. Thus the competition goes on and on. Murranhood is a time when young men develop a reputation that will be central to their identity throughout life, that they were strong, brave, and beautiful—real murran. Yet this reputation is advanced (individually and collectively) not only by asserting the virtue of their age set but by directing criticisms at others (especially the following age set) while defending themselves from counteraccusations.

This competition adds slipperiness to the project of historically reconstructing transformations in eating practices, since elders sometimes exaggerate the extent to which they relied on a pure diet of milk, meat, and blood, ate far from the houses of women, and were in all ways paragons of *nkanyit*. Viewing oral accounts in conjunction with archival sources suggests that transformations in murran eating practices began early in the Lkishilli murranhood—the early 1960s—although in a minor way, such as drinking tea in hiding and perhaps eating maize meal during severe droughts. It is more difficult to pinpoint how and when change accelerated, among whom, and how this differed across areas. Many informants point to *lipis*—the East Coast Fever epidemic of the mid-1970s—as the turning point in the decline of Samburu pastoralism, but the decline has been both steady and uneven in geographical terms and across wealth strata. However, when Lkiroro junior elders, whose murranhood ended around 1990, describe the dramatic changes that have occurred since their murranhood, there is certainly a healthy amount of painting their past as more "traditional" to contrast with the current Lmooli murran. Yet there also is a degree of truth. Consuming gray foods and eating in women's houses have grown more routine among Lmooli murran, even since I began research in 1992. Thus, even if Lkiroro (or the Lkishilli before them) could not be characterized as ur-pastoralists subsisting purely on milk, meat, and blood, gray foods have increased not only in frequency but in the brazenness with which they are consumed by murran.

Elders may exaggerate the failings of Lmooli to enhance their own prestige, but women and even other murran similarly participate in these discourses, though inflected by their particular positions. Murran admit that changes in eating have occurred, though they vary in their explanations. Apart from the minority of Western-educated youths of murran age who essentially reject the *lminong,* murran tend to view their own deviations from historically validated forms of eating mainly through the lens of practical reason: it is simply impossible to eat properly now that livestock have become scarce. Murran excuse their personal transgressions in this way but may not similarly excuse others, often maintaining that some of their peers have gone too far, engaging in inexcusable breaches of right action in their eating.

Women's views are consistent with that of elders, though sometimes tempered by motherly sympathy for murran's problems under the current system. This sympathy is more evident among highland women than lowland women, who are shocked and offended by the laxity of the *lminong* in the highlands. Consider the contempt for highland murran expressed by Naiterru Lenangida, a lowland woman in her fifties— contempt that she maintains is shared just as vehemently by murran from her community: "Our murran despise the murran of Ldonyo [the highlands] when they come here. And when our murran go there, they don't eat that food [in the houses], in the style of that place. They just go and eat privately in hotels, they don't want to chase women from their houses. . . . Those murran of Ldonyo can't do anything. And when enemies come, what can [people of Ldonyo] do, when their murran are just loitering in town chewing gum? So we despise them. Even our murran despise them."

Thus, although the most vehement critics of murran are elders, women and even murran take similar, if usually less strongly felt, positions. Murran are the most central focal point in discourse concerning changing eating practices, only partially because their prestige depends more saliently on their adherence to "tradition" through the exercise of historically validated eating practices. This concern also reflects the

extent to which a murran's eating habits are more than a personal matter, affecting many other Samburu—the families, the local community,
and to some extent all Samburu. The eating habits of murran are now
closely scrutinized not only because their eating is closely regulated and
their moral personhood closely linked to their eating habits, but also
because murranhood has come to stand for tradition among Samburu
of all age and gender categories.

Murran *are* a symbol of tradition, though they are not *just* a symbol.
If murran represent a glamorized past, viewing this as simply symbolic—an icon of identity or perhaps a Hobsbawmian (1983) invented
symbol of the past—is misleading. Certainly, at some level murran's
symbolizing of the past resonates with the picture-postcard image of
braided ochre-smeared warriors, the exemplars and guardians of Wild
Africa—an image that Hodgson (2001) and others have rightfully criticized for both its openly exoticizing elements and its erasure of the
cultural identity of women. Yet, for Samburu of all age-gender sectors,
there is far more significance invested in the meaning of murranhood
than a recycled Western image of the noble premodern. Just as Samburu maintain that murran belong to everyone, all Samburu—elders,
women, and children—are deeply invested as vicarious participants in
the glamour and prestige of murranhood. Although it would be a mis-
take to deny that Samburu are active, knowledgeable participants in
a globalized vision of African warriorhood—young men go to coastal
tourist resorts to market this image, their spears, and more—this is less
significant than the deeply embedded meanings that hinge upon the
exercise of historically validated murranhood.

The significance of murran prestige varies across Samburu actors.
Elders' prestige is constructed vis-à-vis both the ideal and the everyday
practice of murranhood. Everyday murran practices validate the power
and prestige of elders through forms of deference and fealty; the ongoing importance of murranhood to Samburu life constructs the glamour
and prestige that elders attribute to their own murranhood as a living, not anachronistic, meaning. Mothers become true, valid, mature
women through the murranhood of their sons and are integral participants in the rituals of murranhood. The prestige of girls is tied to the
prestige of the murran who are their boyfriends and brothers, and the
failings of murran are felt as their own failings. Boys idolize murran
from a young age, dreaming of the day that they will be like them.

Ostensibly, then, all Samburu are deeply invested in murranhood, in
young men's adherence to historically validated forms of masculinity.

Certainly it is not a timeless past. The glamour of murran is always inflected by a degree of hipness, and has been at least since the early colonial period, when they were first identified as differentiating themselves from previous age sets with new styles of clothing and ornaments and new styles of songs—but always in a way arguably consonant with tradition, to be traditional in a sufficiently up-to-date way. This is a direct reversal from the usual state of affairs in most contexts of change, where the young are the agents of change and the old are pulled along unwillingly, if at all. Since external attempts at social engineering began in the colonial period, elders have always been far more ready to comply than murran. Elders have already had their murranhood, have already made their name. In contrast, murran have always resisted change—perhaps now with more of a tempered reticence—because their present and future reputations are dependent on a culturally validated past.

OTHER EATERS OF GRAY FOODS

If the critiques of murran are vociferous, the failings attributed to them are of a piece with those attributed to other age-gender categories. The criticisms of other groups focus similarly on inappropriate transgression of boundaries caused by the way gray foods are eaten, and secondarily by effects of these foods themselves.

Women are least criticized, and mainly in ways tied directly to the transformation of murran. Women are not held faultless regarding social change, but food is less often seen as the root cause of their failings. Elders sometimes criticize women for acting increasingly as the equals of men—a kind of boundary-violating transgression not dissimilar to murran's eating offenses, yet with women it is tied less to food. Lmomonyot Lempirikany, a vehement critic of the effects of "food of the pot," insists that, as far as the position of women is concerned, the decline of Samburu culture began when the colonial district commissioner announced the coronation of Queen Elizabeth, the ultimate political authority becoming, of all things, a woman. Others tie the problem to *maendeleo* (development). Much of NGO-driven development has been directed disproportionately toward women, such that *maendeleo* sometimes becomes a gender-laden term (Straight 2000; Holtzman 2004).

Where the misbehavior of women is tied to gray foods, it usually involves murran. The inappropriate mixing caused by gray foods mainly involves women—and may lead beyond the cooking pot. Adultery has long been associated with murran who stay close to home. This is ironic, since the murran who stay close to home drinking milk are despised as *naperto nanya malesin* (pesky little calabash drinkers). Yet if the hypermasculine murran of the bush are braver, stronger, and more prestigious, they can be so much "of the bush" *(losoro)* that they lack the ability to speak properly, particularly to women, such that it is the familiar and effeminate murran, uselessly hanging around settlements, who tend to be more successful in seducing married women. Similarly, in the contemporary context, the heavy murran presence in settlements because of gray foods creates conditions conducive to adultery. Thus, Letorori, a Kimaniki elder, employs a bovine metaphor—comparing indigenous Boran cattle to the "grade" or European cows—to argue that gray foods cause greater female promiscuity:

> This thing [new foods] has brought ways that are not good. It's like with cows, like these Boran cows of ours. You see now with the Boran cows, they fight before the bull can mount. As for these "grade" [European] cows . . . they just stand still as the bull mounts. So we get perplexed, why doesn't the bull have to chase the cow? The bull just mounts: "kis." "Kis." "Kis" again: another one is mounted. And Boran cows cannot be mounted like that. And we came to explain that perhaps their food is making them so docile like that, these cows that are just standing to be mounted like that.

Elders are not immune from criticisms related to eating either, but these are also different from those leveled at murran. Structurally they stand in a distinct position in regard to social boundaries and social distance: they are the ones to be avoided, respected, and feared. Consequently, it is largely impossible for them to transgress the spaces of others, though others can impinge on theirs. Changes in eating are problematic for elders mainly in relation to gluttony in commodified eating, selling livestock to buy food (see chapter 9), and most prominently alcohol (see chapter 8). In the livestock economy, there is a long-standing dislike of elders who slaughter too frequently. They are disparaged as *laiyiangak* (literally "slaughterers") who needlessly endanger the well-being of their herds by too frequently slaughtering livestock out of a gluttonous desire to eat meat. Such men could be disciplined by relatives and other elders if this tendency was seen to be out of control. Today, Samburu contend that *laiyiangak* are now *lomirisho* (literally "habitual sellers"), the gluttonous desire for meat being replaced by a gluttonous desire for drink, fed by cash obtained from the too frequent sale of livestock.

While drinking is not bad per se—alcohol is a special food that is the privilege of elders—uncontrolled drinking can lead to uncontrolled sale of livestock, liquidating resources needed for the well-being of the family under an elder's care.

Following murran, the greatest concerns regarding gray foods center on children, and these concerns most closely parallel the criticism of murran, with both physical and moral dimensions. The physical vitality of children is seen to have diminished through their reliance on gray foods, as they are less able to withstand cold weather even though they now wear far more clothing. Children get sick more frequently, contracting diseases that were previously unknown. As Nolmekuri Lekuraki, a woman in her sixties, comments on introduced foods: "It is just dirt, this food of the enemies, in which is put this-and-that. It makes people sick. It makes young children sick when they eat these foods. We did not have these foods, these foods of the enemies."

The belief that children have suffered nutritionally by relying on gray foods is likely true, given that it involves a heavy reliance on maize meal porridge, which often is not even adorned with milk or fat. But equally prominent is the complaint that gray foods have changed children's behavior such that they, like murran, transgress proper social boundaries. Children subsisting on a milk-centered diet came, drank their meal, and went away satisfied to places distant from adults. In contrast, today's children loiter about waiting for hot food, chattering, banging plates and dishes, waking up elders, and being a general nuisance. Nosurai Lekupano, a grandmother in her early seventies, notes the differences between her own children and her children's children: "The children of the past, those who drank milk, were cool. The children of the gray food are hot [boisterous and outgoing]. This gray food burns them away like that. But the children of milk were cool."

The stomach is the seat of Samburu emotions and morality, such that the varying humoral properties of different foods can transform behavior. Thus, while milk is quintessentially cool, producing calmness and good manners, maize meal is hot, making you rude as it burns you up, like an addict in need of a fix. Children of gray food can't sit still, neither listening nor obeying, because they are obsessed with what is on the cooking fire. They are not calm and are not satisfied even by the superior food of milk. Having grown used to maize meal, they must have it, but it never truly satisfies them or allows them to remain calm and cool for a prolonged period of time.

If there are significant similarities, then, between the implications that cooked food holds for murran and children, there are also important differences. Most important, children and murran are not equally constructed as moral beings. Children are not expected to be moral; they are expected to behave. Children are naturally gluttonous and lack the *nkanyit* to be intrinsically motivated concerning proper eating behavior. Children steal food from others and eat all manner of odd things. Parents seek to correct this bad behavior, but childhood is a period of moral maturation when people are just beginning the slow process of acquiring *nkanyit*. In contrast, murran, though in some ways still becoming fully mature, are exemplars of the community. Thus, even if many of the effects of gray foods are broadly parallel, the implications are very different.

There are important similarities and differences in how gray foods affect various age-gender categories, particularly in comparison to murran. The greatest commonality is how food of the pot disrupts the distance between the age-gender categories, which is central to right action and the constitution of moral personhood. If, as Straight (2005) has described it, Samburu conceptualize their social universe through the ways a series of "cuts" differentiate and separate its most crucial divisions, the cooking pot serves as the site for their unseemly remixture.

On one hand, the properties of pastoral foods create inherently better behavior. In the case of murran, meat breeds strength, fierceness, and a sense of shame. More generally, animal foods are satisfying, cooling the stomach and creating an internal state conducive to morality. As Lemayon, an elder in his fifties, relates, people who are satisfied, particularly on the more substantial and cooling foods from livestock, are inherently more moral, while a hungry person may pay little attention to moral boundaries: "[Foods from the animals] make people's hearts fill with spirit, and it gives people a sense of shame. When a person 'gets heart,' it is that spirit which is respect. When you are healthy you have a sense of respect and shame, but when you are thin and hungry you can eat anything. You don't fear anything or anybody."

The humoral qualities of pastoral and purchased foods are mirrored by contrasting forms of sociality associated with their consumption, creating patterns of social distance in marked contrast to the loss of prescribed avoidance induced by gray foods. As the Lkishilli elder Senteku Lekimaroro asserts, reflecting on the time of his murranhood in the 1960s and '70s:

People were respectful at that time. Because someone who is called a warrior could not come near to where they elders are. And so it was for girls. Once she saw old men from afar, a girl would pass at some distance. And women would not go where the warriors were, and boys would not come where the warriors were. . . . But as for now, these foods from the animals are no longer eaten. An uncircumcised girl with a skin skirt will just come now and sit next to an old man. That's how it has become now that people feed on these other foods.

Significantly, the analytically distinguishable threads of humoral qualities of foods and the practical implications of eating various types of food are not closely differentiated by Samburu themselves. This is a consequence of the overdetermination of food, which is a site of such intense and varied significance that threads of meaning and causality become ultimately indeterminate. What we might regard (rightly or wrongly) as distinct phenomena are viewed by Samburu as a single intensely felt and lived dimension of their lives. This affords special power to the forms of memory surrounding food, yet also contributes to the intense ambivalence characteristic of food-centered forms of Samburu memory. The terrain of memory is largely shared but in no sense flat and homogeneous. Variously positioned elders, murran, and women—differing by age, location, wealth, education, and personal disposition or experiences—do not approach these largely shared discourses and meanings with unanimity. It is less the case, however, that they do so in strict opposition to one another, as the terrain of these differences is to a large degree shared and uncontested. Rather, it rests to a great degree in the differing blend of the various meanings and significances of food, as well as the overt trade-offs in contemporary and historically significant forms of eating.

CHAPTER 7

In a Cup of Tea

This is the history of a beverage, tea—not directly as a quintessential product of the capitalist world system, born of plantations and slave labor, and a central cog in the development of world capitalism in Europe and abroad (Mintz 1985; Sahlins 1988; MacFarlane and MacFarlane 2004) but rather—sitting on a dusty hillside in northern Kenya in the faint shade of an acacia tree—the Samburu beverage of choice served, of course, very sweet and piping hot.

Though anthropologists are no longer surprised that even on the fringes of global capitalism our subjects create their worlds from its pieces, the Samburu adoption of tea is particularly laden with contradictions. Within broader political economy, sugary stimulant "drug foods" are emblematic of global capitalism, yet tea is among only a handful of commodities adopted and indigenized within a self-defined Samburu "tradition" constructed in counterpoint to such forces of change, despite the extent to which anxieties concerning change center on food. These contradictions make tea a particularly vivid window for understanding the changing politics of everyday life, regarding both how macrolevel processes of broader political economy are expressed and experienced within everyday realities, and how these become fused to the small-scale politics of daily life: of the domestic group, the community, gender, age, and local stratification. Tea is metonymic of broad-ranging transformations in Samburu life, and the changes surrounding tea over the past sixty to seventy years correspond in intriguing ways to broader processes of change. Tea provides a reading of Samburu history constructed through the agency of Samburu actors determined less by processes of global capitalism than by meanings and relationships constructed by Samburu within that broader context.

Anthropologists have recently paid particular attention to how the very products and practices of global capitalism that apparently threaten cultural diversity can become sources of new diversity, showing the instability of the meaning of global commodities as they are reinterpreted in local contexts.[1] If McDonald's fast food has become a dominant feature in many parts of East Asia (Watson 1997) and Coca Cola has become a fixture in Trinidadian life (Miller 1998), the meanings and uses of these commodities are very different than those imagined in their countries of origin. Yet this approach is not entirely unproblematic, to the extent that it unintentionally accepts the assumptions of globalization proponents (Tsing 2000) through an implied teleology whereby the adoption of Western commodities is a natural, inevitable outcome rather than one constructed in a dynamic interface of active, culturally motivated local agents with broader political-economic forces. There is, in fact, nothing to suggest that non-Western peoples are either natural or undiscriminating consumers of Western commodities, as evidenced in the late nineteenth- and early twentieth-century bead trade, in which Western traders were forced to tailor their wares to the extreme selectivity of indigenous tastes (Straight 2002; Comaroff 1985), and in the total lack of Chinese interest in Western manufactured goods that defined nineteenth-century Anglo-Chinese relations (Sahlins 1988). Nonetheless, there are few accounts of commodities that have *failed* to take hold, and these tend to be relatively minor, confirming the overall inevitability of the adoption of commodities. Thus there are (often quite humorous) examples of poor marketing (e.g., attempts to sell cologne that smells like the flowers used at local funerals [Ricks 1993]) and cases in which *particular* commodities are not adopted principally because other commodities may be used in their place (e.g., using Western-style soap in place of shampoo [Burke 1996]). Even when specific commodities fail to take hold, the assumption remains that local agents are intrinsically consumers. They ascribe new meanings to the choices they make *among* global commodities, but *being a consumer* is assumed to be the inevitable consequence of globalization.

In contrast, the Samburu history of tea suggests that the adoption of global commodities is neither static, predetermined, nor unproblematic, occurring in a context where global commodities are largely peripheral to an economy of subsistence pastoralism and where the commodities adopted have been effectively disassociated from the external forces that introduced them. Commodities Samburu have adopted are few and far between—despite strong encouragement by colonial administrators in particular—and have frequently been reinterpreted as part and parcel of a self-defined traditional culture specifically counterposed to change.

FILTERING "CHANGE" AND "TRADITION"

Entering as a visitor to a Samburu home, one of the first things you will encounter is tea. Passing into the small, impermanent, stick-framed dwelling plastered with mud and dung, through a doorway roughly proportional to the stooped height of the owner of the house who has made it with her own hands, you will be seated on a short, simple, hand-carved wood stool and offered tea. Stoking the fire, which is almost constantly lit atop the three cooking stones in the center of the house, the owner will place in a pot perhaps two cups of water that she has drawn nearby, a cup of fresh milk from the family herds, a handful of tea leaves, and a third of a cup of sugar. It is a process so commonplace and routine that only upon reflection does one question it. Even though Samburu emphasize self-defined tradition in many arenas—dress, adornment, language, ritual, and especially food—they have adopted as a central and naturalized part of everyday life a sugared stimulant "drug food" that perhaps more than any other has come to stand for the spread of the world capitalist system (Mintz 1985; Sahlins 1988).

Interpreting this seeming contradiction requires consideration of how and why Samburu react to varying forms of externally driven change based on their interpretations of "change" and "tradition." Not all forms of change and tradition are valued equally. While some items (such as tea) are not long-standing fixtures, neither are they "invented traditions" (Hobsbawm 1983) that reduce tradition to ideology (Kratz 1992). Although Samburu are typically concerned with maintaining tradition, what they regard as traditional is not necessarily of great historical depth. For instance, ideal male dress now consists of two sheets and a blanket—traditional but in a sufficiently up-to-date manner—in contrast to wearing pants (a distinct and still usually negative marker of culture change) or a single sheet (seen as hopelessly antiquated or *kienyeji*, "local" [Holtzman 2004]). Yet, despite these very different valuations, from a historical standpoint none of these items is more or less traditional. Like both pants and sheets, the archetypal red tartan blanket is manufactured in factories in Nakuru and Pakistan and sold as a "Maasai blanket" in the Nakumatt Superstore off Uhuru Highway in downtown Nairobi.

The result is a self-defined traditional culture that is constructed largely in opposition to broader Kenyan culture but to a considerable degree assembled from its pieces—like Czech beads (Straight 2002), wage labor practices (see chapter 6), or tea. Yet this widespread process of incorporating novel practices and things is neither indiscriminate nor random. For every commodity that has been naturalized as part of Samburu tradition, there are many that have been ignored, rejected, or devalued. The occasional Samburu man might wear a suit and tie for employment or official business downcountry, but he could not wear the same suit for his wedding back home. Similarly, a hundred kilos of sugar might be used for tea at such a wedding, but you will not find a bottle of Coca Cola or even nonindigenous foods commonly eaten by Samburu, such as maize meal. As new items and practices have been introduced, these have met a variety of Samburu responses: outright rejection, grudging acceptance as an unavoidable necessity of contemporary life, and in rare instances, adoption, naturalization, and Samburuization as a part of self-defined traditional culture.

TEA IN CONTEMPORARY SAMBURU LIFE

While the "gray foods" upon which Samburu now depend are denigrated as unappetizing famine foods, the sole exception is tea (*chai*, from Kiswahili), which is both highly valued and integral to self-defined traditional culture. First introduced in the 1930s or 1940s, tea is drunk enthusiastically by all sectors of society and fills key nutritional, social, and symbolic roles: a staple food, the food of hospitality and an essential instrument in creating and maintaining proper social relations, and a necessary feature of ritual occasions.

Both tea and sugar are produced in Kenya, though far from Samburu District. Tea was introduced to Kenya as a cash crop in the colonial era and remains a major source of foreign exchange. In Samburu District, tea leaves are sold in factory-sealed packets of fifty to five hundred grams. Sugarcane is grown in western Kenya and processed in refineries there. Kenyan demand for sugar frequently exceeds national production, however, resulting in intermittent shortages and importation from abroad. The imported sugar is often finer and whiter than Kenyan sugar but less desirable to Samburu, who maintain that it is less sweet. Sugar is shipped to the district in hundred-kilo sacks and sold in bulk in local shops. Near larger towns and centers, women sometimes repackage sugar in small bags containing enough for a few servings of tea to sell to those lacking the money to buy a larger quantity in a shop. Conversely, in remote areas that lack shops, men sometimes load a whole sack onto a donkey to take home and sell to other local residents.

The first of tea's roles is as a dietary staple. This may at first seem odd, since in Western cultures it is a (sometimes noncaloric) beverage. Samburu tea, however, is derived from the British version, where tea has historically been calorically important (Mintz 1985)—although Samburu use considerably more of both milk and sugar. A cup of Samburu tea is roughly one-third milk, although this varies depending on the availability of milk. Water and milk are mixed in a large pot over the cooking fire (typically in a ratio of 2:1) along with a small handful of loose tea, and the sugar is mixed in when the tea boils. A very good cup may be almost all milk, whereas poor families are sometimes forced to drink *turunge*—tea without milk. Tea is not drunk without sugar—in the 1990s the two terms were sometimes used interchangeably. Sugar content averages two to three tablespoons per one-cup serving. One cup (250 milliliters) of tea thus contains 150–200 calories (50 calories in milk and 100–150 calories in sugar). When sugar is available, tea is drunk at morning and evening meals, often constituting the whole meal. It may also be drunk during the day with guests or as a guest in another home. Under ideal patterns of use, then, tea may provide 500–1,000 calories a day—between 25 and 50 percent of all calories consumed. Tea is most often prepared by women, and they typically control the supply of sugar and tea leaves, although elders may sometimes have their own.

Ideal patterns of use are consistent, but there is a geography of tea in terms of actual use, varying according to factors mediating change and development. In highland areas, where government and commercial infrastructure is more developed, most Samburu live no more than an hour or two from a shop selling sugar and tend to follow ideal patterns of daily use. In contrast, many lowland communities are more remote, have less easy access to sugar, and may at times be without tea. As Lesirayon, an Lkishilli elder from near Ndonyo Nasipa, complained to me one evening, perhaps exaggerating a bit in a spirited and spirit-infused rant: "There is only one thing we are missing in this area. There is one thing you should bring. If you want milk, there is plenty. If you want meat, there is also meat. The one thing we don't have is sugar!" Additionally, the lowlands are characterized by a more significant division between relatively wealthy Samburu living far from town and largely stockless pastoralists who have congregated close to trading centers. This division is reflected in the tea drunk by the two groups. Among the former, tea use is limited by access to sugar, whereas the latter experience a lack of milk. Lepalot, an elder from a remote lowland area, expressed utter disbelief to me one day while describing the breakfast he was served when visiting a lowland town. The relative with whom he had stayed served him *turunge*, tea without milk, a substance he found both unpalatable and shocking because of the poverty it represented to him, a man with a hundred cows.

Tea not only provides calories but is perceived to be a key dietary component. During sugar shortages, people feel they are enduring a serious famine, despite having other available foods. I was surprised one day in 1992, while working in the highlands, to meet a friend from my lowland site— more than twenty miles away by road or, for this man, a fifteen-mile walk uphill over fairly rough terrain. His sole reason for this trek was to obtain sugar, which was lacking at his neighboring trading center but he had heard—thankfully correctly—was available at this highland locale.

Providing tea is the most common means of expressing everyday hospitality. Exceptional hospitality may be marked by slaughtering sheep or goats, but a cup of tea is sufficient for the vast majority of guests. Frequent visitors may not be given tea every time they come, and people may come on business that does not require sociability. Repeated failure to give tea may, however, be interpreted as a social slight. Consequently, when tea is not given to a visitor, an explanation frequently is offered, usually concerning a lack of sugar or milk in the home (see chapter 5). In such cases, less desirable foods might be offered as an explicit substitute for tea.

Tea's role in domestic sociality is underlined by the fact that, although sugar may be sold out of the home, prepared tea is not. Samburu make a distinction between those items entwined in sociality and those excluded by virtue of their relationship to market activities. This distinction can be complex and contextual (Holtzman 2001). For instance, Samburu sell both meat and milk to one another but not at home, where norms of sharing and hospitality dictate that such foods are gifts. To sell these items, one must bring them to trading centers to be sold in butcheries or, in the case of milk, in informal curbside markets. Similarly, although sugar is viewed as a commodity governed by the ethos of the market, prepared tea is food and is governed by practices of sociality. Consequently, prepared tea is sold only in towns or centers in designated teahouses—typically but not necessarily shops built with "modern" building materials.

Tea's final role is as an essential component of virtually all ritual occasions, although it lacks religious connotations, and unlike foods such as milk, meat, blood, beer, and fat, it has no direct ritual usage. It is, however, the essential food for ritual occasions, and inadequate sugar—owing to shortages or insufficient cash—commonly delays ceremonies. Tea is served at specific points in many ceremonies, and although not highly ritualized a ceremony would be incomplete without it. Guests are incorporated into the occasion by drinking tea, ensuring their goodwill toward the rituals they have observed.[2] Tea is most important in marriage ceremonies. A few kilos of sugar is frequently given by the groom to the bride's family during marriage negotiations. At the ceremony, the groom must provide the sugar. The amount of sugar is directly addressed in marriage negotiations and is one of the major expenses associated with marriage. Between a third and a half of a hundred-kilo sack is brought to the wedding to provide tea to all in attendance, and sugar is sometimes given out by the cup to neighbors who come requesting it.

Tea, then, has several key roles: it has considerable dietary significance, is the most important instrument for the expression of everyday sociability, and is an integral component of virtually all ritual occasions. Despite being recognized as a relatively recent introduction, it is thoroughly Samburuized—integrated within important cultural roles and not regarded as a foreign element, like other foods and nontraditional items.

THE EARLY HISTORY OF TEA IN SAMBURU

When Samburu first began to use tea cannot be precisely traced. Colonial records indicate that by the early 1950s Samburu were using a small but significant amount of sugar (Colony and Protectorate of Kenya 1952), though sometimes mixed with blood rather than in tea.[3] Spencer (1973) also cites tea as a luxury item that was sometimes purchased by Samburu living in controlled grazing schemes in the late 1950s. Samburu generally place its first use at public meetings organized by colonial authorities in the 1930s and 1940s, gaining widespread usage somewhat later.[4] Many Samburu adults indicate that there was no tea when they were young, and they were exposed to it only as adults. There is, however, likely some bias in these reports because children were not allowed to drink tea at that time, and therefore may not have noticed it until a later age.

By the late 1950s, Samburu had developed a keen interest in tea, perhaps due partially to colonial authorities' active efforts to promote commodities that would encourage livestock sales. Indeed, had all gone as the local colonial administrators hoped, a Samburu history of tea might be just one more version of the well-known story of commodities drawing non-Western peoples into the capitalist world system (e.g., Wolf 1982). Commodities served the two interlocking keystones of colonial policy toward the Samburu—destocking and greater economic integration into the colonial state. In the minds of the colonial administrators, Samburu District was dangerously overstocked with animals that would better serve the colony on dinner plates downcountry. Local authorities frequently turned to forced culling to achieve their ends, in addition to trying to create a desire for goods that could be obtained only through cash. This resulted in authorities' perpetual obsession with attempting to get Samburu interested in often obscure commodities (e.g., Chenevix-Trench 1964) with very little success. There was simply relatively little in the way of consumer goods that Samburu perceived as useful in a pastoral lifestyle they found quite satisfying and, moreover, little they desired enough to induce them to sell cattle. In this context, sugar was a godsend to local authorities, who were delighted to have found something Samburu would willingly sell livestock to obtain, although the frequent failure of supply to equal demand was a source of consternation. In 1953, sugar was allocated to Samburu District at a quota of 127 (hundred-kilo) sacks per month (instead of the 175 requested). The district commissioner reported, "This lack is important, in that everything which assists in the sale of small stock should be encouraged and sugar is much in demand" (Colony and Protectorate of Kenya 1953a).

Why did Samburu want tea when other commodities held little appeal? Many state simply that they tried it willingly when it was offered and found it to be tasty and good. Mintz (1985) has argued that sugars are supremely attractive owing to a basic, even precultural, desire for sweet things, and Jerome (1977) notes that encounters with sweetness are frequently among the earliest components of the enculturation experience of indigenous peoples. Yet, if this speaks to the intrinsic appeal of tea to Samburu, it does not tell us how or why Samburu structured this desire in culturally specific forms, and the Samburu appropriation of tea occurred in close accordance with eating patterns prescribed by the age-gender system, particularly as these related to Samburu interpretations of tea.

Samburu tea use was initially reserved almost exclusively for elders and occasionally extended to their wives. To some extent the restriction to elders is easily explained: they could acquire and control tea because they were more likely to go to towns and public meetings where it was found, and they often marketed the livestock required to buy sugar. Moreover, their political power offered leverage in controlling access to a novel and scarce resource. In addition to obvious aspects of the organization of power, Samburu conceptualizations of tea structured its use. Rather than regarding it as a food, they initially treated it as a luxury item, specifically a substance akin to tobacco. Indeed, in these early stages, tea was governed largely by the same rules as tobacco.

An obvious relationship of tea to tobacco is based on superficial similarities. Some Samburu—such as Lekadaa, a Kimaniki elder who first saw tea in the 1940s—actually thought at first it was a kind of tobacco. Both tea leaves and tobacco are dark and aromatic, and both are mild stimulants. Sixty years later, it is impossible to determine whether the perceived relationship between tea and tobacco was a naïve interpretation of a novel substance based on its similarities to a well-known one, or whether elders may have actively cultivated a perception that justified their own tea use while limiting the expense entailed in buying it for everyone.[5] Regardless, tobacco and tea came to be regarded as similar kinds of substances, with important effects on its use.

TOBACCO IN SAMBURU LIFE

Most Samburu adults use tobacco *(lkumpau)* enthusiastically, mainly chewing it or inhaling it as snuff. Despite its popularity, however, tobacco's cultural connotations are highly ambivalent. Tobacco is tied to a variety of negative effects, yet it is an almost sacred substance, as seen both in its social and ritual use and in myths concerning its origins (see Levi-Strauss 1973 for comparison on the ambivalent nature of tobacco). Tobacco is present at important rituals involving elders, such as marriage and the killing of the *lminong.* Tobacco is distributed to all guests, not merely as hospitality but (like tea use) to incorporate them into the ritual. Even nonusers must accept the tobacco with out-stretched, cupped hands, though upon receipt they may pass it on without formality to someone who does use it. Tobacco is also used in less public rituals, a small amount being burned to fill the air with a purifying smell.

Tobacco's sacredness is embodied in myths concerning its origins. Tobacco is believed to have a supernatural source, growing from a lightning strike in the forest or on graves of the dead. A particularly interesting myth suggests that a boy brought it back from an encounter with the dead. In this story, a herd boy being raised by his dead mother's co-wife is punished for losing his spear when it gets stuck in a hyena that flees down a hole. When he decides to go down the hole in pursuit, he encounters the dead, including his mother. They give him tobacco and instruct him to punish those who have mistreated him—he must give it to them until they are addicted and then never to give it to them again.

Notably, this story incorporates both the sacred nature of tobacco and the negative qualities associated with its use, most important its ability to cause addiction. These negative qualities are summarized in the proverb *Meata lkumpau nkanyit* ("Tobacco has no respect"), particularly for the divisions between ages and genders. Driven by addiction, people may beg for tobacco from those they would otherwise be ashamed to approach. For instance, although young women are expected to avoid elders and to show shame in their company, Samburu believe that tobacco cravings can make them abandon appropriate behavior. Where all other traditional consumables reinforce age and gender boundaries, tobacco has the unique and undesirable ability to foster transgression, although it is unclear how frequently such transgressions actually occur. Samburu regard tobacco-related transgressions as understandable but undesirable. To make matters worse, tobacco is sometimes unavailable. Failing to obtain tobacco, an addict may sleep all day instead of engaging in more productive activity.

TEA AS AN ANALOGUE OF TOBACCO

Early patterns of Samburu tea use closely followed tobacco, evidenced both in explicit connections made by older informants and a marked similarity of use. Early tea use was restricted exclusively to adults, mostly elders. Women were not barred from drinking tea but apparently used it significantly less. Murran did not begin drinking tea until considerably later. As Lenaituwuori, a Kileku elder (initiated 1924), explained, not everyone drank tea when he was young; rather, "it was the Lmirisho and Lterito [the age sets immediately senior to him] who took it just like tobacco."[6]

Children were specifically denied tea at least until the 1960s, and in some areas the 1970s or later. Some suggest that children simply weren't interested in it before milk shortages became commonplace, but this is contradicted by many Samburu who were children at that time and relate stories of having been denied tea or attempting to sneak tea. Lenkopito, an Lkiroro junior elder, relates how during his childhood "we smelled when it was made and we rushed to get at the dregs." Indeed, children's lack of interest in a very sweet, milky beverage seems vaguely plausible only if they had been denied sufficient knowledge about tea to know what it was. Of greater significance was parents' trepidation concerning possible adverse effects on the behavior of children who drank it—that it would make them rude and lazy. The connection here to tobacco—which can make subordinates rude and addicts lazy—is clear. Although some noted a fear that tea might make children rude, fear of laziness was more common. Children are the main herders, and their addiction to a then scarce commodity could have adversely affected their ability to work. An elder who felt bad from not getting tea could sleep all day if he desired; children needed to herd whether they had drunk tea or not. As Naseru Lekutaas, a woman born in the 1930s, stated, "There was [tea when I was young] but we thought it was tobacco, and children were not given it so that they wouldn't become addicted."

Early Samburu tea use was significantly influenced, then, by tea's resemblance to tobacco, a traditional item with strong cultural conceptions governing its use. As sugar and tea became more available and other transformations began to occur in Samburu life, ways of both thinking about and using tea changed dramatically.

FROM TOBACCO TO MILK: THE "EXTENSIFICATION" OF TEA

By the early 1960s, transformations had begun to occur both in the patterns of tea use and the cultural conceptions concerning tea. Most concretely, tea began to be used by ever-widening sectors of society, with consumption spreading from elders to women, children, and eventually murran.

To a degree this may be seen as a classic case of what Mintz (1985) terms "extensification," whereby a prized new commodity moves from a luxury for elites to diffuse, ordinary use by society at large. Such is the scenario in England (Mintz 1985), where over several centuries sugar morphed from a luxury reserved for the nobility to the quintessential food of the working classes. In a classless society like the Samburu, extensification meant that tea moved between stratified age-gender categories. Over time tea became more readily available, as roads gradually improved in the district and between the district and the rest of Kenya. Shops spread to a variety of smaller centers, providing regular access to goods over a much wider area and increasing the likelihood that Samburu men and women of various ages would be exposed to novel items like tea.

Yet, at the same time, the Samburu case calls into question a key assumption of the extensification model. Specifically, the model supposes the desirability of the commodity, either because of its intrinsic properties or because a set of values and meanings attached to it is more or less shared among those initially afforded and denied access to the commodity. This assumption implies an inevitability that when a commodity becomes more accessible, the price drops, or censures removed, it will naturally be adopted by ever-widening sectors of society. Even if, in the case of the English lower classes, the specific uses of sugar and the massive quantities are contingencies of a particular moment of colonialism and industrialization, sugar's basic desirability is viewed as a function of its intrinsic sweetness. Yet the desirability of even a commodity like sugar is constructed through particular, local cultural meanings and social relations that also have the potential to make the commodity undesirable. Lower costs and greater availability may not, for instance, induce one to start providing tobacco to one's children, insofar as we believe it is not good for them. In the same way, greater access to and affordability of tea did nothing, in and of itself, to transform it from a tobacco-like substance, inappropriate for many sectors of Samburu society, into a widely consumed commodity.[7]

A necessary condition for tea's extensification was, then, a reconceptualization of its basic nature. This was not a singularly mental procedure, but was concretely grounded in transformations in the Samburu economy of subsistence pastoralism that began in the 1960s. Samburu universally link changes in tea use to the drastic reductions in their livestock holdings that caused the traditional staple, milk, to be available in ever smaller quantities. Forced to rely increasingly on nontraditional foods—including tea—they reinterpreted the cultural meanings associated with their use.

Milk shortages problematized the use of tea, though tea also offered solutions. As milk became available in lesser amounts, it was not appropriate to divert the dwindling supply to prepare tea exclusively for the consumption of elders. Whereas tea was a luxury for elders, milk was the food of everyone—especially children. Reducing everyone's rightful share—including that of children—to provide a luxury to elders would have been both unfair and contrary to the cultural expectation that men should willingly withstand hardship for the well-being of those under their care. This resulted in more widespread tea use because tea—despite its original associations with tobacco—was found to have desirable qualities as a food item, particularly in the context of a limited milk supply. By using it in tea, a small amount of milk could be stretched significantly and made considerably more satisfying, both because of the greater volume of liquid and because (like tobacco) tea can kill hunger—an effect that is probably due to its caffeine content.[8] In addition, using copious quantities of sugar greatly boosts its caloric content, giving tea a nutritionally significant role.

Despite these material incentives, increased tea use was made possible only by reinterpretation of the basic nature of tea. As long as tea was conceived as akin to tobacco, the use of tea as a food item, fit for the diet of children, was inconceivable. In essence, what had to occur, and what did occur, was a reworking of conceptions of what tea was: Samburu shifted their understanding of tea from something akin to tobacco to something akin to milk, the metaphorical emphasis shifting from the brown, leafy, tobacco-like substance used in the infusion to the milky liquid in which it was infused. Precisely how this transformation occurred cannot be detailed with exactitude, although most informants suggest that it was a slow, perhaps not entirely intentional process that involved an empirical recognition that the effects on children were not, by and large, what had been feared.[9] Children tried tea for one reason or another, through one means or another: surreptitiously slurping up the dregs from their father's cup, being given a taste to satisfy their interest, or simply being subjected to the experimentation of parents curious to find out if the feared effects were true. Lepoora, now a junior elder, described how in the 1970s, as a truculent herd boy in his early teens, he demanded daily that he be given tea. One morning, angry and exasperated at his constant demands, his mother threw a cup of tea in his face. Undaunted and defiant, Lepoora refused to remove the evidence of this insult, herding from sunrise to late afternoon with tea leaves and a brown, gooey film plastered to his face. Thereafter, perhaps feeling that the tea could make him no ruder than he already was, his mother gave him tea.

Interestingly, though tea use became more common because of increasing poverty, it has not been devalued as a consequence—for instance, as a poor milk substitute (although *turunge* is devalued as a poor tea substitute). Several things may account for this. First, in the earliest stage of its use, tea was placed in a category with positive connotations. It was a luxury for elders, a desirable item for the sector of society with the most outward prestige. Consequently, when it became extensified, it already had mostly positive associations. Indeed, there is nothing to suggest that Samburu (now or in the past) have ever regarded tea as less desirable than the milk from which it is made; rather, it is sweet and delicious, and Samburu gladly drink it instead of milk.

Today the shift from seeing tea as akin to tobacco to seeing it as akin to milk is essentially complete. Whereas older Samburu frequently describe early tea use in the idiom of tobacco, younger Samburu rarely make an explicit connection between the two substances, and some flatly reject the idea that there is a connection at all.

TEA AND THE MURRAN

Culturally prescribed patterns of eating are central to murran identity, and anything that suggests a deviation from historically validated eating patterns can be a serious threat to the prestige of that individual, his family, and other murran (see chapter 6). Consequently, the integration of tea into the murran diet was treated with greater circumspection by murran and their families. Tea was both novel and initially categorized as a tobacco-like substance reserved for elders. Whereas allowing children to drink tea hinged largely on an empirical assessment of its effects, a symbolic reconceptualization of tea was essential to render it acceptable for murran. This greater emphasis on murran diet makes the transformation that occurred all the more striking. Like other nontraditional foods considered inappropriate for murran—such as maize meal—tea was gradually accepted as a necessity, if a somewhat odious one. Yet while these other foods continued to be eaten by murran outside the presence of women by being subsumed within the category of milk, tea came to be accepted—although ambivalently—as something murran were permitted to consume in their homes.

When murran began to drink tea is difficult to pinpoint, because they initially drank it in hiding, and informants rarely admit drinking it before it was generally acceptable. The earliest date suggested by informants is the early 1960s, when a catastrophic drought caused a severe decline in the availability of milk.[10] The first age set of murran among whom tea use is held to have been widespread is the Lkiroro (initiated 1976). There were, however, negative connotations associated with tea drinking by Lkiroro murran, because there was not yet consensus on its acceptability, and it could suggest poverty on the part of the drinkers, who perhaps lacked more appropriate pastoral foods. Fearing for their reputations, some families tried to discourage tea drinking by murran sons, especially wealthy families whose sons picked up the habit from poorer age mates. Lengerded, an Lkiroro junior elder from a wealthy family, described how his father came home one day and found him drinking tea with his age mates. Angry at the implication that they had no fitting food to eat, his father immediately snatched a goat from the family herds and sent the lot off to the bush to eat proper food.

Tea has not entirely lost its ambiguity for murran. They now drink tea, without denying that they do so, but they prefer not to drink it in the sight of women. It is generally agreed that since tea is made from milk and used like milk, it may be drunk at home on the condition that it is drunk with an age mate. Murran themselves, however, maintain some level of ambivalence. They are ultimately responsible for their own behavior, and their own prestige will suffer if they fail to observe propriety. I witnessed several spontaneous debates concerning the propriety of murran drinking tea, especially in front of women, usually instigated by a murran concerned about the effects on his social status of taking a cup of tea that was offered to him.

SODA AND THE SAMBURU

> Tribesmen have been seen drinking Coca Cola in the one *duka* at Kauro, 130 miles from Maralal. The *duka* even has a Coca Cola advertisement sign stuck up outside it. It is said that the *duka* owner has ensured the popularity of the drink by describing it as a powerful purgative. (Colony and Protectorate of Kenya 1950)

The history of soda among the Samburu provides an intriguing comparison with that of tea because of similarities and differences in their local and global histories. Like tea, soda is a quintessential drug food of world capitalism—albeit of a later era—with "Coca Colonization"

typically taken to be synonymous with cultural change and Westerniza-
tion (cf. Miller 1997, 1998). Like tea, soda is a sugar-based stimulant
beverage that has entered Samburu life in the context of widespread
political-economic articulation with nonlocal centers of power. Moreover, within wider Kenyan national culture, tea and soda have become
analogues in many ways, carrying similar meanings and interchangeable in many contexts. Soda has had a history among the Samburu that
is nearly as long as tea. Yet soda—despite these global similarities, an
availability in Samburu District roughly comparable chronologically
to tea, and almost universal familiarity among Samburu adults—has
never approached the widespread use, social significance, or indigenization of tea. Consequently, soda's failure illustrates that the adoption
of commodities—even similar ones—is not an inevitable process, and
it suggests some key ingredients in success.

Within Kenyan national culture, soda is used like tea in many
social contexts. Kenyans generally serve tea as a food of hospitality,
although—unlike the Samburu—they may substitute soda. As a guest
in a Kenyan home, one is frequently asked, "Which soda do you take?"
and children are summarily sent to a shop to fetch it. Due to the greater
cost of soda, this is often a symbol of marked hospitality and may
not be repeated on subsequent visits. Further, there are class implications inherent in such offers (e.g., Goody 1982; Weismantel 1991),
since many people cannot afford to drink soda regularly. Offering a
soda shows cosmopolitan hospitality to someone expected to be a soda
drinker. Despite these minor differences, soda—like tea—serves as an
instrument of hospitality, a less expensive and involved substitute for
an actual meal of hospitality.

Soda is also analogous to tea in the sense of *chai*. *Chai* is invoked
regarding money for a bribe, tip, or following a favor, as in the request
"something for *chai* [tea]." The money is not, of course, typically used
for tea. Rather, tea serves as a metaphor for the expression of gratitude for a service that has been rendered. Significantly, soda can frequently be substituted for tea in this context. Instead of *chai,* one may
alternatively ask for "something small for soda." As an instrument of
hospitality, then, soda also serves as a metaphor for a specific type of
hospitality, bribes, or tips.

Within Kenyan national culture, then, soda and tea share a similar,
although not homologous, social-symbolic space. Among Samburu,
however, this connection is salient only among the small minority
who, through education, employment, or some other means, are highly

enculturated in Kenyan national life, and then only with people to whom this form of hospitality is intelligible. For most Samburu, soda use is, at most, sporadic, and its cultural associations are poorly developed, particularly in comparison with tea. Clearly, there are practical considerations behind this. Soda is markedly more expensive than tea. During the early 1990s, a bottle of Coca Cola—the most popular soda—ranged from 5 to 12 KSh ($0.10–0.15), while sugar ranged from 17.50 to 60 KSh ($0.50–1.00) per kilo, with the requisite amount of tea leaves being 5–12 KSh, meaning that the money spent on one bottle of soda could make a far greater quantity of tea.[11] Tea is also much more transportable than soda, since sugar and tea leaves may be brought to remote areas and the beverage prepared with locally available milk and water. In contrast, a prepackaged liquid like soda cannot be transported in quantity to areas without roads.

Acknowledging these practical limitations, however, does not imply that in their absence Samburu would naturally desire soda. Although some Samburu report reacting positively when they first drank soda, many concluded that it "was not tasty." There is a wide range of Samburu reactions to soda and a notable absence of consensus concerning its nature. Soda is, then, like tea, in some ways an exception to the rejection or devaluation of introduced foods. Yet rather than highly valuing it as a part of self-defined tradition, Samburu have constructed it in a position of almost perpetual novelty. Whereas first tobacco and then milk provided idioms through which Samburu interpreted tea, no comparatively appropriate idiom has ever been applied to soda. Soda might be described as "poorly understood," and it remains so to this day among many Samburu, despite sixty or more years of exposure. In a sociocultural context in which maintaining an essence of continuity is central to accepting change, soda has never been fused to any traditional cultural category concerning food and related substances— indeed, there are no categories with which it has an obvious fit—and ways of thinking about soda are therefore limited. As a consequence, to many Samburu, it remains an exotic thing, its properties and even its basic nature somewhat hazy.

Most Samburu—particularly older people and those from remote areas—had little sense of what soda might be when they first drank it. Although their first encounters occurred in various contexts, most were first given soda by more experienced friends or relatives who better knew what it was. Many murran initially believed it to be some type of beer and consequently avoided it, although some were later given some by experienced friends and discovered that it was not intoxicating. Besides fearing that it might be beer, murran also avoided it initially—and in some areas still do—because it was an ambiguous, nontraditional substance that seemed unsuitable for their consumption. Moreover, the perceived "hotness" of carbonation is sometimes seen as having the potential to cause an explosive effect when combined with the natural "hotness" of murran.

The nontraditional nature of soda is reinforced by its absence from Samburu settlements. Samburu commonly encountered soda for the first time on trips from distant settlements to towns. Tired and thirsty after a long journey, they bought a soda or were bought one by a friend or relative. In some cases the purchase was motivated by the belief that soda would be particularly effective in refreshing them and "restoring their blood." In other cases, however, the purchase was driven by the significant contrast between town and Samburu home life. In Samburu settlements, water, milk, or tea would be provided for a weary traveler after a long journey. In contrast, town is a place of money that provides no free means of satisfying thirst. Many suggest that they tried soda for the first time, and in some cases continued to drink it when they came to town, simply because there was no means to get drinking water. Closely associated with town life, it has become familiar in a context specifically defined as outside Samburu culture.

Samburu often first experienced soda in the context of illness, when a relative or friend brought them one to drink after they had been brought to a hospital or clinic for treatment. The primary motivation was not to give the sick person a special treat, since often both the giver and receiver were unfamiliar with soda, and the patient did not find it enticing. Indeed, one of the most common complaints among Samburu who don't like soda concerns its medicinal flavor, noting its similarity to both Western medicines and indigenous herbs. Soda is often believed to have possible curative properties and continues to be commonly bought for people who are sick, which contributed to a soda shortage in one of my research sites during an outbreak of malaria. Soda is not used as a cure per se, but Samburu regard it as Americans might regard the use of vitamins or herbal teas, which are given in the hope of providing some (perhaps unspecified) assistance in withstanding illness rather than vanquishing it entirely.[12]

It is unclear whether Samburu perceive actual benefits for patients who are given soda. It is a source of clean drinking water and easily digestible calories for patients who may be both dehydrated and suffering nutritional stress. There may actually be modest benefits, but there is no indication that Samburu soda use is motivated by these. Although no one could explicitly state reasons for its use by the ill, its status as an unusual, poorly understood substance fits squarely within Samburu ethnomedicine, which is dominated by purgatives that cause either diarrhea or vomiting. The fact that traders initially described soda as a purgative may be significant, particularly given that it is sometimes described as hot because of the carbonation (though other times described as cool and refreshing). There is, however, a general Samburu tendency to believe that new, unusual substances may have curative properties. A good example is *changaa,* a locally distilled liquor that has been widespread among Samburu since the early 1980s. *Changaa* is sometimes used, alone or mixed with rock salt *(magad),* to treat various human maladies or sick calves that do not respond to normal treatment. There is no apparent ethno-pharmacological theory behind this use, which is based simply on the fact that *changaa* is a substance with powerful although not fully understood properties, and it is worth trying when other treatments fail.

Despite an exposure to soda that is similar in duration to tea, and despite soda's similarities to tea in both Kenyan national culture and wider theoretical perspectives, Samburu have not indigenized it to a degree in any way comparable to tea. Indeed, although most Samburu have tried soda and some drink it occasionally, others refuse even to try it. As Lekula, a Kimaniki senior elder, states, "I always see people drinking it, but I have not taken it because it is not food." Sixty or seventy years ago, both tea and soda were novel, foreign substances to the Samburu. Soda largely remains so, whereas tea has become a central item in Samburu life. The reasons for this difference are to some extent economic and practical, a consequence of price and ease of transport. It is also important that the conceptual incorporation of soda by Samburu never fully occurred. Whereas tea could be understood as similar to tobacco and later to milk, soda was never understood as being similar to anything. As it became integrated into Samburu life, it was integrated as something specifically strange and specifically foreign.

What is reflected in this cup of tea is not global capitalism per se, but rather Samburu histories of meanings and relationships in which the global political economy now plays but one, albeit increasingly salient, part. The fact that tea and other commodities are part of a global landscape does not mean that anthropologists must allow "the global" to set our analytical agenda, whether in accepting the assumptions of globalization proponents or in reflexively countering that the presence of Coca Cola does not equal Coca Colonization and that the presence of McDonald's does not equal McDonaldization. Rather we may take tea as a Samburu lens to understand what it means for Samburu, historically and today, to live their lives in a world they forge—significantly but not exclusively—out of the pieces and processes of global capitalism.

There is an uncanniness to tea—at once a central engine in the spread of world capitalism and at the same time nothing more than a nice, hot drink—and there are telling contradictions encompassed in its adoption by the Samburu. Tea is uniquely situated at the confluence of "traditional" Samburu culture and the capitalist world system, against, within, and through which this traditional culture is constructed. Tea came to the Samburu as part and parcel of a process of political and economic integration with the Kenyan state, which has posed considerable material and symbolic challenges to Samburu life, yet at the same time, Samburu have made use of tea as an answer to some of these challenges. The centrality to Samburu of food in forging their social and symbolic worlds renders tea an especially appropriate window on their history, yet this very centrality of food makes their adoption and indigenization of tea all the more surprising.

The Samburu adoption of tea is neither a consequence inevitably dictated by the forces of global capitalism nor a simple matter of choice afforded to new consumers in a globalized market. Samburu agents have, instead, quite selectively made use of this quintessential item of global capitalism in accordance not only with their changing economic circumstances but with interpretations and reinterpretations in a changing politics of everyday life. An icon like tea serves as a reminder that the influx of capitalism and the state is not always best understood within the macro-level concerns of traditional political economy, but sometimes must be seen in the multitudinous ways local agents negotiate this terrain in creating, experiencing, and understanding their worlds. Moreover, the domains that are most crucial to how our subjects live and think about their changing lives, their idioms for understanding their history and their present, may be found most compellingly in the small, practical, mundane routines that form the locus of social relations and constitute the material and symbolic frameworks of their daily lives.

Turbid Brews

ETHNOGRAPHER'S AMBIVALENCE

One of my first main Samburu haunts in the semiformalized hanging out that is participant observation, was in the settlement of the Lengoseks, a large extended family in Nkorika, up the hill from Lodokejek and its Catholic mission. It was a natural fieldwork setting in a number of different ways, not far from the house I was staying in at Lodokejek, and a midpoint between town and the settlement of my friend and sometimes research assistant Robert Lesengei. The settlement was also a major neighborhood center of social activity for many Lkiroro junior elders in the neighborhood, who were my peer group and that of my various research assistants during my two and a half years of fieldwork in the early 1990s, and thus the most natural place for me to make friends and acquaintances. The interest of my Lkiroro age mates in this settlement was partially due to the presence of the four Lengosek brothers. They were fairly wealthy Lkiroros—though their Mekuri father was still alive and living in the settlement, the livestock had already been divided—and, led by the eldest brother, Lendoogi, they formed a dominating social presence in the neighborhood. Alongside these reasons, however, the centrality of the Lengosek settlement in the neighborhood perhaps owed even more to the women—the brothers' mothers, wives, and sister. Virtually all the women in the settlement brewed *busaa,* a locally prepared beer of maize and millet, and given the number of brewers living there, it was rare that a man carrying a coin or two (or, lacking change, a friend ready to help them out) did not find some drink for sale there.

Many of my earliest ideas about Samburu alcohol began to take shape there (Holtzman 1996; 2001), on pleasant afternoons and evenings spent sipping half-liters of busaa from recycled cans of Kimbo vegetable shortening, which was then the standard measure of a unit of sale. There I got to know most of my age mates in the neighborhood, and many of my closest friends during my doctoral fieldwork were the friends and neighbors with whom I shared busaa. Perhaps not entirely surprisingly, then, given the positive nature of these experiences, my first accounts of alcohol in Samburu were relatively sanguine. Certainly, I was careful to see clearly enough through my proverbial busaa-goggles to acknowledge some problematic aspects of alcohol that would be patently obvious to even the casual observer, and which held currency in widespread discourse—occasional drunken violence and a few men who devoted inordinate resources to drinking, at the expense of their families. By and large, however, I emphasized the prevailing (though not unanimous) sentiment of both men and women, that alcohol's positive aspects outweighed any deleterious social consequences, being not just a source of enjoyment and blessings but a central source of income for many Samburu women and an important source of calories for many Samburu men.

When I returned in 2001, Lendoogi—the eldest brother, proud, colorful, outgoing, friendly, wealthy, the emerging household head, and one of the few Lkiroros to have already married three wives—was dead. Whether or not alcohol really had anything to do with his death, alcohol was blamed. Returning home after a drinking bout, he developed severe abdominal pain and died precipitously. Another sometime resident of the settlement from a different family—a Mooli who did not follow traditional murran practices, and therefore drank—was also dead, and here the role of alcohol was far more clear. When his brother—a mild-mannered catechist I also knew fairly well—intervened in the Mooli's drunken attempt to beat their mother, he killed him with a blow to the neck from his short sword, then severed his own mother's arm. After seeing what he had done, he poisoned himself by drinking insecticide.

Certainly many others in the family were not doing poorly—their Mekuri father was still alive and in good health, and most of the women in the settlement were more or less as before, apart from Lendoogi's widows—though their wealth in livestock had clearly diminished significantly. Among the brothers, Norbert, who worked as a teacher, had assumed the role of family head after Lendoogi's death, but sometimes appeared disoriented and inarticulate. Lijah, who worked as a government forest guard, remained industrious and energetic, though much of his energy appeared to be directed to maintaining a steady flow of liquor through his veins, and both he and his two wives were unusually thin. Only the youngest Lkiroro—Kimalen, who drank very little—could be unambiguously characterized as economically and physically well.

My point here is not to transmogrify my earlier views (1996; 2001) of gender-based economic cooperation and interdependence into a morality play on the evils of strong drink, in the ruined shadows of the Lengoseks. If my earlier arguments might potentially be read in a long anthropological tradition of purportedly finding positive social functions in alcohol "even where administrators and health workers find cause for alarm" (Colson and Scudder 1988, 20; see also Karp 1980), I would hasten to emphasize that the positive effects I observed, documented, and analyzed were not imagined, neither by me nor by the Samburu men and women who emphasized them—nor have they disappeared. Thus, although the Lengoseks' demise is both tragic and emblematic of the kinds of problems to which alcohol can lead among Samburu, their alcohol-related misfortune is unusual in both its frequency and its severity. Whether this is due to the personalities of those individuals, the unusually constant availability of alcohol in the settlement, unrelated factors, or just bad luck is hard to say. But among the group that formed my frequent drinking companions in Nkorika, there are no others whose condition appears markedly changed, economically, physically, or socially. There and elsewhere, their wives and other women continue to rely on brewing as an economic livelihood, while the men enjoy the nutritional and intoxicating qualities of alcohol, even in the face of its potential pitfalls.

This chapter aims, then, to neither praise nor condemn alcohol, but to plumb the intense ambivalences that—like my own—characterize Samburu experiences of drinking in contemporary life. As alcohol has taken a central role in a society that until quite recently had very limited access to it, strong drink, in its various forms, has become perhaps the most potently ambivalent signifier in contemporary Samburu life. For instance, Namukare Lekuyie, a woman from Lodokejek in her midforties condemns *changaa*—a locally distilled liquor—as a bringer of death. Yet her condemnation of it is tempered by her vocation as a brewer (just as her husband's equally vociferous condemnation is tempered only slightly by his avocation as drinker): "Even though it kills, it is good because now with all the poor people, it brings them up. It feeds them, they can send their children to school, so there isn't a role that it doesn't enter into. It buys animals, it sends the children of the poor to school even as they enter secondary, so from what we see, we can say that it does a lot of work for people."

Alcohol is indeed a singularly dense site of intense and poignant contradiction, and not merely in the simple choice Namukare emphasizes between economic benefits and social ills. Perhaps even more so than the other transformations discussed in this book, the tensions of alcohol do not simply oppose drinkers and nondrinkers, brewers and nonbrewers, old and young, or men and women; rather alcohol creates forms of personhood rife with moral ambiguities and contradictions. Alcohol is necessary to the efficacy of elders' life-giving blessings but is also a poisonous killer. It is a food that may build bodies or burn them away. It may fill the hearts of elders with unfettered goodness or turn them into stupid, insatiable beasts. For elders, drinking is a moral entitlement but also a frequently immoral act that contravenes the *nkanyit* (respect) which is the basis for such entitlement. Elders are constructed in widespread discourses as ineffectual drunkards, burdened by an anachronistic focus on their herds and by failure to protect their herds from their own predations in the form of livestock sales to get the cash to buy alcohol. For women's part, brewing is typically read as a progressive initiative through which women may gain economic self-sufficiency and provide for their families in an era of pastoral poverty. Yet they are often perceived to be facilitating the social ill of rampant drunkenness, including unsanctioned drinking on the part of women brewers, leading to promiscuity and debasement of the homestead by creating an unsavory barlike atmosphere.

In this chapter, I examine the contradictory subjectivities constituted through alcohol, situated at the confluence of both historically validated forms of Samburu drinking and the transformations entailed in the colonial and postcolonial proliferation of strong drink, with particular attention to transformations in gender and reconfigurations of notions of power and moral personhood constituted through alcohol. In examining these transformations and the contemporary dynamics of alcohol, I suggest that the ambivalence that surrounds alcohol is due not just to the uneasy balance between costs and benefits, but moreover to the fact that it is an intrinsically murky sign, inherently ambiguous because the very nature of alcohol is constituted in a dialogic space in which its basic nature is always debated but never resolved.

COLONIALISM IN A GOAT BAG:
BREWING HISTORIES IN SAMBURU

Chief Lasangurukuri, the British-appointed head of the Lukumae clan in the 1950s, was by all accounts a favorite of the local administration. Like most of the colonially appointed chiefs, he was outwardly compliant, but Lasangurukuri seemed as if he actually meant it. The majority of the Samburu colonial chiefs were viewed by the British administration as ineffectual, unable to direct the people they were appointed to lead, and rooted in tradition to the extent of having little interest in exacting change. In Lasangurukuri, however, the British saw cause for hope. Though he was not formally educated, he had served for a time in the King's African Rifles and had gotten an opportunity to see how people lived outside of Samburu District and Samburu traditions. He was interested in Progress and was considered perhaps the "most forward-looking of the Samburu chiefs." His only fault, as far as the administration notes: he had a tendency to drink too much in his beer hall (Colony and Protectorate of Kenya 1953a).

Lasangurukuri and his beer hall, opened in the administrative center of Wamba around 1952, mark the beginning of widespread recreational and chronic drinking among Samburu. Not being cultivators, they previously had only minimal access to fermentable materials. Beer *(naisho)* was prepared from honey found in the forest or acquired in trade from Dorobo foragers. However, the limited supply of this wild honey made alcohol unavailable on a consistent basis, and beer was used predominantly by married elders only at occasional blessing ceremonies or special meetings. The possibility of recreational drinking—and consequently, chronic drinking and alcoholism—was ostensibly introduced with the opening of Lasangurukuri's beer hall. Serving busaa, a locally brewed maize and millet beer, the beer hall was followed soon after by others in the district headquarters of Maralal and the town of Suguta Marmar, eventually spreading throughout the trading centers in Samburu District.

The active role that the colonial administration played in introducing recreational drinking is surprising and ironic from a number of perspectives. Perhaps most striking, however, is the contrast between colonial attitudes and practices regarding alcohol in Samburu District and those in much of eastern and southern Africa, or the ways ostensibly the same policies were employed for very different reasons and to diametrically opposed ends. Elsewhere in Kenya early twentieth-century colonial policy regarded alcohol as a threat to the peaceful conduct of colonial rule, with administrators reporting a correlation between increased drunkenness and civil unrest (Ambler 1991). The power of alcohol to remove inhibitions could be particularly dangerous not only because of alcohol's ability to subvert the conventions of daily colonial practice but because the perceived limited mental abilities of Africans rendered them particularly vulnerable to the effects of strong drink (Willis 2002). While East African administrators found that it would not be possible to entirely ban drinking by Africans, they found it imperative to control its use, principally through the application of the oft-revised 1930 Native Liquor Ordinance.

The policies toward alcohol embodied in the ordinance were primarily concerned with the dangers that arose as processes such as migration and urbanization disrupted the social fabric of "custom," which was believed to have previously controlled the use of alcohol in "traditional Africa." Stripped of traditional controls, overdrinking might become rampant, posing a physical threat to both drinkers and those around them, and leading to economic exploitation by beer sellers who would unduly drain African communities of their resources (Colony and Protectorate of Kenya 1961). As a consequence, the colonial government developed a multipronged approach to African consumption of alcohol. First, Africans were not allowed to drink European-style beers, wines, and liquor, which were presumed to be stronger than African beers, and therefore more dangerous.[1] More significant was the division of areas into those covered by the Native Liquor Ordinance—mainly urbanized areas where the social fabric was assumed to have been disrupted—and rural areas in which it was assumed that brewing and drinking continued to be governed by custom. In rural areas, brewing and drinking were unregulated, but the sale of alcohol was banned. In urban areas governed by the Native Liquor Ordinance, beer clubs were to be governed by the local authorities (the colonial district officers or the African District Council or African Native Council) and run basically as nonprofit, or parastatal, organizations, on a model first developed in Durban, South Africa, in 1909 (La Hausse 1988) . Profits from the clubs would go directly to the local authority, or in a simplified model, the local authority would collect revenue from licenses or by renting the beer hall to a person allowed to run it for profit. White-owned farms could have clubs for the entertainment of their workers, but the profits were required to go to a fund that would benefit the workers.

What is striking about the colonial promotion of beer halls in Samburu is that—given the rather different context from that which the Native Liquor Ordinance was intended to address—local policy was in marked contrast to the intent of the ordinance. Rather than limiting and controlling alcohol, it actually served to promote it. Samburu in the 1950s was in no way an area of rapid social change crying out for solutions to the problems of migration and urbanization. Even more than today, Samburu was a rural district, with no true urban areas. Though there were a few isolated incidents of illicit brewing, there is nothing to suggest that it posed a widespread problem. Furthermore, rather than having a well-developed brewing tradition closely governed by custom, Samburu had access to alcohol only on a very occasional basis. As such, the effect of colonial policy in Samburu was, in essence, to introduce recreational drinking to an area where it had hitherto been little known.

Although the first beer hall owner, Chief Lasangurukuri, appears to have come upon the idea independently—according to his wife, Lasangurukuri had seen beer halls while in the army and on trips to Nairobi as one of the more favored and "progressive" Samburu chiefs[2]—the local administration had been toying with the idea of beer halls for several years and enthusiastically welcomed the development. This fact is odd from a presentist perspective in which these brews are now illegal, as well as in light of the anxiety with which colonial authorities viewed alcohol. It seems curious that in those particular historical circumstances the colonial administration would see a social good in promoting an exponential increase in Samburu access to alcohol. Yet they did, indeed, see in beer halls the betterment of the Samburu way of life, previously centered exclusively on pastoralism, as well as a possibility of addressing the administration's budgetary issues.

The seemingly peculiar colonial promotion of alcohol becomes somewhat more explicable when read in the context of studies of colonialism through the 1980s and 1990s, which fragmented our understandings of both the colonizer and colonized (e.g., Cooper and Stoler 1992; Dirks 1992; Comaroff and Comaroff 1991). Such studies suggest that rather than being driven by a coherent vision or broadly shared political-economic agenda, colonialism was the product of diverse groups of colonizers and colonized variously empowered to pursue many differing agendas. From this perspective, the colonial promotion of alcohol was less the product of a knowing and powerful colonialism than something pulled out of the proverbial "goat bag" of colonialism—driven by both economic exigencies and ad hoc efforts at social engineering by local administrators who were deeply, but ambivalently, concerned with the betterment of Samburu social and economic life.

The literal goat bag was an off-the-books administrative fund derived from the sale of goat skins, a byproduct of the meat ration issued to government employees, and was used by the perpetually strapped local administration to fund unexpected expenses.[3] Though on the books, beer halls similarly represented unconventional income that promised to meaningfully contribute to a district which was underfunded because of its marginal position in the colony—lacking, as it did, settler populations, large numbers of inhabitants, or valuable resources. At the same time, in the absence of clear-cut material interests, colonialism in Samburu District often took on the air of a moral project, yet one lacking clear moral objectives. Social change was seen as both necessary and undesirable. Although British administrators foresaw the possibility of benefits in the quality of life through Western-style clothing, housing, health, hygiene, and education, there were trepidations about imposing change on what they saw as a basically good, if backward, tribe. The perspective of the district commissioner in 1928 was echoed throughout the colonial period—that while Samburu were "on the whole a law abiding and inoffensive tribe," he had only met two "who[m] I should call truly civilized. . . . They are a released murderer and a prostitute" (Colony and Protectorate of Kenya 1928). In a similar vein, the colonial administrator Charles Chenevix-Trench (1964) notes that in the early 1960s "the trouble is that, when you cut a moran's [warrior's] hair, take away his spear, and cram him into trousers, he rapidly becomes a township spiv, and his last state is worse than the first." The goat bag is thus an apt metaphor for the ad hoc and sometimes idiosyncratic approach taken by the local administration toward social change in Samburu District.

In this context, beer halls were seen as contributing economically to the inadequate budgets of the local administration, but also, counterintuitively, as a means of betterment for the Samburu. The colonial government viewed the pastoral economy with chronic unease, owing both to its unpredictability and the environmental degradation caused by overstocking. The administration believed that Samburu had too many cattle, and sought to reduce them through forced livestock sales, culling, grazing control, and the development of alternative economic activities for the Samburu. Beer halls were regarded as a sound business, and Samburu involvement in them was seen as a step toward turning Samburu into businessmen. Lasangurukuri's beer hall in Wamba appears to be the first and is regarded by many as having been the first business run by Samburu, though a butchery opened by a politically prominent Samburu named Lekalja may have opened a year or two earlier.[4] A beer hall was opened in Maralal a short time later by another chief, Benale Lengerded. Because Samburu did not previously brew busaa, Kalenjin women were brought in from outside the district to serve as brewers in these first clubs.

Busaa clubs steadily proliferated in Samburu District through the 1960s and early to mid-1970s. At their peak, there were clubs in all the major centers of Samburu District, and in most of the minor centers too. This came to an abrupt halt in 1978, following the death of Kenya's first president, Jomo Kenyatta. Beer halls quickly became the focus of one of the first directives of the new president, Daniel arap Moi, as he established himself as moral guardian of the nation. Drinking was characterized as an immoral drain on the productivity and resources of the citizenry. Drinking was bad for society, and running a beer hall was an unworthy profession, because it involved encouraging and profiting from this ill.[5] While initially there was no formal declaration in law, this directive was sufficient to close down Kenya's beer halls. In Samburu District, the closing of the beer halls resulted in moving brewing from towns to settlements. Brewing thus shifted to hidden domestic contexts, where women illegally brewed beer and distilled liquor to sell to Samburu men so as to gain the cash necessary for daily subsistence and other needs, a model that continues to the present. In addition to busaa, changaa (a liquor) grew in popularity after the ban on the clubs. Although it is difficult to date the emergence of changaa, informants suggest it started in the early 1980s, becoming truly popular somewhat later.

THE FOOD OF ELDERS, THE "RATION" OF WOMEN

Brewing plays a central role today in Samburu economic life in nearly all areas. Only in the most remote areas is the role of brewing less significant, though certainly not absent.[6] Women rely heavily on earnings from brewing for daily necessities, as well as for less essential purchases for which their husbands may be unwilling to release cash. They typically sell brews not only to elders in the community but even to their own husbands. Customarily a man is allowed one free glass from his wife's brew, out of respect for him as the *lopeny* (owner) of the settlement, but he must pay if he desires to drink more. Thus brewing allows a woman to get money from men in general, and a wife to get money from her own husband, as well.

Brewing has become an important means of survival for many contemporary Samburu women. As one elder asserted (despite his concern about the problems caused by widespread drinking): "If there was no changaa here, it would bring problems. Problems, problems, problems. There are so many women who don't have anything, they just depend on brewing. Just changaa, just changaa. They would just get problems and die if they couldn't sell it." This contention that many women (and their families) would perish without changaa is only a slight exaggeration. Since less than a fifth of families have sufficient livestock to survive as subsistence pastoralists, and more than 30 percent are nearly stockless, alternative economic activities are a necessity of contemporary life. While men have the option of seeking wage labor, the alternatives presented to women—including the small-scale sale of sugar, tea leaves, and tobacco—typically offer only minimal earnings. In contrast, brewing can provide a level of income that, though not high on an international scale, can allow a woman and her family to live well by local standards. In a survey of eighty-three brewing women in 1993, earnings were equivalent to $12–$20 per month,[7] which compares favorably to remittance levels from wage labor and can provide basic foodstuffs for families with no other alternatives, or discretionary purchases for those who have other sources of income.

Overall, I found during my 1992–94 research period that 42 percent of women had brewed at some time, a figure that—based on informal observation—has not changed dramatically. Brewers are found across all strata of Samburu women, though there are important patterns. Not surprisingly, poverty and not having a husband are the key predictors of brewing. Stockless families brewed at a rate of 62.4 percent, significantly higher than the overall sample, while 57 percent of female-headed households brewed. These two factors often coincide to produce the highest rates of brewing, with 80 percent of stockless female-headed households brewing, compared with 56.8 percent of stockless male-headed households. Brewing can also provide a means of support for woman whose husbands are absent or noncontributing. Thus one woman, whose working husband had not remitted wages from Nairobi

FIGURE 12. A woman with a traditional brewing calabash. Photo by the author.

for a long time, explained that she was "just surviving on the ration of beer [ration lolbusaa]," invoking the metaphor of relief food for the way selling beer allowed her to survive in these difficult circumstances.

By far the most important use of brewing earnings is for basic subsistence. All respondents reported using brewing earnings to buy food, with a mean time of 4.6 days since last using brewing earnings to purchase food, and a median time of 1 day. Brewing cannot, however, simply be reduced to its importance in feeding the poor. In this regard, 22.1 percent of women from the wealthiest families—who are well above subsistence level—also brewed. Although they also purchased food, they were likely to direct more of their earnings toward other kinds of purchases, such as beads, clothes, veterinary medicines, school fees, or even small stock. These women, whose families would eat whether they brewed or not, typically cited a need or desire to circumvent male control of cash to make desired purchases. Just as their husbands might willingly use money from a livestock sale to buy a new blanket or some beads, a wife could freely spend what she earned from selling beer (sometimes even to her husband) to buy what she liked without his consent.

Women's brewing is morally ambiguous, though less highly charged in social debate than men's drinking. At its most positive, brewing is seen as an absolute good, a kind of *maendeleo* (development) through which women are able to take care of their families in the context of pastoral poverty. Those who are less sympathetic may see it as a necessary evil, positive to the degree that it feeds families but a social detriment nonetheless. Others, though acknowledging brewing's role in supporting the poor, nonetheless see it in nearly unambiguously negative terms. As one young elder asserted, "Yes, women rely on it, but it is not a good business." Thus, despite being an effective source of income, it is not a "good" business because it is seen as destroying men's health and mental faculties, resulting in a variety of ills for them and their communities.

The moral valuation of brewers also varies widely. While the majority of brewers are viewed simply like any other upstanding women, there are several potential pitfalls associated with brewing. One of the biggest is that women will begin to consume their own brews. While some drinking is tolerable among older women (particularly those past childbearing age), there exists no justifying ideology, as there is for male drinking, and drinking by younger women is seen in flatly negative terms—again more so than comparable male drinking. Drinking is seen to lead to a loss of responsibility in both men and women, but this can be viewed as more problematic for women because of their direct responsibility for daily care of the home, particularly in looking after small children. Thus, where a drinking man may resemble a roving, ravenous beast, this may be transitory and does not contravene the possibility that he is an otherwise proper elder. In contrast, a woman who drinks is viewed as neglectful of those areas of responsibility that most directly constitute her moral personhood. In addition, brewing can be associated with female promiscuity. While women who brew are in no sense akin to barmaids—who in urban areas of East Africa frequently double as prostitutes—selling alcohol brings a steady flow of drunken men (with money) through the home, which, in a society where adultery is rampant, leads to the obvious consequences. Therefore, although some husbands are quite supportive of their wives' brewing for financial reasons, many find this benefit to be outweighed by the potential for drunkenness and promiscuity. Moreover, brewing typically changes the entire comportment of the settlement. While a quiet, calm home is generally seen as desirable, reflecting the *nkanyit* of the elder who is the *lopeny* (owner) of the settlement, brewing typically means that perhaps seamy drunks roam the settlement at all hours, much like a bar. Consequently, husbands—out of concern for their reputations or for the well-being of the settlement—may forbid their wives to brew, although some women nevertheless do so surreptitiously when their husbands are away.

If women's motivations for brewing are fairly transparent—it is a source of cash with which to feed their families or make discretionary purchases—men's purposes and the effects on their moral personhood are shrouded in considerably greater ambiguity. As with the proverbial calabash behind the calabash behind the calabash that was the focus of chapter 5, men's drinking may be motivated or explained through shifting layers of justification that gain potency from the fact that all these explanations are true—at least to some extent, for some people, sometimes. At one level, alcohol is conceived of as a food, such that its consumption might require no more explanation than why men drink milk or eat meat or porridge. That women are the gatekeepers of the family larder is significant in this regard, as drinking is men's only culturally sanctioned means of self-provisioning. This is significant, culturally and nutritionally, in a society where food can be scarce in absolute terms, and where women and men agree that wives sometimes starve husbands with whom they are at odds.

Yet if alcohol is primarily a food, it is not a food like any other. Rather, it is an ambiguous one, rendering it sometimes less and sometimes more than food. This ambiguity—and the ways it is employed and manipulated—is central to the dynamic surrounding alcohol and its role in the constitution of male morality and power.

FOOD, NOT FOOD

"People say it's a food," my research assistant Benson commented with irritation when I first suggested we explore the nutritional aspects of drinking, "but it isn't." Although most Samburu refer to alcohol as a food, *he* knew it to be a drug—*he* knew better, having been born and raised in the community but now having risen to being one of the few university-educated Samburu, with aspirations to a position in wider Kenyan society. Yes, he agreed, elders say they are eating when they are drinking, but in his view this was a weak excuse used to justify drunkenness.

His reaction did not reflect the dominant Samburu view, and—while far from idiosyncratic—it had clearly been colored by his position as a well-educated cultural critic, as well as by his own family experiences. Aside from his education and hoped-for upward mobility, he had been raised by a mother who brewed and a father who drank heavily, who had at times sold a goat with the excuse of needing fifty shillings to treat a sick child and drunk the rest of the money. His desire to refute the widespread notion that alcohol is food reflects the standpoint of an insider who is opposed to drinking, one pole of usually implicit, sometimes explicit, debates about whether, or how, alcohol is food. In this way "being food" is less a static quality attributed or not attributed to alcohol by varying cultural actors than an assertion, an argument that always suspends disbelief. The social dynamic surrounding drinking is inherently constructed through multiple idioms—just food, more than food, less than food—which are simultaneously available to the actors involved in these contestations but are wholly irresolvable.

Nutritionally, there is good reason, in Samburu cultural gastronomies, to assert that alcohol is food. For those who drink regularly, alcohol provides a major proportion of daily caloric intake, while for others it either significantly replaces or augments other sources of food. Under commonplace conditions of scarcity—with nutritional intake averaging less than two thousand calories a day—the six hundred to eight hundred calories in two tins of busaa or a bottle of changaa easily constitutes between half and a third of the calories an elder might consume in a day. Moreover, as in much of Africa, alcohol is culturally constructed in many senses as a food like any other, at the same time as it is layered with unique qualities and associations. Thus, when Samburu elders request alcohol, or money to buy alcohol, it is common to do so in an idiom of food. They may explain that they have not eaten, and if they are given drinking money, they often give thanks in the idiom of food, *Ashe ta ndaa nikincho* ("Thank you for the food you have given me").

Different forms of alcohol are differently valuated in moral terms, are associated to a greater or lesser extent with food, and are metaphorically associated with different types of food. Busaa, like the traditional honey beer, tends to be thought of in fairly positive terms, while changaa is seen in rather negative terms. Busaa is not highly alcoholic and is largely thought of as food, being very closely associated with porridge, which has similar ingredients and nutritional content. I have, in fact, seen busaa occasionally fed to children when no other food is available, and have been served busaa as a breakfast food. Such use

would be inconceivable for changaa. Certainly changaa is referred to
by its drinkers as food, and occasionally a metaphorical relationship
is made with specific foods, especially tea. Thus, for instance, when I
met with a group of elders in 2002, they asked for some money to buy
tea, before clarifying, "You know, there is the usual kind of tea that
you find at home, and then there is also a special kind of tea that elders
like a lot." These elders were referring to changaa, and in doing so
invoked the metaphor of alcohol not only as food, not even only as the
archetypal food of hospitality, but as a food of hospitality suitable for
those particularly deserving of respect, elders. Yet the food metaphor
only goes so far in regard to changaa—for though busaa is universally
regarded as far superior as food, there are many men for whom only
changaa holds interest, due to its higher alcoholic content. As one elder
asserts, "There are other people who don't want busaa. They just want
changaa. They think changaa is good but busaa is just like *dhubia,* just
like tea with no sugar. But changaa is very good. They say that busaa
is just like tea without sugar, but changaa is good."

The "sugar" referred to here has nothing to do with taste or ingredients, but is a metaphor for its kick, the quick rush of drunkenness
provided by hard liquor like changaa. "Tea without sugar" is, indeed,
a common metaphor for something bland, particularly when bland-
ness is due to the absence of a key ingredient, a phrase also used by
girls to disparage boyfriends' use of the withdrawal method. The more
negative and less foodlike connotations of changaa are also apparent
in the fact that many do not find it to be an acceptable substitute for
naisho in blessings, because of its associations with death and loss. As
Namukare Lekuyie, a woman in her forties, asserts: "As for changaa,
other families won't use changaa for blessings because changaa is bad.
It is like tears. When you make it, doesn't it drip into the pot like tears?
Tung, tung. Even if you buy animals from changaa they won't stay for
long before dying. Changaa kills."

These varying associations of busaa and changaa play a significant
role in the question of whether alcohol actually benefits drinkers nutritionally, a matter of considerable contention. To a great extent, these
debates juxtapose different forms of alcohol and the types of drinkers who are associated with them, pitting the cultural construct of the
moral drinker who grows fat from busaa against the immoral drinker
whose body is burned away by changaa. From a strictly nutritional
standpoint, this dichotomy is problematic, since both contain considerable, and roughly equivalent, calories in the form of alcohol and

210 Histories of Eating

associated carbohydrates. It is likely that this distinction is due less to nutritional differences than to cultural distinctions between the qualities of busaa and changaa and their drinkers. In short, busaa is construed in largely positive terms, and changaa in highly negative ones. As Lemanyishoi, an Lkishilli elder, contends, "Busaa is very good. It's just food, millet and flour. But changaa is terrible." Where busaa is like a cool porridge, thickened with considerable residual grain and filling the stomach while slowly intoxicating, changaa is clear like water or petrol, dripping back into the distillation pot like tears, with no visible nutritional qualities and burning the stomach with its infamous "kill me quick," version of drunkenness. Thus, whereas busaa is an unambiguous food, typically drunk slowly in contexts of camaraderie, changaa is a powerful and ambiguous substance capable of provoking violence, madness, and poor health, useful only in small quantities to treat things like snake bites or unresponsive livestock diseases. Thus, as Lekutaas asserts, "If you drink busaa a bit when you don't have enough food, you will get fat and healthy. You will get fat and healthy if you drink busaa. But changaa isn't good. The only [good] thing about changaa is as medicine, that if you eat something bad, like meat that isn't fully cooked from a cow that died, it will burn it up. It will cook that food in the stomach. But if you drink a lot it's poison."

Surprisingly, drinking—by which informants usually mean, though they do not always specify, drinking changaa—is a common explanation for thinness, despite the large number of additional calories drinkers consume. When informants made this assertion, I sometimes pressed them on this contradiction, usually citing the example of the chief, Lemasara, by far the fattest man in the area and a heavy drinker of all things containing alcohol. The response of Legiso, an Lkishilli elder and prominent born-again Christian living near Lodokejek, was typical: "If you drink and you also eat, then you can grow fat. But the problem is these men who get up in the morning and think about nothing but looking for changaa and never take time to eat."

Yet even this proposition, though plausible, is dubious on several counts. Legiso's assessment was almost certainly based on his brother, a heavy-drinking miscreant, who, though hardworking like Legiso, was mainly driven by a taste for changaa rather than building a wealthy Christian home—and who as a consequence of this hard work displayed a wiry build almost identical to Legiso's, thin but muscled and not unhealthy. Indeed, across the sample measured in the 2002 nutritional survey, there is no correlation between nutritional well-being and drinking. Though this conclusion is not definitive—insofar as it is based partially on self-reported drinking—the anthropometric data does not indicate that drinking truly makes men thin. Moreover, implicit in the association of drunkenness and thinness is a not very subtle blaming of impoverished men for their predicament, much as drug use is construed as the cause rather than the result of urban poverty in the United States. Thus, critics assert that men become thin from roaming around looking for changaa from morning until night, rather than concluding that poverty drives some men to seek alcohol, either in order to relieve stress or as a source of calories. This is not to say that alcohol cannot lead to irresponsible behavior that exacerbates problems associated with poverty. But what is principally at play here is an equivalence made—particularly by Christians and others who look down on drinking—between the moral decay entailed in drunkenness and the physical decay exhibited in thinness. Thinness—though likely not the result of drinking—indexes what they assert is wrong with drinkers: they behave so foolishly, so irresponsibly, as to even neglect eating.

If these negative associations point to why some contend that alcohol is less than food (and thus should not be drunk), its use is, on the other hand, promoted by other ambiguities that make it a kind of food that is only "kind-of-food." One relatively minor point, though intriguing within the logic of Samburu domestic economy, is that being in some senses "not-food" justifies its purchase (at the same time as being food justifies its consumption). Prepared foods are not sold out of homes, nor normally purchased by elders and women unless traveling. Buying prepared food outside the home is considered irrational, since people are entitled to eat freely at home, an attitude that is muted by the fact that alcohol is not-exactly-food. Furthermore, since alcohol is a commodity prepared by women for sale, it is no more freely available at home than anywhere else.

Most crucial here, however, is the sense in which alcohol is construed as an entitlement of elderhood, lessening the connotation that drinking is merely self-provisioning at the expense of other household members (though not diminishing fault if a man's family appears to suffer from neglect or the misdirection of resources). At several levels—both in regard to historically validated Samburu values and postcolonial developments—alcohol is an entitlement of power and constructs power. Yet it creates ambiguities and contradictions that problematize the very basis of this power.

ALCOHOL AND SUBJECTIVITIES OF POWER

"Mr. Hosman!" called out a booming voice, followed by the thunderous knock of a gigantic fist on my front door. "Mr. Hosman!" the voice called out again, followed by repeated pounding. I was out back and didn't hear it at first, while Bilinda refused to answer, not knowing what to expect from the huge, aggressive man on the other side of the door.

It was, of course, just the chief. He was among the tallest men in the area and unsurpassed in girth, well known in his youth for being a real *laingoni,* a bull who was a strong and brave warrior—his physical attributes augmenting a natural ability to command *(aitore).* He was also intelligent and could be a judicious leader, but was at the same time a heavy drinker who often directed his leadership qualities toward other ends when he was drunk. He had first reached our home around 5:00 or 5:30 P.M., dropped off by the pickup truck that provided public transport to Maralal. His home was about forty-five minutes away on foot, and he had some sacks of flour that he couldn't carry. He asked me to drive him, but I demurred, citing the misadventures of a previous occasion. On that occasion, it had gotten late, and he had gotten very drunk while helping to resolve some issues that partially concerned us. Because he was there to some extent on our behalf, and he insisted that a very passable road had been cleared to his settlement, I had agreed to take him even though it was approaching dusk. He had quickly and completely lost this "very passable road," and we refound it only after being redirected by some passing murran attracted by the headlights of a car in the now totally dark bush. Soon after, the Land Rover bottomed out and nearly failed to climb out of a rocky and poorly constructed river ford. Finally, when I found that the rapidly overheating vehicle lacked the traction to climb the slick red-clay slope on the other side of the river, my insistence overcame his incessant commands that we simply continue forward, and he and his female companion had gotten out and walked the rest of the way to his settlement.

I reminded him of that night and suggested that he walk home and send someone to collect the flour sacks the next day or, alternatively, spend the night somewhere nearby and get help in the morning. He reassured me that there would be no replay of the previous events, as we would go the long way, following the main road. This, I knew, was about forty kilometers round trip and would take over an hour. I was not really inclined to comply and, moreover, did not have gas to spare. He reassured me that he would give me two hundred shillings to fuel the vehicle. I told him it cost more like five hundred shillings, and he said he would give me that—a meaningless promise since he had never repaid the five hundred shillings he had borrowed months earlier. Finally, I simply explained to him that I did not even have enough gas, so there was simply no way. He soberly accepted that and went off to rest.

Perhaps an hour later, he was back, hammered. He had gone to a nearby settlement, where he had quickly gotten very drunk. He was now circulating around our host's settlement looking for more drink, food, and the like, and generally being a loud, demanding nuisance. When I found him pounding on the front door calling out my name, he suggested that we load up the sacks in my car and take them to the town, about five kilometers away. Never mind that town was where his original ride was going. For the sake of peace in the settlement, I agreed, dropping him and his flour off at his daughter's shop in town.

In both historically validated and colonial or postcolonial forms of drinking, alcohol is tied to power and privilege, as its use validates and to a great extent constructs power. This relationship is in many ways contradictory: though alcohol use (particularly in its historically validated forms) is justified as a privilege based on the *nkanyit* possessed by elders, for Samburu a fundamental property of alcohol is its potential to subvert *nkanyit*. This is not universal among men who drink—some simply become very talkative, which may or may not lead to breaches of *nkanyit,* while others just drink and sleep—but it is very common. Such individuals become more self-interested, pushy, and greedy than would be acceptable under normal circumstances, when such traits are generally scorned. Behaving in such a way while drunk is certainly not acceptable in a strict sense, but it is typically viewed as an effect of alcohol and not an intrinsic part of the individual's personality. Thus, if pushy and demanding behavior among the sober would be evidence of the damning personality defect of *lobu* (greed)—one of the worst things to be attributed to a Samburu man—such behavior in a drunk is construed largely as an effect of alcohol.

Samburu interpretations of the behavioral changes that often occur among drunks mirror alcohol's well-known capacity in many societies to transform not only actual behavior but socially constructed *expectations* of behavior. Alcohol transforms behavior not because the effects of intoxication alter affect and rationality, but by the potential, well documented in many societies, for alcohol to create alternative sub-jectivities of "the drunk." As Douglas Heath notes, "The drowsiness, clowning, violence, crime, sexual or verbal aggression, maudlin senti-mentality, loquacity, spousal or child abuse, or other concomitants of drunkenness are shaped far more by expectations than by the interac-tion of alcohol with human physiology" (1995, 355). That is, the psy-choactive effects of alcohol are important, but the actual expression of these effects is disproportionately shaped by users' expectations as to how it will make them feel and behave, and observers' expectations of how drinkers behave (Wilson 2005; Garvey 2005; MacAndrew and Egerton 1969). Thus, for instance, in Truk (Polynesia), drunken-ness presages fighting not simply because alcohol makes men violent but because drunkenness creates a subjectivity in which violence is far more normalized (Marshall 1978). More benignly, in Japan alco-hol subverts the norm of orderly, disciplined conduct in interpersonal relations, transforming the behavioral expectations of controlled and status-oriented "salarymen" into raucous karaoke singers or gentle, loving, and relaxed family men.

These transformations in subjectivity express themselves in different ways in historically validated forms of power—the drinking of elders—compared with contemporary postcolonial forms, mainly the drunk-enness of chiefs and to a lesser degree people tied to nonlocal forms of power. Each transformation contains its own set of contradictions, which, though related, are in some sense opposites. Elders' drinking has the capacity to undermine the culturally legitimate authority that justifies drinking, while among such figures as government chiefs, alco-hol becomes an idiom that to some extent explains (if not necessarily excuses) illegitimate uses of power.

In its pre–beer hall incarnations, alcohol, in the form of honey beer, was used exclusively by married men, mainly at blessing ceremonies, weddings, and occasionally meetings. This form of drinking is gen-erally considered to be unproblematic and is sometimes contrasted with commonplace forms of drinking today. Thus, for instance, Nas-eru Lekutaas, a woman in her early seventies, recalled the Lmuget le Nkarna (naming ceremony) during the murranhood of the Kimaniki in the 1950s, noting that even though there were huge amounts of honey beer—every calabash was full of it, leaving no room for milk—people remained peaceful and good-spirited. Busaa is construed in largely the same light and is considered an acceptable substitute for honey beer at ceremonies, though many hold that changaa is not.

Drinking in ceremonial contexts is, indeed, elders' quintessential justification for drinking. Elders are responsible for the most potent blessings (and curses) on a daily basis, but most significantly on important ceremonial occasions. In large ceremonies—such as marriages *(latim)* and circumcisions—elders come without being specifically called and are fed and offer blessings in return, while with smaller ceremonies a handful of neighbors are sought out to ensure that the requisite blessings are performed properly. Alcohol is typically served at such ceremonies, though it may be absent when a large quantity of other food is offered, such as meat from a marriage ox. On a daily basis, elders offer blessings at necessary times or when they wish to show special goodwill—a frequent consequence of giving them something to drink.

Alcohol, then, is centrally tied to the historically and religiously validated source of gerontocratic prestige—the responsibility for giving blessings. As elders, they are construed as being entitled to alcohol, yet their access to alcohol is also construed as part of the public good to the extent that it ensures their blessings will be especially efficacious. This rationale is widely accepted—even those who oppose drinking do not risk the consequences of excluding alcohol from ceremonies at which elders desire it—but it is not lost on some that the notion that it is in the general interest to get elders drunk so they will be happy and bless everyone properly appears more than a little self-serving. Consider, for instance, the exchange between Lekutaas and his wife Naseru concerning the importance of having alcohol at ceremonies, including some recent circumcisions, as they interrupt each other with divergent views on the virtues and necessity of alcohol:

> *Lekutaas:* It helps elders prepare the blessings. Their hearts will be filled with happiness.
>
> *Naseru:* How can they make blessings properly when they are all abnormal?
>
> *Lekutaas:* Their hearts will be filled with happiness. They will give *all* their blessings.
>
> *Naseru:* How they can prepare the blessings properly when they are all staggering and swaying back and forth?
>
> *Lekutaas:* There won't be any blessings left out. They will give *all* of them. There is no one whose hearts will be filled with any bad feelings.

Where Lekutaas presents the "official" view that alcohol plays an important role in creating "good hearts" that will render efficacious blessings, his wife views this explanation with considerable skepticism. Lekutaas views alcohol as creating happiness, which will render blessings particularly effective, while Naseru doubts the supernatural efficacy of a bunch of staggering drunks. These views are not necessarily in flat contradiction—certainly alcohol may strengthen the will to bless even if it weakens the ability—but the discrepancies in their perspectives underline not wholly resolvable tensions. The importance of these tensions is highlighted by the fact that this ability to curse and bless is an underlying motif in elders' demands for alcohol in non-ceremonial contexts, often made explicit by drunken blessings offered should their requests be realized. Alcohol use is thus predicated on assumptions that may or may not be accepted, irrespective of whether they are effectively employed by elders in justifying its use: alcohol is a privilege afforded to elders because of their legitimate authority based on *nkanyit;* alcohol is a necessary ingredient for efficacious blessings; you can never have enough blessings, and so on. At the same time, the rapaciousness and foolishness that is a common transformation in the subjectivities of Samburu drunks undermine the basis for these justifications.

A somewhat different, though related, dynamic regarding alcohol and power is found in relation to state-based forms of power, most notably government-appointed chiefs (Holtzman 2005). There was a very early association between state power and alcohol—indeed, the first Samburu drunks appear to be chiefs. Although frequenting the town and having greater access to alcohol played a role in this development, there are clearly other factors. This is illuminated by the fact that, in contrast, Samburu who began to enter the military in substantial numbers during World War II did not drink because they were murran, for whom drinking is taboo. Indeed, in regard to the history of soda in Samburu (see chapter 7), it is notable that these soldiers often initially eschewed even Coca Cola because they mistakenly took it to be a form of beer. Thus it was not merely opportunity that led to drinking among chiefs, but particular aspects of their personhood that made drinking appropriate. Not only did chiefs belong to an age grade of elders, being thus of the appropriate age-gender segment to drink, but they were by virtue of their chiefness in a position of power and privilege that constructed particular entitlement to alcohol in the Samburu worldview.

Although it would be an overstatement to conclude from the colonial records that there was rampant alcoholism among chiefs, there is significant evidence that the Samburu agents appointed by the British administration quite early began to drink in excess.[8] In 1953, for instance, the outgoing district commissioner recommends that his successor continue with the unusual request he had forwarded to Cardovillis, the Greek merchant who ran the principal shop in the district headquarters of Maralal. Cardovillis was asked to not sell alcohol until *after* the meeting of the African District Council, since sales *before* the meetings had been found to have an adverse effect on the orderly and productive conduct of government business (Colony and Protectorate of Kenya 1953b). In another instance, the paramount chief, Lengerassi, was reported to have become so drunk on a government-sponsored trip to the provincial headquarters of Nakuru that officials locked him in his hotel room to prevent further drinking—only to have him escape through the window. And, as noted above, Chief Lasangurukuri was famously described by the local administration as forward-looking, "but drinks too much at his own beer shop," before becoming fully debilitated by cirrhosis of the liver only a few years later (Colony and Protectorate of Kenya 1953a; 1957).

Today, drunkenness is the rule and sobriety a relatively rare exception among chiefs. Although this cannot be confirmed with definitive quantitative data, virtually every one of the ten or so chiefs with whom I have had substantial contact has been a heavy drinker, and Samburu informants concur in this generalized observation. The relatively rare, albeit increasing, exceptions are converts to Protestant forms of Christianity, who tend to eschew drinking. I suggest that this tendency toward drunkenness is tied to a variety of factors entwined with subjectivities of power in postcolonial Kenya. There are economic dimensions: since chiefs draw a modest salary, they have regular access to cash, which may be used for drinking. Indeed, employed Samburu men generally (though not universally) get drunk when they receive their pay. This phenomenon is far from limited to the Samburu; heavy drinking, particularly after men have received their pay, is widespread throughout Kenya, as well as many other parts of the world.

Even this economic dimension, however, is far from simple. There is more to drunkenness than the experience of intoxication; it also involves social dimensions that are integrally linked to specifically cosmopolitan forms of prestige. That is to say, employed Samburu men do not get drunk on payday simply because *they can:* it is not that they aim for drunkenness whenever they are able and payday is when they actually are able. This may be true for some men but misses important dimensions of drunkenness. Drunkenness serves to *show* they can get drunk; visible inebriation publicly displays a prestige distilled from nonlocal sources of power and money. Thus, when the streets of Maralal fill at the end of the month with drunken teachers, clinic officers, and the like who have come to the district headquarters to collect their pay, they are not simply having a good time and blowing off some steam, though they may well be doing those things; they are also demonstrating to others that they have money and participating in what they understand to be the practice of modern citizens of the Kenyan nation (see also Willis 2002). Drunkenness thus indexes that one is, by virtue of ties to the political or economic apparatus of the Kenyan state, a person of means who can afford (at least on payday) to drink to excess.

In regard to chiefs, in particular, the relationship of alcohol to power may be understood with reference to the nature of state power in postcolonial Kenya. As is commonly noted in both popular and scholarly accounts, widespread corruption and misappropriation of resources is widely viewed by both Kenyans and outside observers as fundamental to the culture of politics (e.g., Haugerud 1995). Certainly this is not to suggest that all officials, whether in Kenya at large or in Samburu District specifically, are corrupt—many are not, and attitudes to corruption have seen significant shifts in the past few years in particular. Widespread corruption has, however, long been recognized as a fundamental part of postcolonial Kenyan governance. Thus, for instance, with the 2003 transition to the new NARC government (following nearly forty years of postindependence rule by the KANU party) aggressive anticorruption measures began to address misallocation of land and other resources at all levels of the national government. In everyday practice, bribery has long been a normalized aspect of interactions with everyone from the police to bureaucratic offices, referred to in common parlance as *chai* or simply *kitu kidogo* ("something small"). Opposition politicians who were seen as being bought off were referred to as having attended "*ugali*-eating sessions," so named because of a specific occasion when an opposition politician claimed all that had occurred in a suspect meeting with the president was a simple traditional meal, but also because of the poignancy of "eating" national resources as a metaphor for corruption, a metaphor that has led Bayart to describe politics in Africa generally as "the politics of the belly" (1993).[9] At the local level, government officials in Samburu District and elsewhere often expect small bribes to complete responsibilities for their constituents, while direct abuse of power is also common, though certainly not universal.

There is, then, a significant disjuncture between indigenous constructions of authority—located in the notion of *nkanyit*—and the forms of authority characteristic of state power in postcolonial Samburu District. Where indigenous authority is constructed as intrinsically disinterested, the authority of state actors is typically, and sometimes aggressively, self-interested. This is not to say that this is the case for all such agents at all times. This is certainly not how their official duties are defined, and individual behavior ranges from close adherence to official prescriptions on the one hand to frequent deviations on the other. All the chiefs I have known had the capacity to exercise their duties with judiciousness at times, though they vary in the extent and frequency with which they exceed these normal bounds, and their reputations in their communities reflect those differences. Chiefs are generally afforded some amount of respect by members of their community, and indeed, no chief would be allowed by their superiors or constituents to function in a way informed by constant and naked self-interest.

How, then, is chiefs' authority constructed, apart from the power afforded by the state? Given that there is an apparent contradiction between the subjectivities constructed in these two modes of power, how are these two modes mediated? At least part of the answer relates to alcohol. Samburu cultural expectations of the effects of alcohol create an alternative subjectivity, which subverts normal patterns of deference and respect and—in the case of chiefs—serves to mediate and blend the effects of drunkenness and state-derived power. That is, alcohol consumption crafts a subjectivity that is at odds with normal, indigenous Samburu expectations of right action, yet largely consonant with the practice of state power in postcolonial Kenya.

It is significant that Samburu tend to discuss the bad behavior of chiefs using an idiom of drunkenness rather than an idiom of greed. Thus, as one young man described a local chief, "Our chief is a terrible drunkard who goes befriending other men's wives." If his defects are deemed to be many, they are read principally (as with chiefs in general) through the lens of the voraciousness associated with drunks. This differs significantly from the tactical greed associated with corruption in Kenya, in which a modernist rationality is applied to the accumulation of ill-gotten resources.[10] But neither is it simple *lobu*, which is an intrinsic aspect of a man's character. Rather, it is in many ways the ravenousness of the drunk, though exercised in new and more muscular ways, with the license afforded chiefs greatly amplified by their ties to state power. Certainly this does not excuse their behavior in the eyes of community members, but to some degree it mitigates and suspends moral judgment, resulting in a less than total delegitimation of their authority.

Is alcohol really a food, or do elders just say that to rationalize their addiction? Are women who brew participating in Progress by finding new ways to support their families in the context of pastoral poverty, or are they contributing to the destruction of their communities by encouraging the waste of resources and destruction of lives in pursuit of drunkenness? Is alcohol an entitlement of the *nkanyit* intrinsic to the subjectivity of elders, or is it a destroyer of *nkanyit* that debases those whose personhood is most centrally constructed through a sense of respect and restraint? In short, is alcohol experienced as a virtue in contemporary Samburu communities, or is it an evil?

The point in posing these questions is not, of course, to answer "yes" or "no" in "objective terms"—all of these answers are true, at least sometimes and in some contexts. The point is not even that different people see alcohol differently, though clearly some do, ranging from those who are completely opposed to it (mainly Protestant converts), to those who see alcohol as largely unproblematic, to those who think that *naisho* and busaa are good, but changaa is bad (and perhaps don't just think this, but *know* it because changaa is all they drink). For virtually everyone, there is some degree of ambivalence toward alcohol, grounded in a balance between its economic benefits and its social ills, between responsible, historically validated forms of drinking and chronic drunkenness, between ritual efficacy and everyday debauchery.

The intrinsic ambiguity associated with the nature and meaning of alcohol renders this ambivalence all the more intense and complex. The most seemingly absolute Samburu moral values are never absolute (see chapter 5) but constructed and applied with guile, creativity, and subterfuge. Morality may come not from being right but from being able to adequately justify one's actions as convincingly close to right—or at least arguably far enough from wrong that no one can definitively prove the error to you or others, regardless of what they might suspect, believe, or be convinced of themselves. What intensifies this dynamic in regard to the turbid brews I have explored in this chapter is the extent to which these ambiguities and ambivalences exist as intensely felt aspects of the conscious, everyday Samburu experience of alcohol as it is debated, employed, and plumbed in everyday discourse, making the social field of alcohol intrinsically one of suspended reality, where the reality that differing actors perceive and know differs explicitly from the one constructed dialogically among them.

CHAPTER 9

Eating Shillings

Money and the Changing Politics of Food

I was in Lesidai in early 2002, and went looking for Lanyaunga Letuaa to interview him about food, including how he acquired his unusual name, "He who eats flour." He welcomed us outside a house where changaa was sold but asked us to wait a few minutes while he finished up some other business. Moving some thirty feet away, he sat with a man around the same age and a younger woman—who, their conversation quickly revealed, were Lanyaunga's father-in-law and his wife Ntinti. In this oddly public forum, they proceeded to discuss Ntinti, who had recently fled to her father's home. Women frequently run away (going *kitalaa*). Though there are no real statistics on this, my informal observations suggest that the estimate of one informant is only slightly exaggerated. He first suggested "about half" go *kitalaa*. This sounded rather low, but he clarified: almost all go at least once, but only half go regularly. They usually head to their father's home, where the husband (and to a lesser degree the wife) must explain their behavior, promise a satisfactory resolution, and pay a fine (*pein*, from English) to the father for troubling him in this way. Thus the three sat to air the grievances that had driven Ntinti away

Ntinti forcefully asserted that she had fled with good cause. Lanyaunga, she insisted, was culpable in the recent death of her infant child, having not fed her properly during her recent pregnancy and after giving birth. First her own vitality faded, and then her baby died when only a few months old. Initially Lanyaunga wholly denied this charge, noting that—being in an area conducive to farming—there was a storehouse full of maize from which she fed freely, but she did not relent. There was maize, but he refused her things like fat that make food palatable and nutritious—a failure she attributed to his (according to Ntinti, false) belief that he had not sired the child. Lanyaunga conceded that he did not, in fact, believe that the child was his, though he fell short of admitting to having intentionally not fed his wife. Though her father attempted to calm the situation, tempers flared and the dispute moved no closer to resolution. In conclusion, Ntinti declared to Lanyaunga, "I will get pregnant again very quickly, but it will never be by you! And I will make sure that the man who sires the child will feed me properly!"

This dispute was telling in several ways, though one can't know how true Ntinti's charges were. Perhaps Lanyaunga, with well-founded or mistaken doubts about the child, did not purchase adequate food for Ntinti. However, it's unlikely that this caused the baby's death. The infant was still nursing, and Ntinti was healthy. She was too thin, particularly by Western standards, but not dangerously so—only slightly thinner than Lanyaunga and considerably better off than his first wife. Yet if the ultimate truth of what transpired between them is unknowable, the terrain upon which this dispute took place marks a significant departure from long-standing patterns of Samburu gender relations surrounding food. For if, in the subsistence pastoralist economy, women are the principal source of food—life-giving milk that passes unmediated from their cows' udders to their own calabashes—money has now become the medium through which much of Samburu food reaches consumers. Not only is money a disproportionately male resource, but eating food purchased with money creates obligations and possibilities that are absent in the context of a pastoral diet, while vitiating others. For instance, a man's obligation to provide adequately for his family no longer simply entails sound herd management, but also includes acquiring and allocating cash adequate for the needs of all family members. Lanyaunga's alleged failing was in not feeding his wife—a marked inversion of a world where women feed their families and the husband is just one more mouth to feed (or not be fed if the two are not on good terms). If money, then, creates male forms of moral personhood not so different from the stereotypical Western breadwinner, it also creates new ways to fail in or evade these responsibilities. Money can be hidden; money can be used in ways other than feeding hungry mouths. Culinary mobility can breed sexual mobility, as men surreptitiously provision women outside the home, and women's secret lovers become the source of their and their children's daily porridge.

Money, then, has significant implications for how Samburu worlds are constituted through food, in terms of the gender relationships highlighted above, but also a host of relationships—intergenerational, among age mates, neighbors, kin—to which food has long been central. As I have argued throughout this book, Samburu may best be understood as a society constituted by alimentary structures, in which the food system is predicated upon, constructs, and reinforces a series of interrelationships and equivalences that fuse seemingly diverse arenas of cultural and social action. Taking food seriously *as food* means accounting for its singular power, derived from meshing a complexly constituted material realm with the symbolic, the ritual, social relations along the lines of kinship, gender and age relations, and a plethora of other domains. Money does not change that fact, but it markedly changes the contours of these relationships, their meanings, and their valuations as compared to a more purely pastoral past.

COMMODIFICATION IN PASTORAL SYSTEMS

Commodification has received considerable attention in many accounts of socioeconomic change in African pastoralist societies. Focusing particularly on the commodification of livestock, these studies offer valuable insights into the implications of cattle's transformation from a commonly held subsistence good to a property structured through the capitalistic logic of individual commodity exchange (e.g., Rigby 1985; Talle 1988; Hodgson 1997, 1999). My focus here differs somewhat, as I emphasize the commodification of sustenance itself, instead of the livestock that form the source of sustenance. Today, focusing on the livestock evokes to some extent a bygone era, when colonial administrators plotted how marketing sugar or umbrellas might entice pastoralists to willingly part with seemingly endless herds of emaciated but beloved beasts, or when anthropologists and other advocates for pastoral peoples argued for the benefits of subsistence pastoralism in opposition to development emphasizing livestock marketing. Commodification has too often been looked at from the top—construing livestock marketers as wealthy capitalist maximizers, and patriarchal ones at that. If there are small numbers of elders (e.g., Talle 1988) who can use livestock marketing to enhance their position in their communities and families, this is not broadly representative.

Most contemporary pastoralists—certainly the Samburu I focus on here—are by and large impoverished, oriented toward and dependent upon a market without which they would not eat. Commodification, then, must be understood in terms of why livestock are sold—principally as a subsistence strategy in an era when subsistence pastoralism cannot meet the needs of any but a handful of the wealthiest families. Viewed from the bottom, livestock marketing is a regular process undertaken to ensure that food is adequate, where the same goat that might otherwise be slaughtered is instead sold, providing far more calories in carbohydrates than it would in protein and fat. Although converting livestock into grain is not new,[1] the ease, frequency, and normalcy with which such conversions occur is an important transformation.

Today, money is less an alternative to the subsistence system than a component of the subsistence system. This is crucial to understanding the dynamics of commodification in Samburu pastoralism specifically, as well as in more general approaches to the anthropology of money. In their seminal collection, Parry and Bloch (1989) critique the notion, introduced by Simmel (1978) and central to Bohannon's (1955) classic analysis of the introduction of money to the Tiv, that, in Bohannon's words, "it is in the nature of general purpose money that it standardizes the exchangeability of every item to a common scale"; in contrast, Parry and Bloch assert, "It is not a priori obvious that by itself money does indeed reduce everything to a common measure" (13). Parry and Bloch take issue with, first, the idea that everything among the Tiv was truly commodified—land, they argued, was not—and, second, the assertion that money, rather than more diffuse changes in the social and economic environment, account for Bohannon's observations. My contention regarding the Samburu is somewhat different. Generalizability is, in fact, crucial to the dynamics surrounding the ascendance of money among Samburu, but *what* money generalizes is not value in a generic sense but a specific culturally and materially charged value: food. Thus, money's central significance is not as an all-purpose medium of exchange but as a medium introducing new dynamics to specific and critical forms of exchange related to basic subsistence.

This implies that livestock are not sold for money in an abstract sense but rather for food, money serving only as an intervening medium. We cannot simply indigenize money as a new dimension of the subsistence system, extracting it from the web of capitalist relations and the implications of these relations. The transformations entailed in commodified eating are paramount, but they lie not in abstract notions of

Capitalism and Capitalist Logic but in particular ways that subsistence is transformed as food increasingly loses its character as an unmediated product of the family herds, acquired freely at morning and evening milkings. As food increasingly becomes a commodity bought with money acquired from the sale of livestock, there are wide-ranging implications for everything from herding strategies to gender and age relations, patterns of sharing, and indeed, how people think about food and constitute their worlds through food.

"HOW IS IT THAT HE CONVERTS THIS BACK TO MONEY?": CHANGING LOGICS OF EXCHANGE

Within the logic of subsistence pastoralism, livestock are three things: they are meat, they are milk, and they are the breeding stock that provides future meat and milk. If this pronouncement may at first glance seem like vulgar oversimplification, my point is very much the opposite. In the non- or marginally commodified pastoralism of even the fairly recent past, the intense social relationships and meanings surrounding livestock—bridewealth, intergenerational relations, "stock friendships"—rested on the building blocks of these three fundamental sources of value. Complex and nuanced human relationships and cultural values were not reducible to the simple material realities of drylands pastoralism (or vice versa); rather, these were mutually constitutive. As Evans-Pritchard famously pronounced for the Nuer, "Their social idiom is a bovine idiom," in which social relationships are not only constructed *through* cattle, but are to a significant degree *about* cattle.

Money does not change that fact but markedly changes the dynamic. In a purely pastoral system, one maintains the proper balance of milk stock, meat stock, and herd reproduction through exchange with stock partners. Thus, one's social-bovine relationships are shaped through the exigencies of the varying values of livestock. Money reworks these values. Aside from the fact that the money for which you exchange your livestock may be exchanged for many things—cloths, beads, school fees, medicine, alcohol, and of course food—the valuation of livestock is structured less by the internal logic of subsistence pastoralism than by their utility in a national economy.

The most obvious consequence is a radical increase in the value of slaughter stock, both in absolute terms and relative to breeding stock. In subsistence pastoralism, male animals are essentially a store of meat, increasing in size but not in number. They are banked until they are needed in times of famine or for social or ritual purposes, or until they can be traded for breeding stock. Breeding stock are more essential, since they perpetuate and increase the herd and, most important, provide the daily sustenance of milk. This transformation is exemplified in two types of exchange that are characteristic of the social and economic relations governed by the subsistence pastoral system: the exchange of slaughter stock for breeding stock, and the exchange of sick animals for goats. The first is fundamental to maintaining key social relations constituted through livestock exchange, proper herd balance, and access to livestock products essential for mundane subsistence and ritual occasions. It also has implications for provisioning murran with meat, a process problematized by changes in the second of these exchange types. In traditional exchange patterns, a large ox could be exchanged for a young heifer. The potential of one animal (i.e., the heifer will reproduce) offsets the difference in bulk. The ox will not bring forth offspring or milk but is a heap of beef that is necessary or desirable in certain contexts. Today, however, few Samburu— particularly in the highlands—will still exchange slaughter stock for heifers because of how these are revaluated by the capitalist market. As Lepariyo, an Lkiroro junior elder, explained: "The people who can exchange a heifer for a bull are very few these days. My father [of the Mekuri age set] is one of the few people who can still do that. But most people can't do it. It is just because of the desire for money."

The reasons for this unwillingness are obvious. Where in traditional exchange, an ox for an heifer is a trade of ready meat for future returns, in the capitalist market each can be exchanged for money but not for equal amounts. Market value is determined by sheer size, by weight. The price offered for breeding stock may be a little higher, assuming that there are buyers interested in rearing their purchases—a newly weaned male may be purchased for 6,000 KSh ($80) or less, while a heifer of similar size will fetch about 8,000 KSh ($105)—but it is mostly the scale that determines value. A large bull or ox might bring 25,000 KSh (approximately $330) or more in 2002, while a young heifer might bring only 7,000–10,000 KSh (approximately $90–$130), such that what had once been viewed as an even exchange was now grossly unfair. Rather than trading one's bull for a heifer, most find it highly preferable to sell the bull and use the money to buy two or three heifers, or use the money for other purposes.

The value of sick animals poses similar issues, but with social implications that can be even more profound. Sick animals, even more than healthy oxen, are quintessentially ready meat. They are the province either of the community as a whole—who typically share in their eating—or of those members for whom slaughtered livestock are particularly appropriate food. These include women who have given birth and murran, the quintessential eaters of meat. Dead or dying animals have traditionally been exchanged for goats at the bargain rate of three or four goats, instead of the standard price of twelve goats for a healthy cow. The ability to sell cows, or meat in a butchery, greatly reduces the desirability of such transactions. In a subsistence context, the value of livestock drops radically once it is reduced to perishable meat, but in a butchery the price of a dead cow is the same as a live one—indeed, the market sets the price of live cows based on their value dead. As a consequence, individuals increasingly aim to get their dying cows to the butchery before their demise. This is, however, far from uncontroversial. Consider, for instance, the case of Lanyasunya (chapter 5), who died of a stomach ailment (purportedly caused by a curse) while the meat of his dead bull still hung in the butchery. A similar incident, though with a different ending, occurred in 1992, when a cow belonging to a young widow lay dying in the bush. She resisted murran offers to buy the cow for three goats, knowing that it would bring a far greater monetary equivalent if it could reach the local butchery. Others argued that this would be an offense to the murran, depriving them of their entitlement. The widow eventually agreed to the deal, owing to that argument and the realization that if the cow died before reaching town it could neither be sold nor eaten by murran—its public death transforming it into food that had been seen by women.

Selling an animal's meat does not necessarily obviate culturally prescribed obligations to share. For instance, as of 2002, when cows were slaughtered for sale in butcheries at the Lodokejek trading center, the lower hind leg of a cow (lwuantan) was still given to elders even though the remainder of the meat was sold. Since meat is usually sold by a community member, the pressure to comply can be great. This does not occur in larger towns, where the animal comes from a distance and there is no sense of community ownership.

If a cow dies in the bush, the sale of meat follows different patterns. If it is dying but not yet totally incapacitated, a buyer can pay four or more goats and take it to a place of his or her choosing, with no obligation to share anything but the lwuantan. In contrast, a dead cow or one so incapacitated that it can't be moved is exchanged for three goats.

The goats do not, however, buy the whole cow, but only large portions of the meat along with the skin and fat. The pieces that are not sold (e.g., ribs, lower hind legs, and major organs) are nearly as substantial as what is sold, and certain portions—though sold—must be given out by the buyer after purchase. These include one *murte* (meat connecting the hind legs and stomach), which is given to a girl from their clan, and one *nkupes* (thigh), which is given to the woman who prepares the skin. Apart from the *lwuantan* (to which elders invariably stake their claim), there are not obvious differences between the parts that are and aren't sold. For instance, the parts not sold are no more laden with meaning. Thus, the *nkiyeu* (brisket), which is used in many ceremonies, is sold, while the liver is not. The key issue is that a substantial amount of the meat can be sold while still reserving a reasonable share for all age-gender sectors—elders, murran, women, big boys and big girls, and young children.

Reactions to the effects of commodification are not homogeneous across age-gender sectors. Murran of the Lmooli age set—whose initiations began in 1990—are seen by elders to have raised troubling issues concerning shifting attitudes surrounding the value of livestock as meat and their value as money, which Lmooli are seen as being particularly attuned to. Although some Samburu construe this is in positive terms, demonstrating the cleverness of the Lmooli, to many it subverts key cultural values by valuing money over the salient relationships and qualities fostered by meat. For instance, widely circulating stories assert that Lmooli are reluctant to eat slaughter stock, preferring instead to (sometimes covertly) sell them rather than feast on meat in the bush. This is particularly problematic because feeding on meat in the bush fosters the strength and vitality essential to murran's role as the defenders of Samburu society, as well as promoting physical beauty and proper patterns of respect and shame.

This system is problematized by Lmooli who are reticent to eat cattle. Indeed, in some instances informants alleged that Lmooli were given cattle to eat and instead sold them for cash, perhaps to purchase beads for their girlfriends. In one account, three elders from the Ipisiki-shu section gave their Lmooli sons calves to trade for a large, fat ox that they would eat at *loikar*. However, once the young men had acquired the ox, they happened upon a mobile livestock trader who offered them 25,000 KSh for the ox—money they spent on a variety of goods rather than eating what they viewed as a large pile of cash. Upon learning of this transaction, Ipisikishu elders met and proclaimed that no one should ever again give Lmooli slaughter stock to eat; indeed, anyone who did so would be cursed.

In a similar vein, Lenanyukie—an Lkishilli elder from the lowland site of Ndonyo Nasipa—relates an instance when an Lmooli was nearly in tears at the financial "waste" resulting from the slaughter of an ox for *lbutan,* a community celebration marking a new birth: "Let's say, for instance, we slaughter the *lbutan* for Nkampit,[2] for a child of about his size. A cow is slaughtered on that day to celebrate, because the women have given birth to a child. . . . Now, when the different age sets are sitting down, a Lmooli comes and exclaims, 'Houch! How much money is that you are eating? You have killed 10,000 shillings today!' So, how is it that he converts this back to money? We don't cry for money."

How is it that he converts it to money? And *why* is it that Lenanyukie does not (or claims to not) understand how or why he does so? Two differing logics seem to be at work, in some senses commensurate and in some senses not. Lenanyukie construes money as a trivial matter, a trifle compared with truly important things: livestock that are an enduring source of livelihood, and the human relationships constructed and maintained through animals. Such a view is consistent with Samburu views of money formed in the context of the colonial encounter, when government administrators strived (with only modest success) to create an acceptance of and demand for cash, and when, as some Samburu today joke, if you dropped money on a path it might be days before someone bothered to pick it up. Lenanyukie sees the reaction of the Lmooli as a dramatic shift in values, favoring bits of paper over what is truly fundamental. Yet whereas Lenanyukie sees a radical disjuncture between those who love people and animals and those who desire money, the Lmooli did not accept this notion of a radical break. If increased interest in the other alluring goods that money can buy—such as beads, cloths, and ochre—is undeniable, such Lmooli and other younger Samburu tend to construe this shift as one of competence over values, of the triumph of practical reason over the folly of antiquated cultural practices. They do not value money over cattle, but they cannot fail to recognize that cattle are also valued in money, and hence equivalent to the things that money can buy. It is not a love of 10,000 KSh in the abstract; rather, where Lenanyukie sees this money as an (albeit large) quantity of a trivial substance, the Lmooli may see it as a gun, or huge quantities of beads, or several months of "gray food."

PROFLIGATE PASTORALISTS, BUDGETING MODERNITY

The simultaneous commodification of livestock and food creates a variety of new equivalences between them and with the money for which they are exchanged. Livestock are now money, and money is livestock, with each taking on meanings and associations of the other. Food is now understood not only in terms of the money used to buy it, but also in regard to the livestock that are sold to acquire the money. Consequently, because food is purchased, it is also "budgeted." Yet this is understood not principally in terms of budgeting finite cash, but in the interests of protecting the herds from which the cash—frequently with some reluctance—emanates.

Many people—even some who are monolingual in Samburu—have come to use the English term *budget* to conceptualize their strategies regarding commodified food. The notion of budget in relation to food has aspects that are both new and old, located in the strategies and ideologies of capitalism and in the praxis of subsistence pastoralism. Having a budget is seen to reflect an internalized embrace of enlightened modernity—practical solutions to contemporary realities—and a measured rejection of aspects of Samburu culture that are incompatible with it. Samburu see "having a budget" as a useful innovation of younger men, to which those from older age sets remain oblivious. It is something that, stereotypically, the "more developed" Samburu of Ldonyo (the highlands) increasingly understand and the *kienyeji* (local) Samburu of the Lpurkel do not.

The modernity Samburu embrace may have very different icons and meanings from Western ones—illustrated, for instance, in asserting modernity by wearing two sheets and a blanket, as opposed to one sheet, which was hopelessly *kienyeji* (local) (Holtzman 2004). Similarly, adopting the term *budget* does not mean their conceptions of it are Western. The notion of budgeting is exhibited in two related contexts with somewhat different references to what it means to be or not be modern. First, informants who saw themselves as modern viewed profligacy in meat-eating as a defining mark of a local *(kienyeji)* lifestyle and mindset. As one highland woman informant asserted, "When we slaughter a goat, we just eat it slowly, bit by bit—even for a month. But those people from the Lpurkel [lowlands], when they slaughter a goat they cannot eat it for two days. They just eat it in the evening, and by the next afternoon the goat is finished. They live a lifestyle of very long ago. The meat will get finished fast, because those people aren't clever."

Whether this reflects actual differences in how livestock are eaten is difficult to gauge. Certainly she exaggerates. I have never seen Samburu, whether in highlands or lowlands, stretch a goat out for a month, though by preparing some form of preserved meat—such as *sirikan* (dried meat) or *ngauwa* (meat preserved in fat)—some small pieces could be consumed as a relish over a long period. More likely, the goat would be sold and eaten as gray food for an extended period. The significant issue is how this purported difference is constructed ideologically. Whereas lowland Samburu are associated with a way of eating characteristic of "a lifestyle of very long ago," highland Samburu, she asserts, eat in a way that is clever, developed, and enlightened, reflecting an understanding of money. Thus, whereas in the "old way" Samburu gorged themselves on meat with no thought of tomorrow, enlightened Samburu budget the meat, eating it slowly, mindful of its value and its cost.

Yet budgeting commodified food also emanates from deeply sedimented understandings drawn from pastoral praxis. Although *loshorro* (porridge) or other gray foods—"foods of the pot"—substitute for or augment milk in daily subsistence, they are also seen as more akin to meat. This does not concern their qualities as consumables—they bear little resemblance to milk or meat, though they are closer to the former. Rather, the equivalence lies in their means of acquisition. While milk is taken from livestock without harm, purchased foods, like slaughtering, are the outcome of the destruction of one's livestock. Just as meat is acquired by killing wealth for food, purchased foods are acquired by dispensing with wealth in exchange for money to buy food. As Leadisimo, a senior elder of the Kimaniki age set, explained: "Today's 'food of the pot' is just like way we slaughtered livestock in the past, the way we slaughtered every time. This 'food of the pot' is like slaughtering because you have to buy it all the time. But you didn't buy the udder of your cow, it didn't bring any expenses. So if a visitor comes and there is milk, they can drink to their satisfaction and go without bringing you expenses, since at the evening milking you will get a lot more."

Whether viewed in the idiom of capitalist modernity or subsistence pastoralism, the "budget" has implications for Samburu social relations, particular in regard to gender. Traditionally, men are supposed to play no role in daily food allocation. Women collect milk at morning and evening, and allocate it as they deem appropriate for the nutritional needs of household members. Men are expected to distance themselves from this role and not interfere in this key feminine responsibility. Today, however, this process has been partially problematized by decreased reliance on milk for daily consumption. Thus, unlike milk—which passes from livestock to woman to consumer—purchased foods often require the intervention of men to provide cash for the purchase of maize meal, fat, or other necessary items. Livestock marketing is done by men, and though there are other important sources of cash—women's brewing or remittances from wage labor—most families regularly rely on livestock sales for food. This can rework women's food-based authority, since the power they express through food can be problematized if they become dependent on men for nutritional resources.

There is as yet no shift toward micromanagement of daily food allocation by men—all informants, male and females at all research sites, continue to assert that men have no role in the allocation of food—but the purchase of food can involve negotiations between men and women. And, particularly among younger men, this involves a "budget." Men are typically reluctant to sell livestock needlessly and do not want to sell more than necessary to procure adequate food. Thus, while informants suggest that older generations simply purchased food (or gave women money to purchase food) and left it to their wives to inform them when more food was needed, younger men typically claim to pay greater attention to their "budget," calculating how long the food purchased from the sale of a goat should last and possibly monitoring if it lasts as long as it should.

The notion of "the budget" creates a novel dynamic in patterns of social life surrounding food. It creates new anxieties surrounding sociality in general, as a result of new incentives to withhold food that were largely absent when the staple food was if not infinite, at least constantly renewed without cost. More generally, however, it creates new avenues for concern and control over food. Where food was previously a solely feminine resource, men are now implicated in the management (though not the micromanagement) of the provisioning process. The potential implications are most highly charged in regard to how gender relations—indeed, gender-based power—are structured through food.

HERDERS, FOOD, AND MONEY: REMAKING
PASTORALIST SUBSISTENCE STRATEGIES

The widespread commodification of food has important implications for herd management strategies. In the subsistence pastoral economy described by Spencer (1965), families typically divided their livestock

into two or three herds—the subsistence herd, the residual herd, and
sometimes the flock of sheep and goats. Family members would typically divide themselves with the livestock, sending a large portion of
the herd with murran to superior grazing in a distant locale, while a
sufficient number of livestock remained at home to feed other family
members. The livestock that were away might be mostly dry stock, but
it was necessary to ensure that milk stock in all places could feed family members.[3] Although the precise configuration observed by Spencer
should not be taken as a timeless mode of herd organization—herding
patterns were significantly shaped by colonial grazing restrictions—the
key point is that two competing goals needed to be balanced in pastoral
subsistence strategies: providing an adequate milk supply for all and
ensuring the long-term vitality of the household wealth in cattle (that
is, balancing short-term subsistence needs with protecting the family's
capital). Additional considerations were the difficulty of mobility and
the comforts of human habitation.

These relationships have been largely disentangled now that Samburu rely heavily on purchased foods. Men can make decisions concerning herd movements with scant reference to human needs, focusing
only on finding the best grazing at a particular moment. Family members may want to have the livestock at home so that milk will be plentiful, exerting pressure to achieve this, but elders are impervious to these
pressures, since they see their role as maintaining the long-term well-
being of the family and its herds rather than serving transitory desires
of the stomach. It is thus common to find families who, despite being
quite rich in livestock, have virtually no livestock at home. Some family
members—usually murran or older boys—may be with the majority of
livestock at a place more favorable for the herds, while the remainder
of the family remains behind eating purchased foods. It is considered
important only to ensure that there are sufficient livestock to provide
milk for tea, yet even this goal is not always met. In 2001–2, Lekeren,
a wealthy elder with approximately forty cows and over six hundred
sheep and goats, kept virtually all his livestock at a second settlement
and at mobile cattle camps in neighboring Laikipia District, leaving
only thirty or so sheep and goats for the use of his second wife, his
brother and his wife, and his mother. Consequently, when returning
home, he often carried a long-life milk packet purchased at a nearby
trading center to use in tea.

Greater sedentarization increases this tendency. In many areas—
especially the highlands—people are increasingly fixed to particular

areas (Holtzman 2004). In the highlands virtually all the land is demarcated into group ranches, in which membership is relatively closed, though sometimes it is possible to move to a new area. In the highest productivity areas, group ranch membership is particularly closely regulated, and in-migration is strictly prohibited. These factors put significant constraints on the mobility of people in highland areas, though the mobility of livestock is less tightly regulated, and in most areas cattle camps can be established by outsiders for a limited time.

There are also increasing incentives for people to remain relatively fixed in place because it allows access to a range of services—simple medical care, easy access to shops and primary education. Access to purchased food is an enabling factor for sedentarization, irrespective of other motivations. It should be noted that shifting a settlement is not a trivial matter, requiring a great deal of labor in taking down houses, packing up belongings on donkeys, moving some distance— possibly with small children or the infirm in tow—and then refencing and reassembling houses on the other end. If this somewhat odious task is avoidable, Samburu see a virtue in avoiding it, even in lowland areas where high degrees of mobility remain the norm. Even though the result may be downgrading the diet from one based heavily on milk to one dependent on purchased food, both women and men may find this preferable to a large expenditure of energy for a short-term shift.

Murran and other herders may exploit the ability of other family members to eat purchased foods in order to keep the family's milk resources for themselves. As long as the cows are away from the settlement, their milk is entirely at the disposal of the herders. Consequently, *lale* (cattle camps) can be a very desirable environment for murran from wealthy families, providing virtually limitless supplies of milk. Ostensibly they are doing a difficult, perhaps dangerous job, but in reality they may seek to string out this job as long as possible to maximize their supply of milk. Thus, for instance, on many visits to Lemarash's settlement in a remote lowland area, we only rarely saw a significant number of cows, despite the fact that he owned between 75 and 150 of them. Indeed, even the vast majority of his 300 or more goats were typically absent. While this was consistent with his goals as a herd manager, his sons, who tended the cows frequently, expressed extreme reticence to bring the animals home, always finding reason to delay their return and perpetually providing negative assessments of the grazing near the settlement, in contrast to the conditions at *lale*. Yes, it had rained at home, they would explain, but the grazing was still better where the animals were at present—perhaps in a few weeks the grass would have grown more, and they could be returned. Certainly these nomadic movements were often better for the livestock than if they remained at home—and herders have a great deal of genuine concern for the animals' well-being, out of an intrinsic love for the animals and a recognition that their present and future well-being depends on them. Yet the self-serving nature of these reports cannot be ignored. Indeed, Samburu agree that herders frequently avoid bringing the animals home, where milk will have to be more widely shared. In light of this, it is not surprising that the group with a consistently high nutritional status were murran from lowland areas wealthy in livestock.

Purchased food, then, has had a significant impact on how livestock is herded. This entails a delocalization of herding away from the residential sites of those dependent upon them for their livelihood. This delocalization has very different implications for different sectors and individuals. To a significant degree it reduces complexity for herd managers, minimizing the potential for conflict between the welfare of humans and that of livestock. It allows herders to more readily monopolize livestock products, while the cattle stay (sometimes almost indefinitely) in cattle camps away from principal sites of human habitation. For women, the implications are more complex. They may have an easier lifestyle, with far reduced—sometimes no—nomadic movement and a more constant source of food. However, dietary quality can be greatly reduced, with relatively less access to dairy products.

CULINARY MOBILITY, SEXUAL MOBILITY

The mobility of food in commodified eating also has implications for patterns of gift-giving associated with adultery. While some suggest that modest gift-giving—mainly food—has long been associated with adulterous relationships, the potential for this is much greater when food can be purchased. Isolated older informants claimed that as murran they brought food (e.g., pieces of meat) to married women with whom they had affairs, but usually food was given by women to their boyfriends. Indeed, one of the few logical reasons cited for women's overmilking (see chapter 3) is to obtain a secret supply of milk for their lovers. Since in the subsistence pastoral economy most food is controlled by women, men cannot easily transfer resources. An occasional surreptitious gift of small stock is hypothetically possible, but this would likely be highly visible, contentious, and at odds with cultural logic.

In contrast, the hidden nature and easy mobility of money makes it easy to transfer outside the home, causing a growing tendency for men's money to find its way into the homes of women other than their wives. This can occur on a small, irregular scale but may also take on a quasi-formalized character, with a handful of men becoming well known for having long-term affairs, similar to an unofficial marriage. This is not problematic in itself. Adultery is widely practiced, and there is a long-standing precedent for elderly polygynous husbands to sanction their wives' affairs, in recognition that their aging bodies are not up to the task of satisfying their wives' procreative and sexual needs. Such men sometimes view the fact that their wives' lovers now bear gifts as a welcome development, since it can offset the expenses of a large polygynous family. Men from poor families may turn a blind eye because of the economic benefits accrued to the family. Lodi Lanyasunya, a Mekuri elder, suggested at least some degree of shift in the attitudes of some men toward adultery and their wives' lovers: "Woooeeee! They were hated, they were hated in those days! As for that time, they were hated. What was done? [*Interviewer*: They were hated.] They were hated in those days. They were hated how? [*Interviewer*: They were hated in those days.] They were hated completely. . . . Nowadays there are those men who say [when they detect adultery], 'Leave it be, so that my children will survive on them.' . . . There are some who are like that and some who hate completely."

Male adultery is largely ignored (except, perhaps, by the woman's husband) unless a man's tendency to "go outside" affects the well-being of his wife and family. This is more than merely a personal or family matter, because elders from the community see it as their responsibility to ensure that their peer's behavior does not result in neglect of his family. For instance, one elder in Lodokejek was well known for his affair with a neighboring widow. This became troubling, however, when it became clear that all his resources—particularly the small government stipend he received—were going to the house of his mistress, while his own family did not have enough food. Consequently, the elders called a meeting and cursed the relationship with the widow, effectively terminating the affair. Unfortunately, however, this did not help the man's family. Shortly after he was forced to end that affair, he took up with the wife of a man who worked near Mombasa on the Kenyan coast. The economic and nutritional effects of these affairs were apparent. Though the man (BMI 21.58) and his mistress (BMI 19.48) were quite well fed by local standards—indeed within or close to American

ideals—his wife's nutritional status was slightly above critical levels
(BMI 16.42).[4]

Although this is an extreme case, which informants emphasized
because of the deviancy of this man's behavior, the commodification
of food makes such behavior a growing possibility for many men (and,
of course, their mistresses). This case was notable because his family
had suffered, even though he was fairly rich, and not simply because
resources were directed outside of his family. He was viewed as someone who should have been a man of consequence in the community,
his success exemplified in his home life. Instead, his home life was an
utter disaster owing to his neglect. Poorer men, though engaging in
similar behavior, are less subject to the judgment of their peers. Thus,
for instance, in inquiring from neighbors why one stockless elder was
fairly well off nutritionally while his wife was quite thin, I was told
that there was little economic cooperation in the family. The husband
and wife survived on their own by selling posts that they cut from the
forest for use in building. While the wife's earnings were used to feed
the entire family (though not usually the husband), the husband took
his earnings elsewhere. Possibly he just fed himself, but more likely
he brought the purchased food to another woman, who then fed him.
Such behavior, though looked down upon, did not prompt the attention attracted by the more prominent man. Destitute, he was already
no one. Moreover, since he had no resources to speak of, he was not
misusing something that should go to his family. He was simply eating
from money acquired by his own sweat—money which, in cultural
terms, his family did not have rights to.

The commodification of food has, however, also begun to recast
gender roles and expectations, with a growing expectation that men
are responsible for seeking and bringing home food. Failure to do
so can be implicated in gender issues that go far beyond food, as
the case of Lanyaunga and Ntinti Letuaa illustrated. Thus, where
food was until recently a distinctly feminine resource from which
men maintained a distance, commodification makes female control
and responsibilities more ambiguous while fostering specific male
obligations. Thus, through commodification, food is becoming a
centerpiece for fundamental transformations in gender obligations,
marriage, and adultery.

These developments have the potential for a largely negative impact
on the lives of women. Although there are two sides to this—"going outside" benefits some women but not men's wives—these developments

generally appear to threaten the benefits women traditionally derive from their differential agency regarding food.

WOMEN AT A LOSS?

The commodification of livestock has been viewed by scholars as having had particularly deleterious consequences for women. Capitalist property relations are seen to consolidate livestock ownership in the hands of men, vitiating the diffuse use rights that women enjoyed in a nonmarket pastoralist system (e.g., Rigby 1985; Talle 1988; Hodgson 1997, 1999). The potential implications of market integration are at least as significant in regard to food as they are for the means of production, livestock, since the commodification of food vitiates the near monopoly of female agency in day-to-day provisioning by making them dependent on largely male-controlled cash to acquire the resources they cook and distribute. Consequently, one would suspect that higher levels of market integration or dependency would lead to an increasingly problematic situation for women, and that women would be better off in families or contexts where the livestock economy is more vibrant, because the dairy products that are their uncontested purview remain central to the diet. On a regional basis, this would mean that women in lowland areas, where the livestock economy remains strongest and the overall economy most purely pastoral, would have a more favorable position than their highland counterparts.

Somewhat surprisingly, exactly the opposite appears to be the case. Although it is a fool's errand to hazard overly generalized statements concerning the overall status of women in any society (Ortner 1996; Hodgson 2001; Holtzman 2002)—there are too many competing and contradictory strands of status, power, and prestige—among Samburu, nutritional status is a highly meaningful measure. Nutrition speaks to the core autochthonous source of female power. Moreover, in a society where scarcity is an ever-looming issue, it provides a salient window into differential access to life-giving resources. Consequently, it is surprising that from the standpoint of nutrition, market integration appears to be advantageous for Samburu women. In a 2002 nutritional survey, women from the remote lowland area of Ndonyo Nasipa, which is wealthy in livestock, had the lowest nutritional status of any group measured—both in comparison to women from other areas and relative to the men from their area. Whereas these women had an average BMI of 17.97, women in the highland area of Lodokejek averaged a BMI of

FIGURE 13. A young wife. Photo by the author.

18.8, and in Lesidai (where agriculture is widespread) they averaged
19.01. In these other areas, women tended to be somewhat better off
nutritionally compared with men. Moreover, women's advantage was
particularly marked as they got older; lowland women were worse
off overall and declined in comparison with men as they aged. Not
only is their average BMI low, but this average is distorted by relatively well-off younger women (especially those in their twenties),
partially masking a rapid decline in nutritional status occurring in
middle age.

Why should women with greater access to livestock products be
worse off nutritionally? In part one must conclude that although they
appear to be wealthy, self-reliant subsistence pastoralists in comparison to the often impoverished pastoralists in less remote areas, their

livestock holdings do not on average allow for sustained subsistence on a purely pastoral diet. Average livestock holdings in 2002 were approximately three tropical livestock units (TLU) per capita. While there is likely some underreporting of livestock holdings, particularly because many livestock were away in cattle camps, close examination of several individual cases indicates that these figures are roughly accurate. Consequently, although a few wealthier families might be able to follow a purely pastoral diet, average holdings are less than half of the 7 TLU per capita widely considered to be the threshold for pastoral subsistence. This overall deficiency in livestock is combined with a tendency for livestock to be unevenly distributed by family members, since large portions of the herds are tended by murran or older boys in cattle camps.

Consequently, despite having rather more robust livestock holdings, these families were still dependent on purchased food. However, unlike women from less remote areas, the process of buying food was much more involved. Consider, for instance, the assertions of Namaita Lemarash, a disfavored second wife (of four) who forcefully expressed her views on the difficulties women face living far from town:

> In Ldonyo [the highlands] you can get a house like this without any animals, and yet the people are very healthy. They are very healthy, such that when you enter a house, it wouldn't even occur to you that they don't have animals. They have better pots than us and better cups. Yet they are the ones who are poor. It's because here in the Lpurkel men are in charge of the animals. So a wife—whenever you want to buy something, you find you have no money. But in Ldonyo a woman can sell milk, or firewood, or even *changaa*.

Part of the issue, then, is access to money. In the highlands or closer to towns, women have options—especially brewing—to acquire money themselves, but in more remote areas their husbands must provide it. Moreover, spending money is hard far from shops. She continues, "People in Ldonyo don't have food problems. You can just rush to Maralal even if you have only ten shillings. Can you take ten shillings to Maralal from here? You cannot even take a hundred to the shop. You cannot even take a hundred shillings and take it to Barasaloi. You must keep it in the house until you add more or sell a goat."

Thus two related factors influence lowland women's access to commodified food: cash is primarily a male resource, and buying food is increasingly difficult as distance to towns increases. Distance creates a pronounced shift in the process of acquiring food. In remote lowland areas, buying food requires a major expedition of two or more days and involves livestock sales and donkeys to carry back the purchased goods. It entails considerable physical effort and some risk. Sometimes it is hard to get a fair price for one's animal, particularly because buyers know that sellers may be in a rush to return home. The time, effort, expense, and risk mean that food is purchased in larger quantities, necessitating significant planning and the heavy involvement of men. Thus, while women in highland areas can acquire money and use it to buy food with relative ease, in lowland areas it is much more complex, requiring the assent and cooperation of men.

The fundamental question is, then, not *whether* market integration is good for the status of East African pastoralist women—a question scholars have considered in regard to historical developments—but rather *how differing forms* of market integration bear on gender relations and women's status. The market may cause problems for women, but it also presents opportunities for resolving these problems. Women's nutritional status in lowland areas is significantly affected by the difficulties they experience, far from centers of trade, to effectively use the market to compensate for a loss of control of nutritional resources concomitant with the broad decline in the livestock economy. It is, somewhat ironically, not market integration but poor market integration that accounts for the lower nutritional status of these women.

"SAMBURU USED TO LOVE ONE ANOTHER": CHANGING PATTERNS OF FOOD SHARING

Samburu see interhousehold food-sharing as having been greatly reduced with the decline in the livestock economy. Many see this as an effect of widespread poverty—few people have enough to share—while others see the decline in the livestock economy as a consequence of the meanness of contemporary Samburu, which leads to reluctance to share. In this view, the decline of the livestock economy is not a consequence of social, economic, political, or demographic changes. Rather, it is a punishment meted out by Nkai (the Samburu deity) in response to selfishness with food. Food, especially milk, is a gift from Nkai that should be shared with others. Since Samburu are increasingly unwilling to share milk with each other, Nkai similarly refuses to share milk with Samburu.

Patterns of sharing are increasingly mapped onto emerging forms of stratification, especially in highland areas. Samburu see sharing as a leveling mechanism but, more important, as a safety net for the poor, particularly because of the relatively high volatility in the livestock economy. A cattle raid could reduce even the wealthiest family to paupers in a single night, while drought and livestock disease regularly recast the fortunes of community members. Today, however, the sharing that persists is seen as quite different, with rich people only willing to share with other wealthy people. In this view, the poor are nonentities, largely disregarded by those who are better off. Sharing is no longer community aid, but rather a means to strategically build and maintain alliances among a local elite. The only silver lining Samburu see is that small-scale earning activities—such as brewing or selling posts—can provide enough money to buy adequate food, thus freeing the poor from odious patron-client relationships with their wealthy neighbors.

In communities where Protestant forms of Christianity have attracted a significant following, sharing is seen to intersect with patterns of religious division. Although converting to Catholicism is not seen as a major transformation,[5] converting to Protestantism usually involves a significant rejection of cultural traditions, marked by changes in everyday practices, including dress, consumption patterns, and integration in community life. Protestant converts are usually wealthier and are now often viewed as more selfish. They often reject traditional patterns of sharing, forming an insular group. Some see them as a wealthy elite, selfish and interested in sharing only with one another. As the Lkishilli elder Lesuyai asserts: "Doesn't this church make some people mean? Those people [of the church] can no longer give food to others. The ones who still share are the ones who aren't in the church. Those of the church have become mean. They have become bad. They say you are not of the group, you don't belong to them." Food sharing, then, reinforces the boundaries of an emerging elite, creating solidarity among the haves rather than benefiting the have-nots.

The general decline in food sharing is accounted for in a number of ways. Population density is often cited, and the overall tripling of Samburu population in the last four decades is exacerbated by a disproportionate concentration of people on Leroghi and closer to towns. High population densities mean that resources are not sufficient for all one's neighbors, and it is socially problematic—and supernaturally dangerous—to share with one neighbor and not another. Thus, while it remains common to feed visitors to one's home, dispensing calabashes of milk or portions of meat is usually impractical. Reduced sharing is also framed by many with specific reference to money. Being money-oriented results in a mindset that is antithetical to appropriate patterns of sharing. As one informant suggested: "Nobody can give you food nowadays—even murran aren't given [food]. . . . It's money that has brought that difference." Lempirikany, a senior elder from the Kimaniki age set, expressed his views more strongly: "As for the shilling, there is now no longer a single person who can share. This shilling has made things terrible, this shilling is bad. We say it's a thing of sorcery. . . . Is it not the one that is breaking everything?"

To an extent, money is viewed simply as money—as a non-Samburu, Western import governed by a less loving ethos than autochthonous models of sharing. One informant noted that, in contrast to food, "there are no ethics about money, because it is a new thing." Samburu make strong distinctions between contexts that are or are not market-oriented. Someone with a lot of sugar would normally be compelled to share it widely, but if it is known that this sugar was acquired specifically for commerce, that expectation is largely absent (Holtzman 2001). Similarly, while sitting one evening with my friend Lenyuki, who was chewing *miraa* (khat), I thought I heard the *miraa* salesman saying he was going to give Lenyuki a small portion as *muro*. *Muro* is one hind leg of a slaughtered animal, which must be given out, and the term can be used metaphorically for sharing a portion of anything—including money. When I asked Lenyuki if he was going to give him *muro*, Lenyuki laughed; surely I had misheard, he told me, for "business people don't know anything like *muro!*"

Yet even these dimensions tied to money can be contextualized in the logic of pastoral sharing, specifically the sharp differences in patterns for milk and meat. Meat sharing has intrinsic extra-household dimensions, and these prescriptive patterns are enforced by the threat of supernatural punishment. Yet informants cite a much greater willingness to share milk than meat—as if generosity with meat occurred only because of prescriptive patterns of sharing and the threat of curses. As the Samburu proverb says, "Meat can never be enough for the people." It is a finite resource, obtained rarely, and only by virtue of a reduction of their wealth in livestock. In contrast, milk, though finite at any given point, is free and renewable, coming to you without expense at the morning and evening milking. And today sharing purchased foods is viewed largely in the idiom of meat sharing, since they are acquired by dispensing wealth. As the Kimaniki elder Leadisimo asserted, "Today's 'food of the pot' is just like way we slaughtered livestock in the past," greatly vitiating hosts' propensity or enthusiasm for sharing.

Indeed, the impact of selling a goat to buy food is little different from slaughtering the animal and exchanging its meat for grain. Consequently, purchased foods are shared frugally, not because they are desirable but because the means of acquiring them are odious. An ironic consequence is that even though pastoral foods are now scarce and purchased foods plentiful, Samburu can be more inclined to give guests tasty and nutritious dairy products than *loshorro*, the thick porridge that constitutes the not very well-liked staple of the diet for most Samburu. Even if milk is scarce and tasty, it is free and will come again in a few hours, while *loshorro*, though undesirable, comes only by reducing one's wealth in livestock. As one junior elder said, "Guests can ruin your 'budget,'" forcing you to sell livestock too soon.

Money also offers a practical and largely legitimate way to avoid sharing. Families living near towns can sell extra milk to regular customers or in informal curbside markets (see Straight 2000). At home there is some obligation to share excess milk with a visitors—and milk is not sold there—but in town it can be sold without an ethical imperative to share. Similar forces compel individuals to sell rather than slaughter livestock. One wealthy junior elder explained what he saw as the foolishness of slaughtering: "It's not so good to slaughter a goat for your wife. If you slaughter for her, the women will come running from all around, and the meat will just get finished quickly. It's better just to sell a goat and buy her some meat from the butchery. You can also use the money to buy her other kinds of food. If you want meat, it is better just to sell a goat and buy a little meat from the butchery instead of slaughtering."

The market, then, offers two mechanisms to avoid sharing. First, in selling an animal, you essentially slaughter without your gain being visible or susceptible to requests from others. You might be asked for money if it is known you have it, but knowledge of what is in your pocket is always indeterminate, and there is much less obligation to share money, unlike meat, which is both obvious and subject to socially sanctioned demands. Second, at butcheries you can buy a small share for a single family (or single person), which is not bound by any obligation to share.

As Parry and Bloch (1989) note, perhaps no single development so potently symbolizes the loss of innocence associated with modernity in Western ideologies of Otherness than the adoption of soulless money by peoples previously bound together by the interconnectedness of gifts. From Aristotle to Marx to Simmel, money is the archetypal executor and symbol of the movement from gemeinschaft to gesell-schaft, to relationships based on cold, impersonal calculation, bringing on the rupture of the social that typifies what is wrong with what we construe as modernity. This view has been problematized by demon-strating that so-called precapitalist societies are not intrinsically more "moral" than those based on money, and the symbolism and material effects of money cannot be reduced to a simple shift based on Western ideological constructions of that transformation. Yet this remains a potent metanarrative for understanding change in African pastoralist societies and elsewhere around the globe. Change is rarely construed as wholly value-neutral, and anthropologists are rightly skeptical—if not outright hostile—regarding ideologically charged discourses that frame change as largely positive, that is, as Progress. Anthropology's accounts of change continue to frame it disproportionately in negative terms, whether it be millennial monsters or the global trade in human body parts, processes of which capitalism, the market, and money are integral parts.

This chapter, like the book as a whole, is more overtly ambivalent in several ways. Certainly there are dimensions of the monetization of Sam-buru subsistence that are mostly negative or have negative implications for at least some Samburu. Yet Samburu's own subjective valuations of the effects of money are just as fraught with affective ambivalence and internal contradictions as would be an outsider's assessment of the objective effects of participation in a money economy on varying Samburu, for these processes are neither unambiguously positive nor wholly negative. Thus, for example, commodified eating would appear to disempower women by vitiating their control of the means of sub-sistence, yet the objective conditions of women in areas where food is less commodified are actually worse. Similarly, if the commodifica-tion of food is an outgrowth of political economic changes that have brought both poverty *and* money, the latter is typically construed by Samburu as a solution to the former, both in the immediate present and in a historical consciousness of change, where drought no longer means death but perhaps just selling goats to buy maize meal until conditions improve. And if some women suffer when their husbands exploit the culinary and sexual mobility made possible by commodified eating, other women prosper for exactly the same reasons.

Throughout the book, I have considered the autochthonous Samburu culinary system as a complex composed of dense webs of causality and meaning, constructing and reinforcing interrelationships and equivalences that tie together seemingly diverse arenas of cultural and social action. I have thus moved toward a perspective that situates food on a level of systemic coherence but rejects both the deus ex machina integration of functionalist paradigms and the Evil Genius implied in a host of power-oriented theories, such as traditional Marxism, Foucault, and Gramscian notions of hegemony. These two broad perspectives are largely mirror images of one another, each investing society with a significant level of coherence emanating from some manner of First Principle. In functionalist paradigms, these are largely aspects of the public good—whether maintaining social order, as in structural functionalist perspectives; successfully regulating the environment, as in cultural ecology; or providing successful adaptation to material conditions, as in cultural materialism. Power-centered alternatives offer a very different vision of the source of this coherence, but depend on models of social and cultural life that can be at least as totalizing. Indeed, with increased interest in Gramscian forms of hegemony and other models that locate power in the mundane, unexamined practices of everyday life, we risk recasting social and cultural life in an excessively integrated framework constructed around the concerns of the politically and economically dominant (Holtzman 2001, 2004).

I suggest, instead, a form of systemic coherence more in line with Althusser's notion of overdetermination. In such a view, food is situated at the intersection of such powerful threads of causality and meaning that ultimate causality and meaning become largely indeterminate. Thus, a sociocultural system is not the product of some grand architecture expressing the First Principle most dear to one's particular theoretical predilections. Rather, it is in a sense a temporary arrangement, a bricolage composed of systems of power, systems of convenience, and systems of need. It is materially symbolic and symbolically material. It empowers women and oppresses women, and also does neither, just as it does to men, children, and the elderly, though not necessarily in equal proportions. Powerful political and economic forces undeniably order significant aspects of social and cultural life—and sometimes life is arranged in such a way that they become unexpectedly powerful, and sometimes these arrangements are rearranged. If they can, actors take advantage of these ambiguities, except when they are disinclined to and don't. It is ultimately an arrangement that works, at least for

Conclusion

It is 2001, and I am relaxing at the house of my friend and former research assistant, Matano Lesengei. He runs off on a short errand—perhaps letting his mother know I am around, looking for milk for tea, or some other such thing—and he hands me his photo album to pass the time while he is away. As I finger through his pictures of old friends, secondary school classmates, and the like, I come across a photo I myself had taken of Matano but that had since slipped from my memory.

It was nearly ten years prior, at the wedding of his brother near Sugata Marmar in October 1992. It was an exciting time—I had been in the field less than half a year, and it was the first Samburu wedding that I attended from start to finish. I was a member of the groom's party, so instead of eating the *rikoret* (marriage ox), I remained with the group of a dozen or so Lkiroro—members of the age set who are my chronological and social peers—feeding in the nearby bush on roasted sheep. It was fun to be included in the group, who amused themselves with the ever-popular game of "play a practical joke on the new anthropologist." I was handed the sheep's lungs, lightly roasted. I took a bite, but they were not very tasty. "Who usually eats the lungs?" I asked. "Women can," someone explained, "but usually we give them to the dogs."

The roasting continued, until somewhere around the second sheep, Matano's eyes lit up and he beamed, "Jon—take a picture of me eating meat!" I quickly agreed and was prepared to snap, but Matano told

FIGURE 14. Matano eating meat at *loikar*. Photo
by the author.

me to wait as he did a costume change. He had been dressed in his
everyday casual wear—a *kikoi* cloth around his waist and a blue nylon
windbreaker on top—his clothing, like himself, fairly standard Samburu neotraditional. Although he was a secondary school graduate, he
was more oriented toward the livestock economy and Samburu culture
than many of his Western-educated peers—partially because his family
remained reasonably well off in cattle, partially because of the influence of his father, a strong-willed elder of the Mekuri age set who often
seemed to lack the stomach to even acknowledge the changes that had
occurred in Samburu life since his circumcision in the 1930s.

Matano began to change. Gone was the windbreaker, replaced by
the *lopon* beads, crossed like bandoliers across his bare chest. Around
his waist he tied a white flowered sheet. On his arms, around his neck,
and on his head he secured an assortment of every type of ornament,
hastily borrowed from our companions. He gripped a long strip of
mutton in his front teeth, looked up with fierce eyes, and as I snapped
the picture, cut off a bite-size chunk with his short sword, just inches
from his lips.

This was the picture that looked up at me now, and I smiled in amuse-
ment, just as I had when I took the picture. What he had wanted wasn't
just a picture of him eating meat. He had wanted a picture of Matano

the meat eater, a murran at *loikar* gorging himself on slaughtered live-stock in the company of his age mates. The picture would memorialize that when he was young, he was a warrior, a real warrior.

That was well and good. Lots of Samburu like those kinds of pictures. The thing that amused me was that most people don't do dress-up to take them, which to me diluted the point of the picture. Looking at him that day and in the picture now before me, I found it funny, though in an endearing kind of way, since the picture we were taking to memorialize who or what he was didn't look like him at all. I had never seen him dressed that way before, and I have never seen him that way since.

Yet if to me the picture was funny because it seemed a fake, to Matano it was different. Certainly there was a playful element, but it was also in earnest. It was not a fake in the sense of if I, let's say, took a picture of him shaking hands with a cardboard cut-out of Bill Clinton, or even in the sense of my own warrior picture, in dark sunglasses and worn-out Adidas, leaning back in a prototypical Samburu pose, legs crossed, spear resting on my shoulder, some beads around my neck. It was even quite unlike the day Barnabas posed with a collection of every weapon he could find, spear, axe, rungu, and bow and arrow, with his dog in the background for good measure. Barnabas neither was nor wanted to be an ochre-smeared Samburu warrior. Matano knew that at his core he really was a warrior, or at least some part of his core really was.

There is, of course, only so far we can psychologize our informants. If we may unpack with relative ease our subjects' ambivalences when they announce them to us, what of the ambivalences we cannot see, or that they themselves have not fully acknowledged—that is the nature of ambivalence. We cannot always know when unspoken ambivalence resides in the unplumbed intricacies of our informants' minds and when the ambivalence is our own, grounded in well-worn dichotomies of Otherness—modern/traditional, Europe/Africa, global/local—which presume contradictions that our subjects may not experience as such. Anthropologists and other scholars have long grappled with the question of how we characterize and explain the subjectivities of interlocutors situated betwixt and between apparently divergent ways of life. Fanon's notion of double consciousness (1967) provides one means for understanding the profound ambivalences that subjects may experience in contexts of change, particularly when characterized by racialized and ethnicized unequal relations of power. Taussig's (1993) notion of mimesis and Stoller's (1995) embodied memories provide related ways of engaging with notions of colonized minds and bodies. Others look past our subjects' immanent or sublimated angst, concerned instead with how they make themselves at home in the worlds in which they reside, regardless of how such worlds may be constituted by radical changes rooted in the historical inequalities of colonialism and the contemporary ones of globalization. Much of the work on religious syncretism may, for instance, be roughly fit in this mold, by defying dichotomies of the traditionalist and the convert. Or, as Kwame Anthony Appiah asserts, the Yoruba do not ride bicycles to emulate Europeans; they do so "because it will take us further than our feet will" (1992, 157). It is fair, then, to consider to what extent our (or my) protracted ruminations on informants' ambivalences and contradictions are merely so many big academic words rooted in our assumptions about who our subjects are or should be, yet concerning experiences with which our subjects may be more or less at ease in their own lives.

Back to Matano. I am reasonably sure that, as characterized by Appiah, he is, in fact, largely at ease with the life he has forged from historically validated elements of Samburu life and those parts of Kenyan versions of global culture that he sees will push him farther. On the one hand, he is a secondary school graduate turned primary school teacher; at the same time, he lives some distance from town in a "traditional" house of mud and dung, and is not only heavily oriented toward the livestock economy but takes tremendous pride in his herd. Yet on second thought, *ease* is perhaps too strong a word. Without forcing my friend too awkwardly onto the Freudian couch of my imagination, I cannot help but believe that a fair portion of his "indigenous" orientation is due to the conscious influence of his strong-willed, stereotypically traditionalist father, as well as the unconscious effects of Matano's complex and not untroubled relationship with him. If Matano had tremendous admiration for his father—who held that the ideals of Samburu life had reached their apex in the massive goat enclosures of the Lterito age set (initiated 1902), the *lpiron* elders who had given his age set fire—the relationship was also far from free of stress. He could be arbitrary, dictatorial, and suspicious. At times he asserted openly that his own sons conspired against him. He sometimes insinuated that Matano's older brother was involved in the still unresolved case of the theft of the family's lucky he-goat in the 1980s. When Matano returned from a trip to Maasailand with an unusually decorated pair of tire sandals, his father accused him of getting them from a Maasai *laibon*, perhaps as an *ntasim* (charm) to attain dominance in the family. For his part, Matano's reverence for his father was tinged with anxiety that his father secretly hated him, that he had had sent him to boarding school because he wanted him to die there, suspecting that Matano was a product of his mother's adulterous affair. It is hard, then, to imagine that Matano's simultaneous subscription to his father's vision of the world and embrace of other ways of being is free of affective ambivalence and contradiction.

It is not the only picture I took of Matano, but it is one of the few that were worthy of the album. Absent is my students' favorite, where in long pants, a sport jacket, and a colorful "Saturday Night Fever"–era shiny shirt, he beams as he stands by the hindquarters of a camel he bought with part of his research assistant's salary. Absent also is the picture of I took of him and his brother, proudly posing in the large field of beans they cultivated near Lodokejek, before their father forced them to migrate to an area more suitable for the goats. If he remains proud of these things, it is not through these that his album memorializes his past. In the album he is a meat-eating murran at *loikar,* where you do not wear a nylon windbreaker.

I have tried in this book to explicate how a people understands their past and how this understanding informs the present, processes that I have suggested are most powerfully constructed through food. This task has been quite deliberately multistranded, exploring varied contexts of memory, various processes and practices that serve as key arenas for thinking about the past. In so doing, I have constructed what I have intended as a more nuanced and ambivalent (and therefore more true-to-life) view of memory and collective memory. I have addressed, or at least opened, a variety of key questions: Why food? What makes food such a diffuse and powerful arena of memory for Samburu? How does food construct the terrain of memory for Samburu in ways that are at once forceful and contradictory, deeply felt but also ambivalent? To what extent does this tell us something predominantly about Samburu, and to what extent can we draw lessons that we can extend to societies around the globe?

Certainly a key piece of the answers to these questions must center on the sensuality of eating, smells and tastes transmitting powerful mnemonic cues that render it a particularly likely and compelling site of memory (Sutton 2001). Yet there is far more than this interpretation, rooted mainly in the gustatory and psychological facets of eating. These facets may be the most significant for those of us for whom food (perhaps even a seemingly endless variety of it) is obtained in relatively simple and reliable ways. But in many contexts this profound sensuousness is layered with the fear and experience of want. Food also serves as a medium for constructing the most significant relationships, the intimate and the public and the avenues in between. Food belongs, as Wiley (2006) recently noted, consummately to both the material and the transcendent, and thus is one of the few arenas that have remained relatively untouched by the often fractious debates concerning the continuing value, or inevitable unbundling, of anthropology's four fields. No one seriously doubts that food is simultaneously, in Levi-Strauss's terms, "good to think," and, in Marvin Harris's, "good to eat." Yet if I have explored these and many of the other things food is "good for," these many strands both exponentially reinforce food's power and run radically at odds with each other. Food creates windows of memory characterized by particular ambivalence and contradiction. For if the power of food—what makes food *food*—resides in its ability to condense diverse strands of causality and meaning in a single whole, this whole is not necessarily, indeed is unlikely to be, a seamless one. Even in objective terms, significant transformations are typically constituted through a diverse mix of gains and losses. And such transformations are rarely understood in objective terms (even to the extent that such a creature exists) but rather in the ways that these are understood through—and in the process remake—culturally constituted subjects, varying by age, gender, wealth, and life experiences.

Thus, for Samburu, porridge *(loshorro),* the simplest of foods—water, maize meal, and if you are fortunate a bit of fat—is in no senses simple. As maize meal has become a key staple in Samburu diet, it has done so as a symbol of both salvation and decay. It has brought diseases that were previously unknown, created ADD-like symptoms in children, and torn culturally important patterns of respect apart at their seams. But times are also good, for this powder, which the oldest Samburu still recall as resembling ashes when it first came to them in the early decades of the twentieth century, has put to rest not only the very real fear of dying of starvation during severe droughts, but even most of the daily worries and struggles of finding food.

Yet, however real these dimensions of *loshorro* are, its meaning can in no sense be encapsulated in these relatively straightforward material trade-offs, particularly for a people whose collective identity, social relations, and—most poignantly—differently positioned forms of moral personhood are deeply and intensely constructed through food. *Loshorro* is not just food, it is "food of the enemies," having become of-Samburu-bodies in the process of collision with a different and viscerally inferior way of life, and it remains "government food," emblematic of their incorporation into the colonial state. New foods are also "poverty foods," metonymic of an era of broad failure in the livestock economy and explanatory of the only good reason that someone would have to shift to such tasteless and unhealthy food. And perhaps most meaningfully, they are also "foods of the pot" concentrating the practice of everyday eating around a single cooking fire; as such, they are "gray foods," indistinct in color and breeding indistinctness, as fundamental patterns of avoidance and social distance are subverted by new ways of eating that bring together members of all age and gender categories. But at the same time these new ways of eating are seen as part and parcel of Development (though no corresponding terms exist, or are even imaginable for *loshorro* itself), representing the Enlightened triumph of practical reason over antiquated cultural restrictions concerning what one eats and whom one eats with. There is not one story here, unless it is the experience of many stories at once, experienced simultaneously in an uneasy, ambivalent mix. The past has many meanings and the present is experienced in ambiguous ways, as persons and identities are redefined and remade and Samburu tastes remain uncertain even to themselves.

Notes

1. MEMORY, AMBIVALENCE, AND FOOD

1. In her work on transformations in Spain, Jane Collier notes a similar ambivalence, and embracing of seemingly opposed identities, for instance among "modern nationalists who embrace both sides of the conceptual opposition between tradition and modernity" (Collier 1997, 210).

2. It should be noted that even the "memory" of a single human being (or of a nonhuman organism) is composed of a variety of different faculties, which arguably have little in common except to the extent that we hold them to function similarly in imparting information, abilities, or emotions derived from past action or experience to a (real or imagined) self.

3. Memory is, after all, the medium through which "facts" are established in oral history, while much of the analysis earmarked as memory in recent anthropological approaches is indistinguishable from history—indeed, in some cases scholars seem to use the terms interchangeably.

4. There are similar parallels with the psychological distinction between explicit and implicit memory.

5. As I will discuss in more detail below, Bourdieu's notion of the habitus is a key formulation of this.

6. There are limits to how far this approach may be pushed. If we take any sediment of the past to be memory—whether it be a continuing religious tradition, foraging terminology, or house structures—the term quickly loses its meaning.

7. Some critics have turned against this critique in recent years (e.g., Farquar 2002; Strathern 1996), some suggesting that "speed-reading" (Ganguly 2001) has resulted in missing the subtlety of his thought. As I will discuss, I am not sympathetic to that perspective.

8. That is, rather than interpreting his work as a kind of quasi-religious text from which we might glean some hidden meaning in countercurrent to its

principal thrust, we should consider what propositions about the world may be derived from his significant insights, in order to further refine their usefulness in social analysis.

2. FOOD AS FOOD

1. The fierce debate between the substantivist and formalist economic anthropologists is a good example of this.

3. THE ALIMENTARY STRUCTURES OF SAMBURU LIFE

1. Well-developed ethnographic and theoretical critiques of the assumption of the primacy of the political sphere are found in Collier (1988) and, in a different sense, Carsten (1997).

2. For comparative perspectives on transformations of the relationship of youths to women in male initiation, see, for instance, Herdt 1982; Godelier 1986; Guttman 1997.

3. Perhaps the only worse offense might be displaying pain during circumcision. That each is based in a denial or control of negative bodily sensations might be fruitfully explored elsewhere.

4. It is, of course, common in other parts of Africa and elsewhere to define womanhood through cooking and food provisioning (e.g., Feldman-Savelsberg 1999).

5. The point is not to diminish these classic examples but to highlight how the unique dynamics of food constitute, rather than symbolize, the relationships I discuss.

4. A SAMBURU GASTRONOMY

1. Laisi are families believed to have origins among the neighboring Rendille, and are held to have supernatural powers.

2. It is extremely unpropitious for cattle to die in the livestock enclosure, such that even sick cattle are brought out for grazing and allowed to die there. Cattle that collapse inside the enclosure are brought outside the settlement to be slaughtered. The path along which they were carried and the place they lay in the kraal are ritually cleansed with leaves.

3. The significance of these is highlighted by the fact that if pictures are taken at a Samburu wedding, the bearing of these cuts into the house is considered to be an essential photographic subject.

4. Cow's milk (66 calories per 100 grams) is calorically similar to camel and goat's milk (both 70 calories per 100 grams), with slight differences in their ratios of protein, fat, and lactose. Sheep milk is far more caloric (102 calories per 100 grams), having greater quantities of both fat and protein (Saveur 2003).

5. Small amounts of honey are also sometimes collected from a flightless burrowing bee, called *nkasuiasui lchobi,* but this is uncommon and the amount insubstantial.

6. This argument is congenial to Whitehead's (2000) far more elaborated analysis of Seltaman food taboos in New Guinea, to the extent that she also relies on multiple strands of causality, though she focuses more on material factors than the nonlogical factors and competing logics I highlight here.

5. THE CALABASH BEHIND THE CALABASH BEHIND THE CALABASH

1. Whether Samburu past behavior actually was more "moral" in their own terms is, of course, a very different question from how an idealized view of the past informs the present.

2. For further discussion see chapter 1.

3. Rappaport does note in passing that there are times when ambiguity is desirable, though this is not the central emphasis of his approach.

4. The hyena features prominently in the folktales of many African peoples (the best-known examples being Beidelman's [1961, 1963] accounts of Kaguru folktales), though with features that typically differ significantly from the Samburu ones described here.

5. See also Gregor 1977, 1985.

6. Samburu insist that a *laingoni lomodio* does not lose control of his bowels out of fear (e.g., as in the English "scared shitless"), but because of an intense emotional urge to fight.

7. In other contexts it is not uncommon to find stories ostensibly about food to actually be stories about human morality in general. Beidelman's (e.g., 1986) Kaguru folktales about eating are seminal examples.

8. Since women allocate food, they are ostensibly outside the realm of possible theft of shares of food. Though women may not allocate food fairly or may retain hidden food for themselves, they have no reason to take back food they have already given.

9. For detailed exegesis of the varieties and causes of unpropitiousness among Samburu, see Straight 2006.

10. Siskind (1973) describes a similar waiting game among the Sharahua.

11. Our friendship has continued since, and he has subsequently given me two goats.

12. A survey conducted independently with husbands and wives in 2002 concerning available foods demonstrated that men's knowledge of what is in the home is highly imperfect, though not entirely lacking.

6. MIXED LIKE A POT OF GRAY FOOD

1. I translate Lemantile's term *nkop* (land or soil) as "world" because he denotes the Samburu social universe, the only lands that are socially and culturally relevant.

2. This is not, of course, an unproblematic assumption. While some (e.g., Piot 1999; Tsing 1993) emphasize the global creation of "local" peoples, Mintz (1998) argues that particular regions have been global melting pots for centuries.

3. Geschiere, of course, does not.

4. In a 1993–94 survey, a staggering 18 percent of adult men were working as watchmen away from home. The survey found that 51.8 percent of adult males participated in migratory wage labor at some time, with 26.3 percent currently active (Holtzman 1996, 2004).

5. For more extensive discussion, see Holtzman (1996)

6. Two exceptions to food-centered explanations of wage labor concern individuals who complete high school in order to seek high paying jobs upon graduation and those employed in jobs so desirable (e.g. the military) as to require no explanation.

7. Murran who have abandoned the *lminong* are an ambiguous category, neither boys nor murran nor elders. They are more accepted in highland areas because of their perceived ties to forward-looking development, but much less so in lowland areas.

7. IN A CUP OF TEA

1. See, for instance, Howes 1996; Miller 1995b, 1997; Rutz and Orlove 1989; Thomas 1998; Wilk 1994.

2. This rather Durkheimian explanation of tea use was provided by informants.

3. This is not a common use today. Colonial records also suggest tea use, but this can't be quantified because tea was also used by non-Samburu "native staff" at the Maralal station.

4. The Lterito age set is widely regarded as the first elders to have tea. This suggests an earlier date, since Lterito became elders in 1912 and *lpiron* fire-stick elders in 1924.

5. It is not uncommon for unusual but desirable foods to be withheld from women and children because of their purported deleterious effects on behavior (e.g., Chibuye et al. 1986; Dembele and Poulton 1993).

6. Tree bark and other plants are prepared in hot-water infusions, and this process may have facilitated the acceptance of tea. Their mainly medicinal purposes differ from tea in social context and cultural meanings. Occasional comparisons are likely retrospective, rather than indicating a significant relationship between early tea use and the use of herbs.

7. There may be important differences in extensification in nonstratified societies. In classed societies, the desirability of commodities parallel at least partially hegemonic valuations of status within the class structure (e.g., rich is better than poor; sirloin is better than Hamburger Helper). In a classless society, however, different age- and gender-based segments may use different items because of their appropriateness to the subgroups' roles and not because of age or gender stratification per se (e.g., men eat tongues whereas women eat liver, but neither tongue nor liver is superior). As commodities such as tea are accepted, their use may follow this age- and gender-appropriate structure rather than one of absolute rank.

8. Interestingly, the standard tea recipe largely preserves the volume of milk Samburu traditionally consumed. Over the past half century, the cattle

to human ratio has fallen from approximately 7:1 to 2:1. Today the quantity of milk available is about one-third what it was in the mid-twentieth century. The tea drunk today contains milk in a ration of 1:3.

9. Some informants still maintain that children who grow accustomed to tea and then do not get it may sleep while herding and neglect the animals.

10. Lkimaniki elders (circumcised 1948) have admitted, however, to secretly eating jaggery in the bush, which they had purchased from Somali traders.

11. Today Coca Cola is by far the most popular soda. The reasons for this are not entirely clear, and—since most Samburu are not avid soda drinkers—may be related to supply rather than local demand. Hillaby (1964) indicates that his Samburu porters in the early 1960s favored Pepsi Cola (now virtually unavailable), and some older informants suggest that their early encounters with soda involved ginger ale. Conversions of prices into U.S. currency are inexact, due to rapid fluctuations in both prices and exchange rates (not necessarily in concert) during the research period (1992–94), which was a particularly volatile time economically in Kenya.

12. Similarly, among the Samburu's southern neighbors, the closely related Mukogodo Maasai, soda is characterized as *lcani,* an "herb" or medicine (Lee Cronk, personal communication).

8. TURBID BREWS

1. The ban was lifted in 1948, though this may have continued to be the de facto policy in some areas for some time thereafter.

2. Oral interview with Mrs. Lasangurukuri, March 1994.

3. Description of the goat bag in Samburu District comes from Ramon Goodwin (personal communication, August 1994), who was a colonial policeman in Samburu District. Access to skins was peculiar to remote areas, where private butcheries were not able to supply the meat, which accounts for why this fund was successfully kept off the books for a prolonged period.

4. The date for the beer hall is based on the statements of informants, including his wife, and its first mention in colonial reports in 1953 Samburu District Annual Report, when it appears to have already been well established. Colonial reports indicate that Lekalja was the first Samburu to be successful in business, but the only mention of his butchery in oral accounts indicated that he followed, and may have been influenced by, Lasangurukuri. As the club is mentioned only in passing in archival sources, it is difficult to fix the exact date of its opening.

5. For example, see "'Cut Number of Beer Hall Licenses' Says Moi," *Nairobi Daily Nation,* October 12, 1978. Since bottled beer was not affected, people suspected that economic motives were involved, particularly given the brewing industry's long-term opposition to *busaa* as a form of unfair competition.

6. Several factors limit brewing in the most remote areas. Brewing supplies are more expensive and difficult to come by, and lower population densities make marketing more difficult, particularly because men tend to be busier and

have less ready access to cash. Brewing is still found in these remote areas, but it plays a less central role in the community.

7. A conversion of 1993 Kenya shillings into dollars is problematic, because this was a period of rapid devaluation of the currency. The dollar equivalent here is higher than my earlier figure from the same survey (Holtzman 2001) because this better captures the comparative buying power at that time and in 2005.

8. There is no evidence to indicate that British sought to promote drinking among Samburu chiefs, despite Willis's (2002) discussion of the use of the privilege of access to European alcohol in cultivating African elites elsewhere in Africa.

9. For instance, see "There Is Revolution in the Air, but Do the Young Know It?" *Daily Nation,* November 19, 2002. Ugali is the national food of Kenya, a thick polenta-like substance made from maize meal and eaten with a variety of sauces, stews, or relishes.

10. Among Samburu, applying a modernist rationality to greed is mainly associated with the relatively small number of converts to Protestant denominations, who have largely rejected indigenous Samburu values and local social relations.

9. EATING SHILLINGS

1. Samburu and other pastoralist groups engaged in trade with agriculturalists in both the precolonial and colonial eras as a response to famine.

2. *Nkampit* is the Samburu word for a forest monster, and here refers to my son William, then about two and a half.

3. Certainly other foods could be used to supplement or replace milk during famine, but would not have been the staple food during normal circumstances.

4. Body Mass Index (BMI) is a standard measure of nutritional well-being, calculated by height in meters squared, divided by weight in kilograms (height^2 * weight). It is considered to be highly comparable across gender. A BMI of 20 is considered to be healthy in developed countries, while 18.5 is often cited as a cut-off when activity levels decrease and morbidity increases.

5. Catholic conversion is often quite casual and does not require significant behavioral changes.

Bibliography

Akyeampong, Emmanuel K. 1996. *Drink, Power, and Culture Change.* Oxford: James Currey.

Allison, Anne. 1991. Japanese Mothers and Obentos: The Lunchbox as Ideological State Apparatus. *Anthropological Quarterly* 64: 195–208.

Althusser, Louis. 1962. *For Marx.* Trans. Ben Brewster. New York: Penguin Books.

Ambler, Charles. 1991. Drunks, Brewers and Chiefs: Alcohol Regulation in Colonial Kenya. In *Drinking: Behavior and Belief in Modern History,* ed. Robin Room and Susanna Barrows, 165–83. Berkeley: University of California Press.

Antze, Paul, and Micheal Lambek, eds. 1996. *Tense Past: Culture Essays in Trauma and Memory.* London: Routledge

Appadurai, Arjun. 1981. Gastropolitics in Hindu South Asia. *American Ethnologist* 8: 291–305.

———. 1986. *The Social Life of Things.* Cambridge: Cambridge University Press.

———. 1988. How to Make a National Cuisine: Cookbooks in Contemporary India. *Comparative Studies in Society and History* 30, no. 1: 3–24.

———. 1996. *Modernity at Large: Cultural Dimensions of Globalization.* Minneapolis: University of Minnesota Press.

Appiah, Kwame Anthony. 1992. *In My Father's House: Africa in the Philosophy of Culture.* New York: Oxford University Press.

Arhem, Kaj. 1987. Meat, Milk and Blood: Diet as Cultural Code among the Pastoral Maasai. Upsala Papers in Social Anthropology, University of Upsala.

Bahloul Joelle. 1996. The Architecture of Memory. Cambridge: Cambridge University Press.

Baker, Keith. 1990. *Inventing the French Revolution.* Cambridge: Cambridge University Press.

Batsell, Robert. 2002. "You Will Eat All of That!" A Retrospective Analysis of Forced Consumption Episodes. *Appetite* 38: 211–19.

Bayart, Jean-François. 1993. *The State in Africa: The Politics of the Belly.* London: Longman.

Beidelman, Thomas O. 1961. The Hyena and the Rabbit: A Kaguru Representation of Matrilineal Relations. *Africa* 31: 61–74.

———. 1963. Further Adventures of Hyena and Rabbit: The Folktale as a Sociological Model. *Africa* 33: 54–69.

———. 1982. *Colonial Evangelism.* Bloomington: Indiana University Press.

———. 1986. *Moral Imagination in Kaguru Modes of Thought.* Bloomington: Indiana University Press.

Berdahl, Daphne, M. Bunzl, and M. Lampland, eds. 2000. *Altering States: Ethnographies of Transition in Eastern Europe and the Former Soviet Union.* Ann Arbor: University of Michigan Press.

Berdahl, Daphne. 1999. *Where the World Ended.* Berkeley: University of California Press.

Bohannon, Paul. 1955. Some Principles of Exchange and Investment among the Tiv. *American Anthropologist* 57: 60–70.

Botman, H. Russell, and Robin Peterson, eds. 1996. *To Remember and To Heal.* Cape Town: Human and Rousseau.

Bourdieu, Pierre. 1976. Marriage Strategies as Strategies of Reproduction. In *Family and Society,* ed. R. Forster and P. Ranum. Baltimore, MD: Johns Hopkins University Press.

———. 1977. *Outline of a Theory of Practice.* Cambridge: Cambridge University Press.

———. 1987. *Distinction.* Cambridge, MA: Harvard University Press.

———. 1998. *Practical Reason.* Stanford, CA: Stanford University Press.

Bozolli, Belinda, and Mmantho Nkotsoe. 1991. Women of Phokeng. Johannesburg: Ravan Press.

Brown, Michael. 1996. Resisting the Rhetoric of Resistance. *American Anthropologist* 98: 729–35.

Buckser A. 1999. Keeping Kosher: Eating and Social Identity among the Jews of Denmark. *Ethnology* 38: 191--209.

Burke, Timothy. 1996. *Lifebuoy Men, Lux Women: Commodification, Consumption and Cleanliness in Modern Zimbabwe.* Durham, NC: Duke University Press.

Butler, Judith. 1990. *Gender Trouble.* London: Routledge.

———. 1993. *Bodies That Matter.* New York: Routledge.

Carrier, James, and Josiah McC. Heyman. 1997. Consumption and Political Economy. *Journal of the Royal Anthropological Institute* 3, no. 2: 355–73.

Carsten, Janet. 1997. *The Heat of the Hearth.* Oxford: Clarendon.

———. 2000. Introduction: Cultures of Relatedness. In *Cultures of Relatedness: New Approaches to the Study of Kinship,* 1–36. Cambridge: Cambridge University Press.

Casey, Edward. 1987. *Remembering: A Phenomenological Approach.* Bloomington: Indiana University Press.

Chatwin, Mary Ellen. 1997. Socio-Cultural Transformation and Foodways in the Republic of Georgia. Commack, NY: Nova Sci.

Chenevix-Trench, Charles. 1964. *The Desert's Dusty Face*. Edinburgh: W. Blackwood.

———. 1993. *The Men Who Ruled Kenya*. London: I. B. Taurus.

Chibuye, Peggy , M. Mwenda, and C. Osborne. 1986. CRZ/UNICEF Study on Childrearing Practices in Zambia. Lusaka: Zambia Association for Research and Development.

Clark, Gracia. 1989. Money, Sex and Cooking: Manipulation of the Paid/Unpaid Boundary by Asante Market Women. In *The Social Economy of Consumption,* ed. Henry Rutz and Benjamin Orlove, 323–48. Monographs in Economic Anthropology No. 6. Lanham, MD: University Press of America.

Classen, Constance. 1997. Foundations for an Anthropology of the Senses. *International Social Science Journal* 153: 401–12.

Cole, Jennifer. 2001. *Forget Colonialism? Sacrifice and the Art of Memory in Madagascar*. Berkeley: University of California Press.

Collier, Jane. 1997. *From Duty to Desire*. Princeton, NJ: Princeton University Press.

Colony and Protectorate of Kenya. 1928. Isiolo District Annual Report. Nairobi: Kenya National Archives.

———. 1930. Native Liquor Ordinance. Nairobi: Kenya National Archives.

———. 1934. Samburu District Annual Report. Nairobi: Kenya National Archives.

———. 1948. Samburu District Annual Report. Nairobi: Kenya National Archives.

———. 1950. Samburu District Monthly Intelligence Report, October 1950. Nairobi: Kenya National Archives.

———. 1952. Samburu District Annual Report. Nairobi: Kenya National Archives.

———. 1953a. Samburu District Annual Report. Nairobi: Kenya National Archives.

———. 1953b. Samburu District Handing Over Report, 1953. Nairobi: Kenya National Archives.

———. 1957. Samburu District Monthly Intelligence Report, August 1957. Nairobi: Kenya National Archives.

———. 1957. Samburu District Handing Over Report, August 1957. Nairobi: Kenya National Archives.

———. 1961. Report of the Working Party on the Manufacture and Sale of Liquor. Nairobi: Kenya National Archives.

Colson, Elizabeth, and Thayer Scudder. 1988. *For Prayer and Profit*. Stanford, CA: Stanford University Press.

Colvin, Christopher. 2003. "Brothers and Sisters Do Not Be Afraid of Me": Trauma, History and the Therapeutic Imagination in the New South Africa. In *Contested Pasts: The Politics of Memory,* ed. Katharine Hodgkin and Susannah Radstone, 153–68. London: Routledge.

Comaroff, Jean. 1985. *Body of Power, Spirit of Resistance*. Chicago: University of Chicago Press.

Comaroff, Jean, and John Comaroff. 1991. *Of Revelation and Revolution, Volume 1.* Chicago: University of Chicago Press.

———, eds. 1992. *Ethnography and the Historical Imagination.* Boulder, CO: Westview.

Comaroff, John, and Simon Roberts. 1981. *Rules and Process.* Chicago: University of Chicago Press.

Comito, Jacqueline. 2001. Remembering Nana and Papu: The Poetics of Pasta, Pane and Peppers among One Iowan Calabrian Family. PhD diss., University of Iowa.

Connerton, Paul. 1989. *How Societies Remember.* Cambridge: Cambridge University Press.

Cooper, Fred. 1992. *Dialectics of Decolonization.* Ann Arbor: University of Michigan Press.

Cooper, Fred, and Ann Stoler, eds. 1992. *Tensions of Empire: Colonial Cultures in a Bourgeois World.* Berkeley: University of California Press.

Counihan, Carole. 1984. Bread as World: Food Habits and Social Relations in Modernizing Sardinia. *Anthropological Quarterly* 57, no. 2: 47–59.

———. 1999. *The Anthropology of Food and the Body: Gender, Meaning and Power.* New York: Routledge.

———. 2004. *Around the Tuscan Table: Food, Family, and Gender in Twentieth Century Florence.* London: Routledge.

Counihan, Carole, and Penny Van Esterik, eds. 1997. *Food and Culture: A Reader.* New York: Routledge.

Crush, Jonathan, and Charles Ambler. 1992. *Liquor and Labor in Southern Africa.* Athens: Ohio University Press.

Csordas, Thomas J., ed. 1994. *Embodiment and Experience. The Existential Ground of Culture and Self.* London: Cambridge University Press.

Daily Nation. 1978. "Cut Number of Beer Hall Licenses" Says Moi. October 12, 1978, Nairobi, Kenya.

———. 2002. There Is Revolution in the Air, but Do The Young Know It?" November 19, 2002. Nairboi, Kenya.

Daniels, E. Valentine. 1996. *Charred Lullabies.* Princeton, NJ: Princeton University Press.

De Boeck, Filip. 1994. "When Hunger Goes around the Land": Hunger and Food among the Aluund of Zaire. *Man* 29, no. 2: 257–82.

Deacon, Harriet. 1998. Remembering Tragedy, Constructing Modernity: Robben Island as a National Monument. In *Negotiating the Past,* ed. Sarah Nuttall and Carli Coetzee, 161–79. Oxford: Oxford University Press.

Dembele, U., and M. Poulton. 1993. Research Work on Early Childhood Attitudes, Practices and Beliefs in Kolondeba, Southern Mali. Paper Presented at the Workshop on Childrearing Practices and Beliefs in Sub-Saharan Africa. Windhoek, Namibia.

Dettwyler, Kathleen. 1993. *Dancing Skeletons.* Long Grove, IL: Waveland.

Diner H. 2003. *Hungering for America: Italian, Irish and Jewish Foodways in the Age of Migration.* Cambridge, MA: Harvard University Press.

Dirks, Nicholas, ed. 1992. *Colonialism and Culture.* Ann Arbor: University of Michigan Press.

Ditton, Jason. 1980. A Bibliographic Exegesis of Goffman's Sociology. In *The View from Goffman,* ed. Jason Ditton, 1–23. New York: St. Martin's.

Donham, Donald. 2001. Thinking Temporally or Modernizing Anthropology. *American Anthropologist* 103: 134–49.

Douglas, Mary. 1966. *Purity and Danger.* London: Routledge and Kegan Paul.

Empson, William. 1930. *Seven Types of Ambiguity.* New York: New Directions.

Englund, Harri, and James Leach. 2000. Ethnography and Meta-Narratives of Modernity. *Current Anthropology* 41, no. 2: 225–48.

Erikson, Erik. 1966. The Ontogeny of Ritualization in Man. *Philosophical Transactions of the Royal Society of London. Series B, Biological Sciences* 251: 337–49.

Evans-Pritchard, E.E. 1937. *Witchcraft, Oracles and Magic among the Azande.* Oxford: Oxford University Press.

———. 1940. *The Nuer.* Oxford: Oxford University Press.

Fajans, Jane. 1983. Shame, Social Action and the Person. *Ethos* 11, no. 3: 166–80.

Falk, Pasi. 1994. *The Consuming Body.* London: Sage.

Fanon, Frantz. 1967. *Black Skin, White Masks.* New York: Grove.

Farquar, Judith. 2002. *Appetites: Food and Sex in Postsocialist China.* Durham, NC: Duke University Press.

Feldman-Savelsberg, Pamela. 1999. *Plundered Kitchens, Empty Wombs.* Ann Arbor: University of Michigan Press.

Ferguson, James. 1999. *Expectations of Modernity.* Berkeley: University of California Press.

Fiddes, Nick. 1991. *Meat: A Natural Symbol.* New York: Routledge.

Foucault, Michel. 1984. *The Foucault Reader.* Ed. Paul Rabinow. New York: Pantheon.

Fratkin, Elliot. 1991. *Surviving Drought and Development: Ariaal Pastoralists in Northern Kenya.* Boulder, CO: Westview.

———. 1994. Pastoral Land Tenure in Kenya: Maasai, Samburu and Rendille Experiences, 1950–1990. *Nomadic Peoples* 34/35: 55–68.

Frazer, James. 1922. *The Golden Bough.* New York: Macmillan.

Freud, Anna. 1930. *The Psychoanalytic Study of the Child,* Volume 2. Madison, CT: International Universities Press.

Fumagalli, Carl T. 1977. A Diachronic Study of Socio-Cultural Change Processes among the Samburu of Northern Kenya. PhD diss., State University of New York, Buffalo.

Gabbacia, Donna. 1998. *We Are What We Eat: Ethnic Food and the Making of Americans.* Cambridge, MA: Harvard University Press.

Galaty, John G. 1982. Being "Maasai," Being "People of Cattle": Ethnic Shifters in East Africa. *American Ethnologist* 9: 1–20.

Galaty, John, D. Aronson, and P. Salzman, eds. 1981. *The Future of Pastoral People.* In *The Future of Pastoral People,* ed. John Galaty, Dan Aronson, and Philip Salzman. Nairobi: Institute of Development Studies.

Ganguly, Keya. 2001. *States of Exception.* Minneapolis: University of Minnesota Press.

Garvey, Pauline. 2005. Drunk and (Dis)Orderly: Norwegian Drinking Parties at Home. In *Drinking Cultures,* ed. T. Wilson, 87–106. New York: Berg.

Gavaghan, Terence. 1999. *Of Lions and Dung Beetles.* London: A. Stockwell.

Geertz, Clifford. 1973. *The Interpretation of Cultures.* New York: Basic Books.

Geschiere, Peter. 1997. *The Modernity of Witchcraft.* Charlottesville: University Press of Virginia.

Geurts, Kathryn Linn. 2002. *Culture of the Senses: Bodily Ways of Knowing in an African Community.* Berkeley: University of California Press.

Gilsenan, Michael. 1976. Lying, Honor and Contradiction. In *Transaction and Meaning: Directions in the Anthropology of Exchange and Symbolic Value,* ed. Bruce Kapferer, 191–219. Philadelphia: Institute for the Study of Human Issues.

Gitlitz, David, and Linda Kay. 1999. *Drizzle of Honey: The Lives and Recipes of Spain's Secret Jews.* New York: St. Martin's.

Godelier, Maurice. 1986. *The Making of Great Men: Male Domination and Power among the New Guinea Baruya.* Cambridge: Cambridge University Press.

Goffman, Erving. 1969. *Strategic Interaction.* Philadelphia: University of Pennsylvania Press.

Goody, Jack. 1982. *Cooking, Cuisine and Class.* Cambridge: Cambridge University Press.

Gordon, Robert. 1992. *The Bushman Myth.* Boulder, CO: Westview.

Gottlieb, Alma. 1992. *Under the Kapok Tree: Identity and Difference in Beng Thought.* Chicago: University of Chicago Press.

Grandin, Barbara. 1988. Wealth and Pastoral Dairy Production: A Case Study from Maasailand. *Human Ecology* 16, no. 1: 1–21.

Gregor, Thomas. 1970. Exposure and Seclusion. *Ethnology* 9: 234–50.

———. 1977. *Mehinaku.* Chicago: University of Chicago Press.

———. 1985. *Anxious Pleasures.* Chicago: University of Chicago Press.

Gulliver, Paul H. 1955. *The Family Herds: A Study of Two Pastoral Tribes in East Africa, the Jie and the Turkana.* London: Routledge and Kegan Paul.

Gupta, Akhil. 1998. *Postcolonial Developments.* Durham, NC: Duke University Press.

Gupta, Akhil, and James Ferguson, eds. 1997. *Culture, Power, Place: Explorations in Critical Anthropology.* Durham, NC: Duke University Press.

Guttman, Matthew. 1997. Trafficking in Men: The Anthropology of Masculinity. *Annual Review of Anthropology* 26: 385–409.

Halbwachs, Maurice. 1992. *On Collective Memory.* Trans. Lewis Coser. Chicago: University of Chicago Press.

Handler, Richard, and Jocelyn Linnekin. 1984. Tradition, Genuine or Spurious. *Journal of American Folklore* 97: 273–90.

Hannerz, Ulf. 1987. The World in Creolization. *Africa* 57: 546–59.

Harris, Marvin. 1966. The Cultural Ecology of India's Sacred Cattle. *Current Anthropology* 7: 51–59.

———. 1986. *Good to Eat.* New York: Simon and Schuster.

Haugerud, Angelique. 1995. *The Culture of Politics in Modern Kenya.* Cambridge: Cambridge University Press.

Heath, Douglas, ed. 1995. *International Handbook on Alcohol and Culture.* Westport, CT: Greenwood.

Hensel, Chase. 1996. *Telling Ourselves: Ethnicity of Discourse in Southwestern Alaska.* Oxford: Oxford University Press.

Herdt, Gilbert. 1982. *Rituals of Manhood: Male Initiation in New Guinea.* Berkeley: University of California Press.

Herren, Urs. 1991. Socioeconomic Strategies of Mukogodo Households. PhD diss., University of Bern.

Hillaby, John. 1964. *Journey to the Jade Sea.* New York: Simon and Schuster.

Hobsbawm, Eric. 1983. Introduction: Inventing Traditions. In *The Invention of Tradition,* ed. Eric Hobsbawm and Terrance Ranger, 1–14. Cambridge: Cambridge University Press.

Hodgkin, Katharine, and Susannah Radstone, eds. 2003. *Contested Pasts: The Politics of Memory.* London: Routledge.

Hodgson, Dorothy Hodgson. 1997. Embodying the Contraditions of Modernity: Gender and Spirit Possession among Maasai in Tanzania. In *Gendered Encounters,* ed. Maria Grosz-Ngate and Omari Kokole, 111–30. London: Routledge.

———. 1999. Pastoralism, Patriarchy and History among Maasai in Tanganyika, 1890–1940. *Journal of African History* 40: 41–65.

———. 2001. *Once Intrepid Warriors.* Bloomington: Indiana University Press.

Hofmeyr, Isabel. 1994. *"We Spend Our Years as a Tale That Is Told."* Johannesburg: Wits University Press.

Holtzman, Jon D. 1996. Transformations in Samburu Domestic Economy. PhD diss., University of Michigan.

———. 1997. Gender and the Market in the Integration of Agriculture among Samburu Pastoralists in Northern Kenya. *Research in Economic Anthropology* 18: 161–205.

———. 1999a. Cultivar as Civilizer: Samburu and European Perspectives on Cultivar Diffusion. *Ethnology Monograph Series* no. 17: 11–19.

———. 1999b. Household, Gender and Age Sets: Domestic Processes and Political Economic Organization among the Samburu of Northern Kenya. In *At the Interface: The Household and Beyond,* ed. Nicole Tannenbaum and David Small, 41–54. Lanham, MD: University Press of America.

———. 2000. *Nuer Journeys, Nuer Lives: Sudanese Refugees in Minnesota.* Needham, MA: Allyn and Bacon.

———. 2001. The Food of Elders, the "Ration" of Women: Brewing, Gender and Domestic Processes among Samburu Pastoralists in Northern Kenya. *American Anthropologist* 103: 1041–58.

———. 2002. Politics and Gastropolitics: Gender and the Power of Food in Two African Pastoralist Societies. *Journal of the Royal Anthropological Institute.* 8, no. 2: 259–78.

———. 2003a. Age, Masculinity and Migration: Gender and Wage Labor among Samburu Pastoralists in Northern Kenya. In *Gender at Work in*

Economic Life, ed. Gracia Clark, SEA Monographs. Walnut Creek, CA: Altamire.

———. 2003b. In a Cup of Tea: Commodities and History among Samburu Pastoralists in Northern Kenya. *American Ethnologist* 30, no. 1: 136–55.

———. 2004. The Local in the Local: Models of Time and Space in Samburu District, Northern Kenya. *Current Anthropology* 45, no. 1: 61–84.

———. 2005. The Drunken Chief: Alcohol, Power and the Birth of the State in Samburu District, Northern Kenya. *Postcolonial Studies* 8: 83–96.

———. 2006a. Food and Memory. *Annual Review of Anthropology* 35: 361–78.

———. 2006b. The World Is Dead and Cooking's Killed It: Food and the Gender of Memory in Samburu, Northern Kenya. *Food and Foodways* 14, nos. 3–4: 175–200.

———. 2007. Eating Time: Capitalist History and Pastoralist History among Samburu Herders in Northern Kenya. *Journal of East African Studies* 1, no. 3: 436–48.

Howes, David, ed. 1996. *Cross-Cultural Consumption: Global Markets, Local Realities.* New York: Routledge.

Humphrey, T., and L. Humphrey, eds. 1988. *We Gather Together: Food and Festival in American Life.* Ann Arbor: UMI Research Press.

Hutchinson, Sharon. 1996. *Nuer Dilemmas.* Berkeley: University of California Press.

Jackson, Michael. 1982. *Allegories of the Wilderness: Ethics and Ambiguity in Kuranko Narratives.* Bloomington: Indiana University Press.

———. 1995. *At Home in the World.* Durham, NC: Duke University Press.

James, Wendy. 1988. *The Listening Ebony.* Oxford: Clarendon.

Jerome, Norge. 1977. Taste Experience and the Development of a Dietary Preference for Sweet in Humans. In *Taste and Development: The Genesis of Sweet Preference,* ed. J.M. Weiffenbach, 235–48. Washington, DC: U.S. Department of Health, Education and Welfare.

Jing, Jun. 1996. *The Temple of Memories.* Stanford, CA: Stanford University Press.

Johnsen, Nina. 1997. Maasai Medicine. PhD diss., University of Copenhagen.

Johnston, H.H. 1886. *The Kilimanjaro Expedition.* London: Kegan, Paul, Trench.

Jordanova, Ludmilla. 2000. *History in Practice.* London: Arnold.

Kahn, Miriam. 1986. *Always Hungry, Never Greedy: Food and Expression of Gender in a Melanesian Society.* Cambridge: Cambridge University Press.

Karp, Ivan. 1980. Beer Drinking and Social Experience in an African Society: An Essay in Formal Sociology. In *Explorations in African Systems of Thought,* ed. I. Karp and C. Bird, 83–119. Bloomington: Indiana University Press.

Kasfir, Sydney. 1999. Samburu Souvenirs: Representations of a Land in Amber. In *Unpacking Culture: Art and Commodity in the Postcolonial World,* ed. Ruth B. Phillips and Christopher Steiner, 67–83. Berkeley: University of California Press.

Kelly, T. M. 2001. Honoring Helga, "The Little Lefsa Maker": Regional Food as Social Marker, Tradition and Art. In *Pilaf, Pozole and Pad Thai,* ed. Sherri Innes, 19—40. Amherst: University of Massachsetts Press.

Kielmann, A., N. Kielmann, A. Jansen, D. Njama, G. Maritim, R. Mwadime, and K. Saidi. 1994. Nutritional Profile of the Population in a Food-for-Work Project Area: A Case Study from Samburu District, Kenya. *Food and Nutrition Bulletin* 15, no. 3: 215–26.

Kipury, Naomi. 1983. *The Oral Literature of the Maasai.* Nairobi: Heinemann.

Kratz, Corinne. 1992. "We've Always Done It Like This . . . Except for a Few Details": "Tradition" and "Innovation" in Okiek Ceremonies. *Comparative Studies in Society and History* 35, no. 1: 30–65.

Kugelmass, Jack. 1990. Green Bagels: An Essay on Food, Nostalgia, and the Carnivalesque. *YIVO Annual* 19: 57–80.

La Hausse, Paul. 1988. *Brewers, Beerhalls and Boycotts: A History of Liquor in South Africa.* Johannesburg: Ravan Press.

Lakoff, George, and Mark Johnson. 1999. *Philosophy in the Flesh: The Embodied Mind and Its Challenge to Western Thought.* New York: Basic Books.

Lane, Christel. 1981. *The Rites of Rulers.* Cambridge: Cambridge University Press.

Lee, Richard B. 1979. *The !Kung San: Men, Women and Work in a Foraging Society.* Cambridge: Cambridge University Press.

Lenane, Dean. 2002. English Culinary Atrocities. Exquisite Corpse, Cyber Issue 11.

Lentz, Carol, ed. 1999. *Changing Food Habits: Case Studies from Africa, South America, and Europe.* Amsterdam: Harwood Academic.

Lesorogol, Carolyn K. 1991. Pastoral Production and Transformations among the Samburu of Northern Kenya. MA thesis, University of California–Los Angeles.

———. 2003. Transforming Institutions among Pastoralists: Inequality and Land Privatization. American Anthropologist 105, no. 3: 531–42.

Levi-Strauss, Claude. 1969. *The Raw and the Cooked.* Trans. John and Doreen Weightman. New York: Harper and Row.

———. 1973. *From Honey to Ashes.* Trans. John and Doreen Weightman. New York: Harper and Row.

Little, Peter. 1992. *The Elusive Granary.* Cambridge: Cambridge University Press.

Little, Michael, and Brooke Johnson. 1986. Grip Strength, Muscle Fatigue and Body Composition in Nomadic Turkana Pastoralists. *American Journal of Physical Anthropology* 69: 335–44.

Llewelyn Davies, Melissa. 1981. Women, Warriors and Patriarchs. In *Sexual Meanings,* ed. Sherry Ortner and Harriet Whitehead, 330–58. Cambridge: Cambridge University Press.

Lockwood, W., and Y.R. Lockwood. 2000. Finnish American Milk Products in the Morthwoods. In *Milk: Beyond Dairy,* ed. H. Walker, 232–39. Proceedings of the Oxford Symposium on Food Cookery. Totnes, U.K: Prospect Books.

Long, Andrew. 1992. Goods, Knowledge and Beer: The Methodological Significance of Situational Analysis and Discourse. In *Battlefields of Knowledge: The Interlocking of Theory and Practice in Social Science Research and Development*, ed. N. Long and A. Long, 147–70. London: Routledge.

Lupton, Deborah. 1994. Food, Memory, and Meaning: The Symbolic and Social Nature of Food. *Sociological Review* 42, no. 4: 664–87.

———. 1996. *Food, the Body, and the Self.* Thousand Oaks, CA: Sage.

MacAndrew, C., and R. Edgerton. 1969. *Drunken Comportment: A Social Explanation.* Chicago: Aldine.

MacFarlane, Alan, and Iris MacFarlane. 2004. *Empire of Tea.* Woodstock, NY: Overlook Press.

Malkki, Liisa. 1995. *Purity and Exile.* Chicago: University of Chicago Press.

Malinowski, Bronislaw. 1922. *Argonauts of the Western Pacific.* London: Routledge.

Mankekar, P. 2002. "India Shopping": Indian Grocery Stores and Transnational Configuration of Belonging. *Ethnos* 67, no. 1: 75--98.

Marcus, George, and James Clifford. 1985. The Making of Ethnographic Texts: A Preliminary Report. *Current Anthropology* 26, no. 2: 267–71.

Marcus, George, and Dick Cushman. 1982. Ethnography as Text. *Annual Review of Sociology* 11: 25–69.

Marshall, Mac. 1978. *Weekend Warriors: Alcohol in a Micronesian Society.* New York: McGraw Hill.

Mauss, Marcel. 1967. *The Gift.* New York: W. W. Norton.

McIntosh, William Alex, and Mary Zey. 1989. Women as Gatekeepers of Food Consumption: A Sociological Critique. *Food and Foodways* 3, no. 4: 317–22.

Meigs, Anna. 1984. *Food, Sex and Pollution: A New Guinea Religion.* New Brunswick, NJ: Rutgers University Press.

Merker, Moritz. 1910. *Die Maasai.* Berlin: Verlagsbuchhandlung Dietrich Reimer.

Miller, Daniel. 1995a. Introduction to *Worlds Apart: Modernity through the Prism of the Local*, ed. Daniel Miller, 1–22. London: Routledge..

———. 1995b. Consumption and Commodities. *Annual Review of Anthropology* 24: 141–61.

———. 1997. *Capitalism: An Ethnographic Approach.* Oxford: Berg.

———. 1998. Coca Cola: A Black Sweet Drink from Trinidad. In *Material Cultures: Why Some Things Matter,* ed. Daniel Miller, 169–88. Chicago: University of Chicago Press.

Minkley, Gary, and Ciraj Rassool. 1998. Orality, Memory and Social History in South Africa. In *Negotiating the Past,* ed. Sarah Nuttall and Carli Coetzee, 89–99. Oxford: Oxford University Press.

Mintz, Sidney. 1985. *Sweetness and Power.* New York: Viking.

———. 1996. *Tasting Food, Tasting Freedom.* Boston: Beacon.

———. 1998. The Localization of Anthropological Practice: From Area Studies to Transnationalism. *Critique of Anthropology* 18, no. 2: 117–33.

———. 2003. *Devouring Objects of Study: Food and Fieldwork.* David Skomp Distinguished Lecture in Anthropology, April 30, 2003, Indiana University, Bloomington.

Mueggler, Eric. 2001. *The Age of Wild Ghosts: Memory, Violence and Place in Southwest China*. Berkeley: University of California Press.

Murphy, Robert. 1971. *The Dialectics of Social Life*. New York: Basic Books.

Narayan, Umal. 1995. Eating Cultures: Incorporation, Identity and Indian Food. *Social Identities* 1, no. 1: 63–86.

Nestel, Penelope. 1985. Nutrition of Maasai Women and Children in Relation to Subsistence Food Production. PhD diss., University College, London.

———. 1989. Food Intake and Growth among the Maasai. *Ecology of Food and Nutrition* 23: 17–30.

Netting, Robert McC. 1964. Beer as a Locus of Value among West African Kofyar. *American Anthropologist* 66: 375–85.

Nout, M. J. Robert 1981 Aspects of the Manufacture and Consumption of Kenyan Traditional Fermented Beverages. PhD diss., Landbouwhogeschool te Wageningen, The Netherlands.

Ohnuki-Tierney, Emiko. 1991. *Rice as Self: Japanese Identities through Time*. Princeton, NJ: Princeton University Press.

Ong, Aihwa. 2003. *Buddha Is Hiding*. Berkeley: University of California Press.

Orlove, Benjamin. 1994. Beyond Consumption: Meat, Sociality, Vitality and Hierarchy in Nineteenth-Century Chile. In *Consumption and Identity*, ed. Jonathan Friedman, 119–46. Switzerland: Harwood Academic.

Orlove, Benjamin, and Arnold Bauer. 1997. Chile in the Belle Epoque: Primitive Producers, Civilized Consumers. In *The Allure of the Foreign*, ed. Benjamin Orlove, 113–49. Ann Arbor: University of Michigan Press.

Ortner, Sherry. 1984. Theory in Anthropology since the Sixties. *Comparative Studies in Society and History* 26: 126–66.

———. 1989. *High Religion: A Cultural and Political History of Sherpa Buddhism*. Princeton, NJ: Princeton University Press.

———. 1995. Resistance and the Problem of Ethnographic Refusal. *Comparative Studies in Society and History* 37, no. 1: 173–93.

———. 1996. *Making Gender: The Politics and Erotics of Culture*. Boston: Beacon.

Packard, Randall. 1989. The "Healthy Reserve" and the "Dressed Native": Discourses on Black Health and the Language of Legitimation in South Africa. *American Ethnologist* 16: 686–703.

Pandolfo, Stefania. 1997. *Impasse of the Angels*. Chicago: University of Chicago Press.

Parry, Jonathan, and Maurice Bloch. 1989. *Money and the Morality of Exchange*. Cambridge: Cambridge University Press.

Partenan, Juha. 1991. *Sociability and Intoxication: Alcohol and Drinking in Kenya, Africa and the Modern World*. Finnish Foundation for Alcohol Studies, vol. 39. Finland: Gummerus Kirjapaino Oy.

Peters, Karl. 1891. *New Light on Dark Africa*. London: Ward Lock.

Piot, Charles. 1999. *Remotely Global: Village Modernity in West Africa*. Chicago: University of Chicago Press.

Plotnicov, Leonard, and Richard Scaglion, eds. 1999. *Consequences of Cultivar Diffusion*. Ethnology Monograph series, no. 17, University of Pittsburgh, Department of Anthropology.

Pollock, Nancy. 1992. *These Roots Remain: Food Habits in Islands of the Central and Eastern Pacific Since Western Contact.* Laie, Hawaii: Institute for Polynesian Studies.

Pottier, Johan. 1999. *Anthropology of Food: The Social Dynamics of Food Security.* Malden, MA: Blackwell.

Powles, Julia. 2002. "Like Baby Minnows We Came with the Current": Social Memory amongst Angolan Refugees in Meheba Settlement, Zambia. Paper presented at the Association of Social Anthropologists of Great Britain and the Commonwealth, Arusha, Tanzania.

Pratchett, Terry. 2001. *The Thief of Time.* New York: HarperCollins.

Psathas, George. 1980. Erving Goffman and the Development of Modern Social Theory. In *The View from Goffman,* ed. Jason Ditton, 170–209. New York: St. Martin's.

Ranger, Terence. 1983. The Invention of Tradition in Colonial Africa. In *The Invention of Tradition,* ed. Eric Hobsbawn and Terence Ranger, 211–62. Cambridge: Cambridge University Press.

Rappaport, Roy. 1979. "The Obvious Aspects of Ritual." In *Ecology, Meaning and Religion,* 173–221. Berkeley, CA: North Atlantic Books.

———. 1999. *Ritual and Religion in the Making of Humanity.* Cambridge: Cambridge University Press.

Richards, Audrey. 1932. *Hunger and Work in a Savage Tribe.* London: Routledge.

———. 1939. *Land, Labour and Diet in Northern Rhodesia.* Oxford: Oxford University Press.

Ricks, D. 1993. *Blunders in International Business.* Oxford: Blackwell.

Rigby, Peter. 1985. *Persistent Pastoralists.* London: Zed.

Rosaldo, Renato. 1989. *Culture and Truth: The Remaking of Social Analysis.* Boston: Beacon.

Roseberry, William. 1996. The Rise of Yuppie Coffees and the Reimagination of Class in America. *American Anthropologist* 98: 762–75.

Rubel, Paula, and Abraham Rosman. 1978. *Your Own Pigs You May Not Eat.* New Haven, CT: Yale University Press.

Rutz, Henry. 1989. Culture, Class and Consumer Choice: Expenditures on Food in Urban Fijian Households. In *The Social Economy of Consumption,* ed. Henry Rutz and Benjamin Orlove, 211–51. Monographs in Economic Anthropology No. 6. Lanham, MD: University Press of America.

Rutz, Henry, and Benjamin Orlove, eds. 1989. *The Social Economy of Consumption.* Monographs in Economic Anthropology No. 6. Lanham, MD: University Press of America.

Sahlins, Marshall. 1972. *Stone Age Economics.* Chicago: University of Chicago Press.

———. 1976. *Culture and Practical Reason.* Chicago: University of Chicago Press.

———. 1988. Cosmologies of Capitalism: The Trans-Pacific Sector of "the World System." *Proceedings of the British Academy* 74: 1–51.

———. 1993. *Waiting for Foucault.* Cambridge, MA: Prickly Pear Press.

Samuel, Raphael. 1994. *Theatres of Memory.* London: Verso.

Sangree, Walter. 1966. *Age, Prayer, and Politics in Tiriki, Kenya*. London: Oxford University Press.

Saul, Mahir. 1981. Beer, Sorghum and Women: Production for the Market in Rural Upper Volta. *Africa* 51, no. 3: 746–64.

Saveur. 2003. Mother Milk. 68: 48–61.

Schneider, Harold K. 1959. Pokot Resistance to Change. In *Continuity and Change in African Cultures*, ed. William Russell Bascom and Melville J. Herskovitz, 144–67. Chicago: Phoenix Books.

———. 1970. *The Wahi Wanyaturu*. Viking Fund Publication in Anthropology no. 48. New York: Wenner Gren Foundation for Anthropological Research.

Scott, James. 1985. *Weapons of the Weak*. New Haven, CT: Yale University Press.

Seremetakis, C. Nadia. 1996. *The Senses Still*. Chicago: University of Chicago Press.

Shack, William. 1971. Hunger, Anxiety and Ritual: Deprivation and Spirit Possession among the Gurage of Ethiopia. *Man* 6, no. 1: 30–43.

Shaper, A. G. 1962. Cardiovascular Studies in the Samburu Tribe of Northern Kenya. *American Heart Journal* 63: 437–42.

Shaw, Rosalind. 2002. *Memories of the Slave Trade*. Chicago: University of Chicago Press.

Shipton, Parker. 1994. *Bitter Money*. Washington, DC: American Anthropological Association.

Simmel, Georg. 1950. The Sociology of Georg Simmel. Trans. Kurt Wolff. Glencoe, IL: Free Press.

———. 1978. The Philosophy of Money. London: Routledge and Kegan Paul.

Singer, E. 1984. Conversion through Foodways Enculturation: The Meaning of Eating in an American Hindu Sect. In *Ethnic and Regional Foodways in the United States: The Performance of Group Identity*, ed. Keller Brown and Keith Mussel, 195–214. Knoxville: University of Tennessee Press.

Siskind, Janet. 1973. *To Hunt in the Morning*. New York: Oxford University Press.

Smith, Andrea. 2004. Heteroglossia, "Common Sense" and Social Memory. *American Ethnologist* 31, no. 2: 251–69.

Sobania, Neal. 1980. The Historical Tradition of the Peoples of the Eastern Lake Turkana Basin. PhD diss., University of London.

Spencer, Paul. 1965. *The Samburu*. London: Routledge and Kegan Paul.

———. 1973. *Nomads in Alliance*. Oxford: Oxford University Press.

———. 1988. *Masai of Matapoto*. Manchester, U.K.: Manchester University Press.

Stoler, Ann. 1986. Plantation Politics and Protest on Sumatra's East Coast. *Journal of Peasant Studies* 13, no. 2: 124–43.

Stoller, Paul. 1989. *The Taste of Ethnographic Things*. Philadelphia: University of Pennsylvania Press.

———. 1995. *Embodying Colonial Memories*. New York: Routledge.

Straight, Bilinda. 1997a. Altered Landscapes, Shifting Strategies. PhD diss., University of Michigan.

————. 1997b. Gender, Work, and Change among Samburu Pastoralists in Northern Kenya. *Research in Economic Anthropology* 18: 65–92.

————. 2000. Development Ideologies and Local Knowledge among Samburu Women in Northern Kenya. In *Rethinking Pastoralism in Africa,* ed. Dorothy Hodgson. London: James Currey.

————. 2002. From Samburu Heirloom to New Age Artifact: The Cross-Cultural Consumption of Mporo Marriage Beads. *American Anthropologist* 104, no. 1: 1–15.

————. 2005. Cutting Time with Beads. In *The Qualities of Time,* ed. Wendy James and David Mills. London: Berg.

————. 2006. *Miracles and Extraordinary Experience in Northern Kenya.* Philadelphia: University of Pennsylvania Press.

Strathern, Andrew. 1971. *The Rope of Moka.* Cambridge: Cambridge University Press.

————. 1996. *Body Thoughts.* Ann Arbor: University of Michigan Press.

Suggs, David. 1996. Mosadi Tshwene: The Construction of Gender and the Consumption of Alcohol in Botswana. *American Ethnologist* 23, no. 3: 597–610.

Sutton, David. 2001. *Remembrance of Repasts: An Anthropology of Food and Memory.* London: Berg.

Swedenburg, Ted. 1991. Popular Memory and the Palestinian National Past. In *Golden Ages, Dark Ages: Imagining the Past in Anthropology and History,* ed. W. Roseberry and J. O'Brien, 152–79. Berkeley: University of California Press.

Swedenburg, Ted, and Smadar Lavie, eds. 1996. *Displacement, Diaspora and Geographies of Identity.* Durham, NC: Duke University Press.

Talle, Aud. 1988. *Women at a Loss: Changes in Maasai Pastoralism and Their Effects on Gender Relations.* Stockholm: Stockholm Studies in Social Anthropology.

Taussig, Michael. 1980. *The Devil and Commodity Fetishism in South America.* Chapel Hill: University of North Carolina Press.

————. 1993. *Mimesis and Alterity: A Particular History of the Senses.* New York: Routledge.

Thomas, Philip. 1998. Conspicuous Construction: Houses, Consumption and "Relocalization" in Manambondro, Southeast Madagascar. *Journal of the Royal Anthropological Institute* 4, no. 3: 425–46.

Tsing, Anna. 1993. *In the Realm of the Diamond Queen.* Princeton, NJ: Princeton University Press.

————. 2000. The Global Situation. *Cultural Anthropology* 15: 327–60.

Verdery, Katherine. 1999. *The Political Lives of Dead Bodies.* New York: Columbia University Press.

Walens, Stanley. 1981. *Feasting with Cannibals.* Princeton, NJ: Princeton University Press.

Watson, James, ed. 1997. *Golden Arches East: McDonald's in East Asia.* Stanford, CA: Stanford University Press.

Weiner, Annette. 1983. *Women of Value, Men of Renown.* Austin: University of Texas Press.

Wertsch, James. 2002. *Voices of Collective Remembering.* Cambridge: Cambridge University Press.

Weismantel, Mary. 1988. *Food, Gender and Poverty in the Ecuadorian Andes.* Philadelphia: University of Pennsylvania Press.

———. 1991. Tasty Meals and Bitter Gifts: Consumption and Production in the Ecuadorian Andes. *Food and Foodways* 5, no. 1: 79–94.

Weiss, Brad. 1996. *The Making and Unmaking of the Haya Lived World.* Durham, NC: Duke University Press.

White, Luise. 2000. *Speaking with Vampires.* Berkeley: University of California Press.

Whitehead, Harriet. 2000. *Food Rules.* Ann Arbor: University of Michigan Press.

Wiley, Andrea. 2006. The Breakdown of Holism and the Curious Fate of Food Studies in Anthropology. *Anthropology News* 47, no. 1: 9, 12

Wilk, Richard. 1994. Consumer Goods as a Dialogue about Development: Colonial Time and Television Time in Belize. In *Consumption and Identity,* ed. Jonathan Friedman, 97–118. Switzerland: Harwood Academic.

Willis, Justin. 2002. *Potent Brews: A Social History of Alcohol in East Africa, 1850–1999.* Oxford: James Currey.

Wilson, Gail. 1987. Money: Patterns of Responsibility and Irresponsibility in Marriage. In *Give and Take in Families,* ed. J. Brannen and G. Wilson, 136–54. London: Allen and Unwin.

Wilson, Thomas, ed. 2005. *Drinking Cultures.* New York: Berg.

Wolcott, Harry. 1974. *The African Beer Gardens of Bulawayo.* New Brunswick, NJ: Rutgers Center for Alcohol Research.

Wolf, Eric. 1982. *Europe and the People without History.* Berkeley: University of California Press.

Wood, Nancy. 1999. *Vectors of Memory: Legacies of Trauma in Postwar Europe.* New York: Berg.

Young, James. 2000. *At Memory's Edge: After-Images of the Holocaust in Contemporary Art and Architecture.* New Haven, CT: Yale University Press.

Young, Michael W. 1971. *Fighting with Food: Leadership, Values and Social Control in a Massim Society.* Cambridge: Cambridge University Press.

Index

Text: 10/13 Sabon
Display: Sabon
Compositor: IBT Global
Printer and binder: IBT Global

CPSIA information can be obtained
at www.ICGtesting.com
Printed in the USA
JSHW041423120122
21959JS00001B/18